FALSE START IN AFRICA

Books by the same Author

La Culture du Riz dans le Delta du Tonkin   1935
Misère ou Prospérité Paysanne?   1936
Le Problème Agricole Français   1946
Les Leçons de l'Agriculture Américaine   1949
Voyages en France d'un Agronome   1951 and 1956
Economie Agricole dans le Monde   1953
   (Types of Rural Economy   1957)
La Nécessaire Révolution Fourragère   1955
Révolution dans les Campagnes Chinoises   1957
Evolution des Campagnes Malgaches   1960
Terres Vivantes   1961
   (Lands Alive   1964)
Reconversion de l'Économie Agricole:
   Guinée, Côte d'Ivoire, Mali   1961
Sénégal et Madagascar
Sovkhoz, Kolkhoz ou le problématique Communisme   1964
Cuba, Socialisme et Développement   1964 and 1969
Chine surpeuplée, Tiers-monde affamé   1965
Développement Agricole Africain   1965
Le difficile Développment Agricole de la République
   Centrafricaine   1966
(with Bernard Rosier) Nous allons à la famine 1966
   (The Hungry Future 1969)
Réforme agraire et modernisation de
   l'agriculture au Mexique   1969

False Start in Africa

René Dumont

Translated by Phyllis Nauts Ott

Introduction by Thomas Balogh

With an additional chapter by John Hatch

ANDRE DEUTSCH

FIRST PUBLISHED MAY 1966 BY
ANDRE DEUTSCH LIMITED
105 GREAT RUSSELL STREET
LONDON WCI
COPYRIGHT © 1966 ENGLISH TRANSLATION
BY ANDRE DEUTSCH LIMITED
SECOND IMPRESSION JULY 1967
THIRD IMPRESSION OCTOBER 1967
REVISED EDITION AUGUST 1969
ORIGINALLY PUBLISHED IN FRENCH UNDER THE TITLE
L'Afrique Noire est Mal Partie
© 1962 BY EDITIONS DU SEUIL, PARIS
ALL RIGHTS RESERVED
PRINTED IN GREAT BRITAIN BY
EBENEZER BAYLIS AND SON LTD
THE TRINITY PRESS
WORCESTER AND LONDON
233 95816 9

To Osendé Afana, author of *L'économie de l'Ouest-Africain*, who was captured taking medical supplies to a village and decapitated 15 March 1966.

INTRODUCTION

by T. Balogh, Fellow of Balliol, Oxford

I was asked by the Publishers early in 1964 to write an introduction to Professor Dumont's classic analysis of the problems of new Africa. I wrote this preface early in the summer of that year, before the General Election, the establishment of a new Ministry of Overseas Development and my own assumption of official duties. Nothing that I say in the introduction should therefore be taken as reflecting the official view of Her Majesty's Government towards the issues dealt with in the book.

London, April 1965

The bewildering violence of the 'wind of change' in Africa has converted the most universally colonial continent into the greatest jumble of independent states. Their existence is in most cases due neither to the exigencies of geography nor to ethnic unity. They are the ultimate results of the disastrous rivalry and the chase for colonial aggrandisement of the 'great Powers' at the end of the nineteenth century. They are also the inheritors of the imperial institutions, especially in administrative structure and education, which suddenly lost such socio-economic relevance as they had ever possessed.

Accordingly, the test of intellectual freedom and courage also underwent a startling change. In the 'bad' old imperial days non-conformity meant striving for increasing political rights and equality, it meant demanding the education of the inhabitants for this purpose having due regard to the backwardness of the traditional sectors.

It meant a ceaseless struggle to equip the administrative machine with planners and experts instead of paternalistic administrators with no relevant technical knowledge. It meant a determined fight against the snobbish deprecation of such expertise as existed; against the superior attitudes of the conventional anthropologists protecting their stock-in-trade of quaint, if barbarous habits (including sex-initiation, which in many parts involved female circumcision) and consequently maintaining traditional barriers in the way of social progress towards political equality. It meant a shift in education towards technical education – including administration; and more especially towards agricultural education through a vast development of agricultural services coupled with rural education. It meant a shift of research and care from cash-crops needed by the metropolis to food-growing essential to the health of inhabitants. Little success was achieved in this struggle during the existence of colonial systems.

The test of fearless nonconformity has radically changed with the change in political structure. The 'Establishment' both here and in France (and even in the United States despite its anti-feudal roots) has, with that sudden, instinctive and uniform turnabout so characteristic of its power to survive, transformed large parts of an erstwhile rebellious and constructive heterodoxy into conventional wisdom; but this new orthodoxy has in its turn lost much of its relevance because the new situation of partitioned and balkanized independence demands new methods of implementing unchanging goals. Regional planning for common markets; a universal national service for peaceful investment and progress based on the organization of a rural education service – making use of co-operatives and agricultural extension rather than a new drive for literacy – and a complete reform of higher education with closest attention to the time-pattern of socio-economic development plans: these are the main points of the solution now needed, which could not have been achieved under the old régimes. It means also fighting against the adoption by the new rulers of metropolitan attitudes to education and to agricultural development. This demands a decisive curtailment of the secluded privileged existence – amounting to apartheid – maintained by the new tiny administrative African *élite* which was the direct result, paradoxically enough, of the thoughtless demands for equality with the expatriate administrators. These demands were made without realizing the implication of this 'equality' with expatriates on the relation of the new rulers to the mass of poverty-stricken peasants. It means a reform of destructive land tenure systems, including the system of unconditional private ownership, which seems to lead to exploitation rather than progress. All these are new requirements, hardly likely to be popular with articulate Africans.

On the other hand, progress is also dependent on a reform of the attitudes and approach of the 'rich' countries. In particular it depends on the co-ordination of technical and resource aid, both bilateral and multilateral, and on a change in the attitude of national and international agencies.[1] It demands a re-education of experts so that they can operate successfully in the new framework.

The basically paternalistic superiority of the erstwhile champions of classical learning of Oxbridge and the Sorbonne finds its new expression in an uncritical and ultra-polite acceptance of whatever emerges as a consequence of the administrative, educational and socio-economic failures of the defunct imperial systems. The new constructive nonconformity criticizes the mistakes of the new régimes and is intensely conscious of their origin in the very nature of those imperial systems it has always attacked.[2] In accepting, indeed pandering to the defects of the hotch-potch of the new régimes, the conventional wisdom of the Metropolitan Establishments defends its own colonial record while parading in a misleading décor of modernity.[3] The same (lack of) expertise and sociological comprehension that caused so much mischief is often doled out under the guise of technical assistance. *Plus ça change . . .*

Professor Dumont is a shining example of how constructive thought can be fused with a fearless political attitude. He has been a

[1] One example of an attitude, widely held at present, that is harmful in its effects on economic progress, is that of hostility to peaceful universal national service. This hostility is based on a view of labour relations derived from experienced integrated industrialised countries, and leads to increased trade union organization which tends to destroy progress in the poor areas that need changes in primitive agriculture and industrialization.

[2] It is this consciousness of responsibility which separates progressive critical thought from such well-meaning conservative critics of new Africa as Dr Little, not to say the white racialists.

[3] The so-called Ashby Report on Higher Education in Nigeria is a typical example of this ill-thought-out 'modernity'.

matchless champion of the most disinherited, oppressed, exploited, wretched and physically most ailing class in the world, the primitive peasant who is living in primeval misery at a time when the privileged population are able to flourish while wasting an untold mass of resources on national rivalry in the arms and space-race; resources amply sufficient, if well applied, to lift Adam's curse and to eradicate poverty from the face of the earth. His merciless investigation of the feudal battening of a tiny minority on the toil of the multitudes in the Mediterranean, in Latin America and in Asia, has earned him the detestation of the callous profiteers who benefit from the mal-distribution of private property. His equally famous analysis of the defects of Soviet, Cuban and Algerian collectivism[1] were no less disliked by the respective rulers of those countries.

But Professor Dumont is much more than an intrepid enemy of exploitation and mal-administration. He is one of the few agronomists who combine a professional technical knowledge with a sense of social and economic balance alien to technocratic enthusiasts, who so often dominate, to the detriment of world socio-economic development, both the international and national agencies for technical assistance. He is not one of those agricultural economists who took refuge in their speciality because they were incapable of being economists. He is an agronomist with a real socio-economic sensibility.

In the present volume Professor Dumont analyses the basic problem of new-ex-French-Africa[2] south of the Sahara.

It is a tale of failure, as the title indicates; failure, on the whole, due to the historical framework in which liberation has taken place. Despite vociferous pan-Africanism it is a tale of fragmentation into units – apart, perhaps, from the Congo and Nigeria (both of which are menaced by strong centrifugal forces) – hardly viable and

---

[1] Unfortunately not available in English translation. The most important: *Révolution dans les campagnes chinoises*, 1957; *Évolution des campagnes Malgaches*, 1960; *Terres vivantes*, 1961; *Problèmes d'agriculture USSR*, 1963; *Des Problèmes Generaux de l'économie Agraire Cubaine*, 1962.

[2] Mr Hatch's chapter shows how similar the imperial impact was on the ex-British territories. The difference was that the British territories were dominated by an outdoor-loving non-intellectual public school Oxbridge-type, conscientious (apart from the Kenyan pro-settler attitude) in protecting their wards; the French were dominated by literary Sorbonne products longing to get back to Paris and thus rather less willing to incur the displeasure of metropolitan vested interests.

certainly unable to sustain self-supporting development towards quasi-European standards of life. In many territories there is actual impoverishment in comparison to Colonial days. Even where progress has been achieved it was achieved through industrialization. This, however, reached those narrow limits set by the lack of adequate markets. The creation of markets, however, depends on regional unification and planning, and on that rural socio-economic revolution which is necessary to secure any appreciable increase of purchasing power of the overwhelming mass of population which remains – and for scores of years will remain – dependent on agriculture.

On the other hand, the destructive forces of tribalism can only be overcome by strong, i.e. localized, *nationalistic* drives, themselves fatal to the emergence of viable units, because these would have to transcend the old colonial sub-divisions, sub-divisions which are incompatible with economic independence. There is as yet no hard evidence that a new supra-national approach is emerging (as contrasted with verbal asseverations of pan-African loyalty). It is not the trend towards one-party states that is the really disturbing phenomenon in Africa. A competition of political parties for popular favour is hardly compatible with the effort and sacrifice demanded by the investment requirements of a rapid social and economic development. The ominous feature of contemporary Africa is the fact that the great opportunities vouchsafed to the charismatic leaders who emerged during the process of decolonization for co-operative development based on sacrifice have not been firmly grasped.

It is in this respect that Professor Dumont's book presents a completely pathfinding analysis. I have seen him at work in Senegal during a week of fact-finding which left us and our Senegalese hosts breathless and exhausted. There could be no doubt that Dumont's technical knowledge, his patent sympathy for the underdog, his ruthless sincerity won admiration even among those whom he criticized mercilessly.

It was an extraordinary lapse that his work was not immediately translated into English (or read at whatever cost of effort in the original French); it is hardly less important for Britain in its fumb-

1*

lings for a new approach to independent Africa, than it was for France. It implies a revolutionary reassessment of our advice and technical assistance in education, agriculture, animal husbandry and above all in the search for a social framework – in administration and institutions – within which the overdue reforms can be successfully put through. If one considers, for instance, the adverse effects on Africa of the Oxbridge approach to higher education, one can only wish we had had a Dumont in the 1940s, when our mistaken policies took shape.

August, 1964

CONTENTS

Charts

LIST OF ABBREVIATIONS

BDPA – Bureau pour le Développement de la Production Agricole
CAR – Central African Republic
CFA – Formerly the Colonies Françaises d'Afrique, now the Communauté Financière Africaine
CFDT – Compagnie Française pour le Développement des Textiles
CGOT – Compagnie Générale des Oléagineux Tropicaux
CINAM – Compagnie d'Études Industrielles et Aménagement du Territoire
CRAM – Communes Rurales Autochtones Malgaches
ECA – Economic Commission for Africa
FAC – Fonds d'Aide et de Coopération
FAO – Food and Agricultural Organization of the United Nations
FEANF – Féderation des Étudiants d'Afrique Noire en France
FERDES – Fonds d'Équipement Rural et de Développement Économique et Social
FIDES – Fonds d'Investissements pour le Développement Économique et Social
FRIA – Compagnie Internationale pour la Production de l'Alumine (operating in the Fria dislrict of Guinea)
INEAC – Institut National d'Études Agronomiques du Congo
IRAM – Institut de Recherches et d'Application des Méthodes de Développement
IRAT – Institut de Recherche d'Agronomie Tropicale et des Cultures Vivrières
IRHO – Institut de Recherches pour les Huiles de palme et Oléagineux
ORSTOM – Office de la Recherche Scientifique el Technique Outre-Mer
PSU – Parti Socialiste Unifié
PUF – Presses Universitaires de France
SEMA – Société d'Études de Mathématiques Appliqués
SERESA – Société d'Études de la Réalisation Économique et Sociale en Agriculture
SFIO – Parti Socialiste, Section Française de l'International Ouvrière
SMIG – Salaire Minimum Interprofessionel Garanti
SMP – Secteurs du Paysannat Marocain
SOGEP – Société Générale d'Études et de Planification

AUTHOR'S INTRODUCTION

' "False Start in Africa". Your title is too brutal. It is going to offend the Africans, you know how touchy they are.' 'You'll be pandering to typical colonial prejudices.' 'Worst of all, by criticizing the new nations and their leaders you will vindicate the colonialists, who felt the Africans were not ready for independence.'

I am aware of these pitfalls and many more besides. And so I hesitate in starting to write this book as I have never done with my others. In recent years I have fought bitterly with South American landowners and Indian moneylenders, who parcel out land to share-croppers. But there my adversaries were exploiting the peasantry, and were formidable obstacles to development and progress in their countries. I had a rousing battle with Chilean friends at the University of Santiago in January, 1960.

But when I confront a young African official, who was perhaps my student, my position is more difficult. If he persists in a course which retards his country's development, and hangs on to his privileged status, he is only following a path we laid out for him. If he believes wholeheartedly in the French educational system, I, as a former professor, am scarcely in a position to reproach him for it.

In May 1961 a number of farmers north of Brazzaville said to me: 'Independence isn't for us; it's only for the city people.' I heard the same criticisms that year in Dahomey and Madagascar, but in more specific terms. That October I spent a day in the lower Mungo region of the Cameroons. Rebel recruits there are from ten to twenty-five years old, sometimes only eight years old, according to the President of the Council, Charles Assalé. I read a speech given the month before by the Mayor of Nkongsamba at a reception of Monsieur Assalé. I reproduce the last part of it here, unedited.

'Lastly, the effects of terrorism and counter-terrorism. The terrorist attacks and the massive reprisals which follow them have placed the ordinary population in a strategic position, have made of them a flock of sheep oppressed on both sides, wandering and without a master, and have given them a complex, a widespread feeling of citizens diminished, living between two forces, between two oppressions . . .

'To the great shame of our nation, a speaker declared on September 3rd, 1961, to the sustained applause of the audience and without being contradicted, that recolonization, or the return to power of the whites, would receive an overwhelming majority in a referendum to decide between maintaining independence and recolonization.

'So we are not yet at the stage, at least locally, where independence is a means of effective evolution of the masses. Rather, the masses have the impression that national sovereignty has created a privileged class which has cut itself off from them.

'We are fully aware that those in public office, as arms of the central government, constitute for the time being the *élite* of the country, and for this reason they have a mission to stimulate and further general progress.

'While we publicly pay homage to those in this group, and they are many, whose devotion and disinterested service are without limit, at the same time we strongly regret that a good number of our officials, scorning a real sense of public office and duty, are only interested in the advantages and privileges of their positions . . .

'We are not making a complaint against anybody, we are simply stating that at the rate we are going now, we are headed towards a worse colonialism, that of class.' I must emphasize that the speaker was loyal to the government; he concluded thus: '. . . We have told you of the feeling of perplexity spreading among the people, and our anxieties about the practices tending to create an ill-fated régime.'

I can hardly rejoice at such a statement, if it indeed proves that the old upper-class chief administrators were right. I have always declared to my African friends that the independence we all fought for would be the beginning of their troubles. The journal *Esprit*

devoted its June 1957 issue to the 'Childhood Diseases of Independence'. One cannot attain to the dignity of manhood without first
shouldering its problems. The time has come to face these 'childhood diseases' squarely, and realize that they are not 'shameful'. It
is urgent that they be cured quickly, as a first step towards economic
development. Purely political independence is a preliminary. Real
independence can only be achieved through economic development.

As an agronomist and grandson of a peasant, I feel called upon to
defend the underdeveloped and often oppressed peasants, the true
proletarians of modern times. Only a massive effort on their part can
'take the brake off' the economy in backward countries, bring them
out of stagnation and start accelerated development. Oppression
alone, regardless of what has been said about China, can never
release the enthusiasm necessary for such an effort.

Confronted with the new 'class colonialism', I have only three
alternatives. I can say nothing; as I do not like to offend Africans,
this would be the easy way out. I could resort to flattery, as many did
during the independence celebrations in 1961–1962. Or I could
simply omit some of my more unpleasant conclusions, which would
be another form of lie. In this context let me quote a man from the
Cameroons who, during the discussion following my second lecture
in Yaoundé in October, 1961, told me in substance: 'What you are
saying is not pleasant to hear, but we can accept it from you because
we know that it is inspired by friendship.' I thank this unknown
friend for giving me the courage to undertake one of the most
ungrateful tasks I have ever set myself.

Unlike the followers of Moral Rearmament and similar dogmatic
creeds, I do not pretend to 'ultimate' truth. I realize that it is
unattainable; perhaps in that respect I am unfortunate. But those
who claim to possess it, from the OAS to Stalinists, are dangerous
impostors, for they use it to justify all their crimes. As far as I am
concerned, the search for fractions of truths, provisional and relative
though they may be, is a deeply satisfying task. But it has to be done
objectively, by those who willingly admit their fallibility before
setting out to teach others.

I bear part of the responsibility for the present situation in Africa,
which is one of the principal reasons I must speak up now. I was

consulted by many of the new African governments between 1958 and 1961: the Malagasy Republic, Guinea, the Ivory Coast, Mali, the Republic of the Congo (Brazzaville), Chad, Dahomey, Senegal and the Cameroons. After a trip to Cuba, I helped draft the new plan for Ruanda-Urundi. My responsibility would be even greater if I did not point out to the Africans how dangerous their attitude is. I speak of those who believe that political independence is sufficient, who underestimate the importance of economic development, or who simply sit back to enjoy their new privileges.

I must thank all those who have helped me, particularly the African peasants and the African students who attended my lectures in the winter of 1961–1962. Their criticisms, often very sharp, have been most useful. And thanks also to the friends who criticized the manuscript: it needed it.

I shall first explore a question posed by Domenach, namely, whether tropical Africa is in fact, as many have written, a continent with a curse on it. (The book will deal only with tropical Africa. It will touch briefly here and there on the former Belgian colonies. The experience of English-speaking Africa is discussed as a whole in the last chapter, by John Hatch.) Europe, who got off to the first start in economic development, has lost its political supremacy, but its economy is moving again. A part of Asia, particularly Japan, China and Siberia, is developing rapidly. In the Western hemisphere, magnificently rich in resources, North America is heavily industrialized, and a serious beginning has been made in South America. In a world in the process of transformation, is the African continent to be the only one condemned to stagnation, without future and without hope?

I shall go on to discuss why tropical Africa, after a tentative precolonial start, seems to be marking time. The Europeans, of course, bear most of the blame. Slavery and colonialism, both political and economic, are their responsibility. But the Africans have taken over now. The industrial and agricultural development of the continent, one as indispensable as the other, are meeting a number of obstacles, some rooted in tradition, others uniquely modern. But it is possible to revolutionize the savannah and forest regions. There are enormous agricultural possibilities in the forests of Africa, while the potential for the savannah rests in combining cultivation with livestock raising.

Such an extended technical transformation will demand fresh thinking, and a complete recasting of methods used to train, organize and activate the peasantry, as well as of credit and co-operative organizations. Full employment is a priority, and can be immediately achieved by convincing peasants to donate labour to development schemes, which I call 'labour investments'.

I will then discuss the halting pace of recent African evolution, which runs the risk of leading to 'South-Americanization'. But I shall end on a comforting note. The necessary European and world co-operation, combined with more effort on the part of the Africans, can set the situation to rights quickly, conquer underdevelopment in twenty years, and give the lie to the title of this book.

POSTSCRIPT

Amid the general euphoria — as widespread in France as in Africa — at the time of independence, a writer had to be rather arrogant to say that Africa was off to a bad start, especially because the start was barely outlined at all and because we, the colonizers, were most responsible. Nevertheless, I preferred to run the risk of annoying some of my African friends rather than show my disrespect by flattering them or withholding my essential ideas. That would have been a hypocritical form of neo-colonialist segregation. Confronted by the 'childhood diseases of independence', I thought it was important to try to diagnose their cure. The tone I adopted was sometimes clumsy, but I was trying to defend the tropical peasantry (the true proletarians of modern times, even though, ironically, they own their tools of production). However, I knew too little about history or about African sociology and psychology to be able to do a thoroughly satisfactory piece of work. Consequently, I overestimated pre-colonial civilization and under-estimated the problems of development. Africa must simultaneously learn to use writing and money, the plough and the centralized state (which Asia has known for a long time), while striving to grapple effectively with the Industrial Revolution.

Those who were put off by the title of the book—and they still outnumber the actual readers—have occasionally stated that it did not put forward 'any constructive criticism'. This, however, was not the opinion of President David Dacko, who asked his ministers to read it before inviting me to the Central African Republic. Nor was it that of Robert A. Gardiner, executive secretary of the United Nations Economic Commission for Africa, who, in July, 1964, asked me to conduct, for presentation before the ECA, a study of the technical and economic problems hindering or promoting African agricultural development.[1] If African governments ask me for another study, perhaps I shall write about how 'Africa must make a good start' despite all its impediments.

The time has not yet come. Several years after this book was first published, the facts bear witness—alas, only too well—to the title, although a contradiction would make me very happy. Between 1957 and 1963, production for commercial exploitation in Dahomey sharply declined. Cotton production is collapsing in the Central African Republic. Upper Volta is making no progress, and Guinea and Mali are bogging down. Even when the situation is better, as in the Ivory Coast or the Cameroons, development is not benefiting everyone.

Since 1959, according to ECA research, the production of food-stuffs in Africa has risen at a rate of about 1·7 per cent per year, slower than the population increase of 2·5 per cent. Even if these figures are debatable, the meaning of the difference between them is not: Africa will increasingly have to import foodstuffs.

Africa's traditional agrarian economy is floundering under our generally indifferent eyes. But Paul Bairoch has shown us that, since the end of World War I, the annual productivity of Afro-Asian peasant labour has declined by about one-fifth. In the first part of this book, I shall focus attention on the Europeans and Africans responsible for this stagnation. Next, I shall study the reforms that appear to be most urgent if the continent is rapidly to approach independent, self-sustaining development. Trying to avoid paternalism,

---

[1] My report was published as *Le développement agricole africaine* in the collection Tiers-Monde (Presses Universitaires de France, Paris, 1965). A year after publication, the 1,000 copies to be distributed by the Commission were still with the printer.

I shall attempt, nevertheless, to detail the requirements for economic take-off, whatever the political framework. The reluctance noticeable since 1959–1962 toward all forms of 'risky' premature socialism will be re-inforced by the facts.

This study is geared to provoke public opinion. Although I am campaigning for more aid to our brothers in difficult circumstances, I shall not stop criticizing them in a brotherly—occasionally rude—manner. The situation becomes more serious in an Africa where the 'generosity' of the rich countries is as unsatisfactory as the 'devotion' of local leaders to the national interest.

Because of the population explosion, not only Africa but the entire Third World has made a false start. The basic problem of the countries of the Third World is that their levels of mechanization and understanding do not allow them to go beyond a certain rate of progress. But, ironically, progress in medical science has, by lowering the mortality rate, inflicted on them a population explosion with which they cannot cope. All this forced me, with Bernard Rosier, to cry out in alarm, 'We are headed for famine!'[1] Let us hope, for the future of our civilization, that this second call will be heard.[2] Let us admit that this hope diminishes every day.

---

[1] *Nous allons à la famine*, by René Dumont and Bernard Rosier, Editions du Seuil, Paris, 1966; published as *The Hungry Future*, by André Deutsch, London, and Frederick A. Praeger, New York, 1969.

[2] Having predicted a famine in India for 1966 in our United Nations report (published in New Delhi in November, 1959) and in the *New Statesman* (London), December 19, 1959, we ask that this time we be taken seriously.

CHAPTER ONE
There is no curse on Black Africa

I. PROBLEMS IN THE TROPICS: DISEASES, MALNUTRITION, SOIL AND CLIMATE

None of the great modern economic powers – Europe, the United States, the Soviet Union, China or Japan – has developed under tropical conditions. Tibor Mende doubts that such development is possible. In his book, *The Tropical World*, Pierre Gourou discusses the many obstacles that faced tropical countries after the Second World War. Because of the unhealthiness of the climate, there is a vast number of endemic diseases unknown in temperate zones. Yellow fever, yaws, leprosy and sleeping sickness are among the scourges that have been widely and effectively attacked, but have not yet disappeared. Malaria is on the wane. The most difficult problems are with bilharzia, which irrigation projects help to spread, filariasis, onchocerca and similar diseases.

There is a wide variety of intestinal diseases which render the unfortunate victim almost totally helpless. The colonials who have suffered from dysentery will bear me out.

Sanitary conditions and disease control methods are still mediocre, despite recent improvements. They are, of course, greatly hindered by widespread malnutrition, caused largely by the poor quality of food, sometimes even by insufficient quantities of food. Too often, the inhabitants of the savannah region have serious food shortages in the period preceding their one cereal harvest. The problem is aggravated when a cash crop, such as peanuts or cotton, replaces the food cereals, like sorghum and millet. This has happened in Senegal, where preliminary studies for the Plan revealed how widespread privation is before the harvest. When the soil of an over-populated area is exhausted, want becomes chronic, as is the case with the Kabrais in North Togo, the Kirdis in the Northern Cameroons, and the Boukombe regions in Dahomey. If seasonal variations which are extreme normally are increased in any way, chronic want becomes real famine. This occurred in Mali (the former French Sudan) in 1913–1914, and in Ruanda-Urundi in 1943, where there were 36,000 deaths.

The most serious and widespread nutritional lack is protein, particularly protein of animal origin. This applies especially in the great forest region.[1] The population there may eat more regularly than in the savannah, but lives on tubers (manioc, yam, taro or macabo, sweet potato) and plantains, all of which are greatly deficient in nitrogen. The situation is even more serious for those 'critical groups' of the population most sensitive to the deficiency, such as pregnant women and nursing mothers. In areas where custom forbids consumption of certain foods, often those containing nitrogen, or where the best portions are reserved for the men, it can mean catastrophe.

Infants being weaned often go directly from their mother's milk to manioc, a starchy tuber that contains no nitrogen, and contract kwashiorkor, a fearsome disease. Many die of it, and those who recover are physically and mentally scarred the rest of their lives.[2]

There are other important deficiencies, particularly in mineral salts (calcium, phosphates, iron, etc.) and vitamins, sometimes fats, particularly far inland and in Madagascar. The lack of Vitamin A results in night blindness; it is easy to treat with the right palm oils.

In order to raise the level of foodstuffs rapidly, in quantity and above all in quality (and it is indispensable for the increased efforts that must be demanded of African workers), the land must be made to produce more. Higher productivity is held back by natural tropical conditions, which are often inferior. Tropical soil on the average is poorer than that in Europe and North America, with the exception of soils that derive from volcanic rocks and recent alluvial

---

[1] Guinea, Upper Volta, Gabon, the Congos, Sierra Leone. The average per capita yearly consumption of meat is 1 to 3 kilograms. 'Eggs and chickens are in principle only for gifts.' (From an excellent study made by the F A O on Africa, November, 1961, hereafter cited as F A O Africa.)

[2] See the study of Professor R. Debré in *La Faim*, the Report of the *Rencontres Internationales de Genève*, September, 1960.

deposits. Most important, it is far more exposed to degradation by the intense rainfall, which causes serious leaching and carries off the mineral elements and humus. This makes the rivers a muddy brown, as in Scandinavia. Combustion of organic material is also more rapid.

Often this process leads to total destruction, as is the case when iron or laterite shields are formed; the protective topsoil has been carried off, and they are completely desiccated by the exposure of their surface and the alternation of the rainy and dry seasons. A number of villages in the eastern part of the Central African Republic are thus surrounded with a ferric 'halo', which will become iron ore one day, but can never be of any use to agriculture, even in the far distant future. In lower Guinea 'boval' have formed which are irreparably infertile.

Erosion, of course, is another type of total soil destruction. It is aided by the stripping of the topsoil produced by brush fires or by continuous and unintelligent planting. Madagascar provides a good example of how a handful of men can destroy enormous stretches of earth. Herders burn the tall grass on the savannah in order to grow a small second crop in the dry season. In my opinion the erosion thus caused far outweighs the profits on their cattle-raising. In other words, the combination of cattle-raising and deliberate brush fires will either bring no economic benefit or result in a deficit: plant life is impoverished, the land is destroyed, lines of communication are damaged, and eventually fertile alluvial land is covered over and ports silted up (as happened at Majunga), a process accelerated by the increased cartage on the rivers.

Men bear the brunt of the responsibility for such erosion. Dry cultivation of rice (*tavy*) on cleared forest land is frequently done without adequate rotation on the slopes of the eastern coast of Madagascar. This prevents anything but the sparse 'savoka' vegetation from coming up again, mostly as a result of the leaching out of fertilizing elements. I cannot be too vehement about the evils of deliberate brush fires. In the leached out Sahel region, south of the Sahara, where there are a good many herders, foresters like Grosmaire estimate that more than 80 per cent of the feed available in the dry season is destroyed by these fires. Even when there are no herders, brush fires are lit for a single hunt in order to move around more easily, and also to destroy the ticks. Sometimes they are even lit for the sheer visual pleasure they afford.

The instability of tropical soils is often increased by climatic conditions. This is not always true, however, since the absence of winter weather allows a continuity of vegetation impossible in temperate countries, provided the dry season is not too long and an adequate supply of water is available, or has been made available. This is difficult to do, since the rivers are swollen by torrential rains and hard to harness, particularly for agriculture. The lowlands, both valleys and littorals, are hard to drain. As P. Viguier[1] has pointed out, the dry season in the tropics generally corresponds to the long Scandinavian winter. During both there can be no vegetation or agricultural activity, which creates seasonal unemployment. This is difficult to reduce with current techniques and equipment.

2. THESE PROBLEMS INTENSIFIED IN AFRICA

In Brazil, north of Parana, the *terra rossa legitima* produces two to five tons of Arabica coffee per two and a half acres, without fertilizer. The western coast of Africa produces only 400 pounds to slightly under one ton of Robusta coffee. The difference does not hold true everywhere, however. The volcanic soil surrounding Cameroon Mountain is on a par with the best *terra rossa*: its nitrogen content is ·005 per cent and it is 13 per cent organic material. The hills of Ruanda-Urundi are often fertile, as are a good number of the highlands in East Africa, where the climate is temperate. Throughout the tropics, the recent fluvial or marine alluviums can produce rich rice fields. The high Merina plateaux near Tananarive easily produce over a ton of rice per acre, despite the fact that the soil has been overworked. Particularly fertile are the *baibohos*, areas of fluvial deposits in Madagascar, above all in the north-western part of the island. In those that are covered with thick mud during submersion in the rainy season, the ton per acre can be easily surpassed in the dry season without irrigation or fertilization.

The soils in Africa form a patchwork of very varied quality, but

---

[1] *L'Afrique de l'Ouest Vue Par Un Agriculteur*. Maison Rustique, Paris, 1960.

on the whole they are inferior to those in tropical South America. They are worse than those of South-East Asia, but better than those of southern India and the eroded hills of southern China. Too often, they derive from archaean rocks, gneiss, sandstone and granite. Sandy soils lacking in precious elements preponderate over clay and limestone soils. Some varieties of schist are justly reputed, but they do not begin to compare with recent volcanic rocks as primary soil material.

From Dakar to Chad and to Congo (Brazzaville), as in southern and western Madagascar, production is modest on the most prevalent soil varieties under present cultivation systems.[1] In general, the climate in tropical Africa is less favourable to agriculture than the more 'maritime' climate of South-East Asia, the Pacific and Caribbean islands, and the coastal zones of South America. None of these are exposed to the tsetse fly, the great scourge of cattle-raisers. No other continent has such a large proportion of deserts, which include the Sahara and the Kalahari. The vast areas bordering them, such as the Sahel and Sudanese regions (see map), are desiccated by the desert wind, the harmattan, and thus much more arid, despite equal rainfall, than the drought area in north-eastern Brazil. Less than half of Africa between the latitudes of 30° north and south has adequate rainfall – say about eighty or more centimetres – to support intensive agriculture. This region is situated mostly in Central Africa and along the west coast.

In the Equatorial and Guinean belts, the great rain forests, excessive rainfall can be a drawback as soon as monthly precipitation exceeds eight inches. The lack of sun cuts down on oil palm harvests brutally, as they like to have 'their feet in the water and their heads in the sun'.

3. THE VICIOUS CIRCLE CAN BE BROKEN

The soil is fragile, without a doubt, and the climate unpredictable, but the situation is by no means desperate. Pierre Gourou has

---

[1] 'The soil in humid areas is poor in nutritive elements and humus, shallow, leachde out, not very productive. . . . Arid soil is often shallow, badly drained or saline in depressions, very heavy, of mediocre texture, and of limited productivity because of the lack of water . . . erosion is serious.' F A O Africa, pp. 12–13.

pessimistically written that laterite is utterly barren, but he is perhaps unaware that the well-known red clay of Matanzas, the richest earth in Cuba, is loose laterite. It is so productive that the cost of growing sugar there is about the lowest in the world.

The other geographer who writes that 'Madagascar has the colour of a brick, and also the fertility' deserves to be hung in effigy. His 'witticism' has long discouraged anyone who wanted to develop the *tanety*, the hills in the centre and west of the island. By intelligent association of cultivation and cattle-raising (I shall discuss this later as applied to the Sakay region), one can produce two or three times as much with the 'bricks' as with the 'rich' meadows in the Auge country in France. The latter are poorly maintained, and their reputation is highly overrated.

Agriculture with high yields and uninterrupted planting is a relatively recent phenomenon even in Europe, where the 'disgraceful fallow system', as Arthur Young called it,[1] was still practised on a large scale in the nineteenth century.[2] Often it is more difficult to attain continuous cultivation in tropical than in temperate climates. Until very recently agriculture in Africa has been in the hands of technically less developed people – in some areas it still is – who have only a few crude tools. This explains why they have always resorted to brush fires to clear the savannah and forests, and enable the grasses to grow back for their animals. Techniques of storing hay and silage are unknown. The idea of storing feed belongs to European agrarian civilization, and is only beginning to gain currency in Africa.

The African has lacked food, livestock and carts to carry manure and fertilizer cheaply. He has therefore had to let the land lie fallow for long periods, during which grasses, trees and bushes grow up, in order to 'remake' the fertility of the soil. It is a vicious circle of low-yield agriculture, on unfertilized land, cultivated by underfed workers. This 'itinerant' agriculture has been called a happy relationship of man and nature. I for one do not find it very satisfactory.

---

[1] Arthur Young, *Travels in France.* Cambridge University Press, 1929.
[2] Khrushchev condemned it at a plenary meeting in the USSR in March, 1962.

4. AGRICULTURE AND UNDERDEVELOPMENT

Needless to say, such underdevelopment in agriculture seriously affects the entire economy.[1] It is inseparable from the lack of industry and underdevelopment in general. Agrarian backwardness always inhibits and sometimes prevents entirely any possibility of rapid economic expansion. Indeed, the agricultural revolution in England, the enclosures in the sixteenth to eighteenth centuries, and the rapid progress made by agriculture in the United States in the first half of the nineteenth century were well before, and greatly facilitated, the Industrial Revolution in those countries. In the same way, the virtual stagnation of the great landed estates in South America has prevented the development of industry there. The Land Tax of the French physiocrats,[2] like the heavy tax levied in Japan after 1869, was also an essential prerequisite to agricultural progress, and thus to general development.

In all relatively over-populated areas, the pressures of population make itinerant agriculture absolutely unacceptable. South Dahomey, northern, south-west and south-east Nigeria, the Bamiléké country in the Cameroons, the Kabrai, Kirdi and Serer regions in Senegal, Mayumbe (north of Matadi in the Congo), Ruanda-Urundi, north-central Tanganyika, and the 'reserves' of Kenya and South Africa — all these areas are too crowded to cling to their archaic systems of production. The rhythm of growth in West Africa, as in other retarded regions, is taking on the proportions of a 'population explosion'. Areas of over-population are rapidly spreading out, and soils are being badly eroded.

But the greater part of Africa is under-populated, and therefore does not yet have its back to the wall, like so many valleys and deltas in the Far East. It is not forced to adopt immediately the most intensive methods of cultivation, whether or not these surpass the economic optimum, and in this it is fortunate. This necessity may have seriously endangered agricultural progress in China.

---

[1] 'An increase in the productivity of the rural sector is the only way to assure that economic progress will become widespread.' F A O Africa, p. 3.

[2] In the middle of the eighteenth century the 'physiocrat' school of thought considered that as all income derived from land, land only should be taxed. 'Georgism' (after Henry George) was influenced by this concept, and the movement is still important in Denmark.

But under-population has its disadvantages as well. Throughout French-speaking Africa there is a series of islands of intense agricultural and economic activity, separated by vast, almost empty spaces. The cost of maintaining roads and railroads, and of transportation in general, is correspondingly higher when there are only one to fourteen inhabitants per mile, which is true in French-speaking Africa, as against forty-nine in Nigeria and 114 in France. It slows down passage to a modern money economy, without which one cannot have a modern agricultural system.

African problems can be summed up in one word: underdevelopment. Most of this study is therefore applicable to other backward tropical countries. Without industry, without resources of energy except manpower, without modern methods of cultivation and consequently without high yields, without buying power for the products of future industries, a new vicious circle forms. It should be attacked by industrialization, certainly, but it can be broken more effectively and quickly through agriculture. Progress in agriculture should not be considered as a preliminary to industrialization, but an indispensable corollary. The essential bases of an agricultural revolution are irrigation schemes, organic and mineral fertilizers, effective erosion-prevention, and the utilization of new and economical sources of energy; above all, close association of agriculture with livestock-raising. In order to accomplish this, the labour surplus must be put to work, which has not been done so far.

The conclusions of this short summary are very obvious. In Africa, natural conditions, although clearly more difficult than in Europe and America, can certainly be conquered, particularly in view of the enormous reserves of energy and minerals, and the advances possible with modern agricultural techniques. Men alone are responsible for the economic backwardness of Africa. The question is which ones, Africans or Europeans. Too many Europeans, quick to call the African 'primitive' (if not a lazy thief and liar), place the entire blame for African backwardness on him. We forget too easily that the white man exploited the African shamelessly for centuries, through slavery, colonialism and economic exploitation. Although the metropolitan countries have recently expressed a desire to stimulate economic development in Africa, emphasizing their 'generous' aid programmes, these remained for a long time – and still are – badly conceived and administered. Before I make any positive proposals, or make my criticisms of the new African leaders, I would like to discuss briefly the part played by Europe. It was often criminal in the first phases, and lately has been somewhat incoherent, despite a certain measure of good will.

CHAPTER TWO
Slavery, Colonization and Economic Exploitation

1. PRE-COLONIAL CIVILIZATIONS

African civilizations reached a kind of apogee in the fourteenth and fifteenth centuries, earlier around Benin. African blacksmiths knew how to work gold, copper, bronze and even iron, the latter as early as the time of Christ. They thus surpassed the oceanic civilizations, like those of pre-columbian America, in technical development. The system of cultivation practised at the time, working the earth with hoes after clearing it with fires, and rotation of fallow lands, is still used today with rare modifications. However, new crops have been introduced, mainly from America, like corn, manioc, peanuts, yams and, later, cocoa, which are the main foods in many regions.

Agricultural progress was greatly hindered by the absence of carts, wheels and animals to pull them.[1] The Mediterranean swing-plough would have represented a great advance over the African *daba*, or hoe. The soldiers and caravans who so often and easily crossed the Sahara at that time unfortunately did not think to bring along the basic tools of their agrarian civilization to the Nigerian and Senegalese valleys. Africa is still suffering from this oversight. The only energy available until the present day, and it is generally still true, is that of individual men and women, particularly the latter, who are weakened by sickness, parasites and malnutrition. Formerly, 'fraternities' of different age groups meant that the youth of an area could be mobilized for urgent agricultural work.

The civilization was also characterized by the existence of some

---

[1] Carts on wheels were known in Nigeria (see H. Lhote, *Fresques du Tassili*), and horses and oxen were frequently used in the savannah, though not in the forest regions because of the tsetse fly. The Belgians domesticated the elephant in the forest areas, as was done in Ceylon.

slavery, the absence of private landed property, the insignificance of trade, the concept of leisure as a full-time activity,[1] the importance of hoarding, whether it was gold, or jewels or cattle, and an almost complete lack of construction, in a permanent sense. No irrigation projects have been achieved comparable to those in Szechuan, which were accomplished before the Christian era. However, no one knows where agrarian African civilization would be today if it had been able to follow a normal development, in peaceful contact with European techniques. Alas, this development was brusquely arrested, and we are still paying for the crimes of our white ancestors, who believed that they were free to do anything, endowed as they were with 'innate superiority'.

2. THE RACE FOR SLAVES ARRESTED DEVELOPMENT

Territorial conquests in the Americas in the sixteenth and seventeenth centuries were often accompanied by the extermination of the native populations. This is what occurred in North America. Elsewhere, in Brazil for example, contact with Europeans decimated the Indians, who rapidly succumbed to the diseases transported with their conquerors. Their civilization was one of hunting, fishing and gathering food. They were less robust than the Africans, less resistant to diseases of all kinds, and they made poor slaves. Nevertheless, north-east Brazil, starting at the end of the sixteenth century, and the Caribbean in the seventeenth century, were the principal sources of overseas wealth for France, because of sugar cane production. Consequently, France preferred to cede her 'acres of snow' in Canada, the second largest country in the world, for a few little islands in the Antilles, where one could make a quick fortune.

In order to develop and exploit the rich lands of the Americas, from the Potomac to southern Brazil, the profitable slave trade was established. Estimates of the number of Africans taken as slaves from the sixteenth to the nineteenth centuries, with the maximum being taken in the seventeenth and particularly the second half of the

[1] In periods of less demographic intensity, or periods which follow an age of advanced civilization, a civilization of leisure comes into being which gives pre-eminence to social relations and customs, difficult to modify later. Thus, it has been said that it is hard to put the English to work.

eighteenth, vary from ten to twenty million. Demand ran very high: slaves were so badly treated that reproduction alone could not maintain their numbers at a constant level. Overwork and insufficient food meant a fearsomely high mortality rate. Santo Domingo, which received more African slaves than any other area, took in 2·2 million in less than fifty years. In 1763 Governor Fénélon estimated that only 600,000 were left.[1] Most of them were taken from Benin in the seventeenth and first half of the eighteenth centuries, and then from the Congo and Angola, in the second half of the eighteenth century.

One remembers also all the other victims of the slave trade, killed during the raids or the wars they brought on, or who died during the long march to the coast, in the camps awaiting transportation, and above all during the long sea voyage. The human haemorrhage thus inflicted on Africa is estimated by writers to be between 60 and 150 million men. As a result, the African continent, which in the eighteenth century had about the same population as Europe, or a fifth of the world population, today only has about a twelfth.[2]

The damaging effects of the slave trade went much further. Internal wars became profitable and multiplied, blocking political and economic development and the evolution towards large empires, and helping to dismantle those already in existence. If the Europeans had traded with the Africans on an equal basis, they would have brought them, in exchange for African products, carts and wheels, materials which could increase production. If they had also provided some education and training, the simple art of harnessing oxen, for example, instead of searching for slaves and easy money, the situation in Africa today would certainly be very different.

History cannot be remade; but this particular trade cannot be set down as a fruitful one for either side. In exchange for the slaves, gum, ivory, gold and other 'real' riches, Europe introduced Africa to knick-knacks and trinkets, loincloths, jewels and tobacco, gunpowder and firearms (obsolete models) and, worst of all, alcohol. 'From the time of the first contacts between Europeans and Africans

---

[1] Père Dieudonné Richon (a Capuchin monk), *La Traite et l'Esclavage du Congolais par les Européens*. Paris, 1929.

[2] There was a flourishing slave trade on the east coast, centred in Zanzibar, which dealt with the Middle East, but the numbers of slaves involved were far less.

on the coast, alcohol was one of the choice items in trading.'[1] Out of 193,000 francs worth of goods brought to Cotonou in the last three months of 1890 from Marseille, 134,000 francs worth were alcohols and wines (108,000 francs worth was rum). When he ceded his territory to Louis Philippe in 1843, the King of Assinie received, among other things, 'six containers of eau-de-vie of 200 litres each and two cases of liqueurs'.

3. COLONIZATION AND COLONIAL AGREEMENTS

The wars of colonial conquest, particularly towards the end of the nineteenth century, intensified an already grave situation. The military, in search of booty, promotion and personal glory, left massacres and ruin in their wake which, for the most part, served no political or military purpose. Even the trading companies protested, fearing with reason that little profit could be derived from a waste-land.

On July 28th 1895, Jules Ferry declared without a twinge of conscience that 'The Declaration of the Rights of Man was not written for the Blacks of Equatorial Africa'. General Meynier wrote more honestly: 'From the first day of their encounter, Europeans affirmed the principle of their superiority over the black race. . . . They have forced the Africans into slavery, justifying it on the basis of superior strength. . . . To open markets for their trade in Africa, they have stamped out the last vestiges of African civilization. If one compares their methods with those of the Berbers and even the Arabs, the parallel to this day does not favour the Europeans.'[2]

Doctor Bartoume-Moussa, of the Central African Republic, writes that 'the situation of the Central African Republic, gravely affected by the slave raids of the Arabs, was worsened in 1900 by forced portage and paddling on the rivers, the extortions of guards, the recruitment of labourers for the construction of the Congo-Ocean railroad, the harvesting of rubber and wax, cultivation of cotton, malnutrition and sleeping sickness.'[3] Apropos of portage, André

---

[1] H. Bismuth and C. Ménage, Report to the Haut Comité d'Etude et d'Information sur l'Alcoolisme (Dans les Etats Francophones d'Afrique Occidentale), Paris, 1960.

[2] Captain H. Meynier, L'Afrique Noire. Paris, 1911.

[3] From an unpublished report made in 1960.

Gide, in *Voyage au Congo*, wrote of the terrible price paid by the Mangia tribe for colonial trade. He felt that an official report written in 1902 by the regional administrator spoke for itself: 'For the last year the situation has been getting more and more difficult. The Mangias are worn out, and have no longer the ability or the will to do anything. They prefer anything, even death, to portage. . . . Dispersion of tribes has been going on for more than a year. Villages are breaking up, families are scattering, everyone abandons his tribe, village, family and plot to live in the bush, like a wild animal, in order to escape being recruited. No more cultivation, no more food. . . . Famine occurs, and in these last months the Mangias have been dying by the hundreds of hunger and misery.'

A fairly conservative author (he proposed as late as 1952 that French Equatorial Africa be called 'Equatorial African France') has written of the huge concession areas in the Congo: 'Time has condemned the refusal of the monopoly companies to make long-term investments, and to comprehend the vital necessity for them, even more than the principle of the monopoly company itself. The failure on the social level was that of the concessionary régime; the economic error was to have believed in fabulous riches, easily obtainable, and in very cheap manpower; on a more modest level, to have believed in huge ivory production; to have misunderstood its role as a sign of wealth and a means of saving; to have taken for the flow of production what was in reality the liquidation of assets. . . . The railroad works lasted fifteen years. Undertaken without much mechanical equipment, confided to jobbers whose manpower was supplied by forcible recruitment and the transfer of Ubangi and Chad tribes with horrifying indifference to matters of hygiene and food, they exacted a murderous toll. . . . André Gide's voyage revealed many of the less excusable abuses and hastened the liquidation of the concessionary régimes and of portage.'[1]

Let me end here with a quotation from an Englishman of the Romantic period: 'The barbarisms and the atrocities perpetrated by the so-called Christians in every area of the world and on all the peoples they have been able to subjugate have no parallel in any

[1] H. Zieglé, *Afrique Equatoriale Française*. Berber-Levrault, 1952.

other era of world history, in any other race, however savage, coarse, pitiless or shameless it may have been.'[1]

After the conquest, the era of colonial 'peace' began, characterized by servility. Only the most extreme docility was tolerated by the Europeans. I lived through it in Tonkin from 1929 to 1932. However, the period was not without its benefits. Teaching began – very tentatively, I admit – to spread. By 1945 it had reached more than 5 per cent of the average population in the French territories. The battle against the great endemic diseases was carried out with undeniable successes, reversing the population trend, which had been stagnant, at times regressive. Gabon had a million inhabitants at the beginning of the century, and does not have half that number now. Unfortunately, agricultural production did not progress as quickly, except for several cash crops. The desire to improve the nutrition of the Africans and to develop industry was not much in evidence. On the plantations, conflicting types of advice were given the African peasants. Often when there is a rapid turnover in an office, each administrator wants to impose his own particular ideas, often based on scanty technical knowledge.[2]

For a long time technical services were maintained on a skeleton basis. There was one engineer, later two, in Tonkin from 1929–1932 in charge of raising the level of rice cultivation for a million families, on $2\frac{1}{2}$ million acres of rice fields. Forced labour in the mines and on the plantations for a pitifully low wage hardly encouraged the men to work harder. I shall discuss later the error involved in forcing crops on people, as was done with cotton in French Equatorial Africa.

On the credit side, railroads, ports and roads were built, facilitating the growth of trade on a less unilateral basis. New crops, such as peanuts, cotton, coffee, cocoa, bananas and others were substituted for wild, uncultivated food supplies. Imported goods began to include a larger number of more useful products, such as sugar and cotton goods. But the proportion of alcohol brought to Africa grew steadily, and the economic framework was still that of 'treaty trade', and economic exploitation, defined by Jean Dresch[3] as follows: 'In

---

[1] W. W. Howitt, *Colonisation and Christianity*. London, 1838.
[2] Their mentality derives from that prevalent in the 'Arab Bureau', well analysed by Vincent Monteil in *Esprit*, November, 1961.
[3] 'Questions Ouest-Africaines', *Boletim cultural da Guiné Portuguesa*, January, 1950.

essence, it consists of taking out of a country its export products and selling imported products to the native population which has received money for the exports. It is a very elementary circle in which the market, in so far as is possible, is in the hands of the mother country, and the colony is condemned to produce only raw goods without manufacturing them at home.' He has also shown the important role played by capital invested in trade (38 per cent), which easily surpassed that of plantation investments (18·8 per cent), of exploitation of the forests (12·5 per cent) and of the mines (7·5 per cent) in the French colonies in Africa in 1945.[1] It is often thought that trade of this kind belongs to a period that has run its course, as if it has disappeared. A quick trip to Madagascar in the summer of 1961 convinced me that this is far from the case.

4. ECONOMIC EXPLOITATION – THE MALAGASY EXAMPLE

In December of 1949, in the northern Congo (then Belgian), I picked up an alarm clock I wanted to buy in a little Greek shop. The proprietor quickly grabbed it out of my hands, saying: 'That's a treaty article, it only works for a few days.' But it was sold to the Congolese at the same price as good European clocks. The next month, in Chad, I calculated that one hour of work for a cotton labourer would bring him about three-tenths of an inch of ordinary cotton cloth; a hundred hours for a yard, and three hundred hours or fifty days for a miserable little swatch three yards long.

In 1960 Father Boltz formed a 'pre-co-operative' association at Ambalavo, near Fianarantsoa in Madagascar, in order to protect 'his' peasants from the veritable 'gang' of raw rice buyers. Since the membership card read '*Coopérative d'achat et de vente Patrie*' (Fatherland Buying and Selling Co-operative), the buyers managed to insinuate, not without success, that the Father wanted to 'sell' the Fatherland. For a while they overpaid for the rice in order to ruin the co-operative, resorting to the classic trick of leaning on the scales. They were known to give out a cake or an apple, rare treats for poor peasants, for each basket of rice. The report of Father Boltz reads, in summary: 'Extraordinary as it may seem, the sub-prefecture rose

[1] *Bulletin de l'Association des géographes français.* March–April, 1946.

against us, to protect far from legitimate interests. . . . The police subjected us to endless investigations. We paid ten CFA[1] francs for a kilogram of raw rice, but as soon as we stopped buying the price fell to eight and seven francs. On the other hand, we had to pay twenty-three francs for peanuts which sold formerly for fifteen francs or less.'

The co-operative also sells consumer goods. 'A coverlet sold by the association for 2·005 francs cost 4·5 francs in the Chinese shops.' I wrote in *Afrique-Action*, October 21st 1961, that the chief buyer in Fianarantsoa for the *Société Rochefortaise* refuses to weigh the pigs when he buys them, saying ' "It isn't done". His estimate usually runs 20 or 30 pounds below the real weight, this for pigs weighing 150 to 200 pounds.' As a result of the article the Director of the Fianarantsoa branch of the Société was replaced. Times are changing at last.

During the summer of 1961 I sought in vain for a long time – and I cannot even divulge how I finally obtained it – for a book by R. Gendarme entitled *L'Économie de Madagascar*. Although it was published by the *Centre d'Études Économiques*, a part of the *Institut des Hautes Études*, now the University of Madagascar, and contained a preface by the Director of Higher Education, the work disappeared in a few days from book-store windows in Tananarive. It was said that the Malagasy Government had forbidden its sale, but government officials to whom I spoke denied this. Others attributed it to the intervention of a VIP in France, or to massive purchases on the part of the great trading associations, whose parasitic role is clearly shown in the book, which is an excellent work. The French editor refused to put the remaining 300 copies on sale and consequently the book cannot be found in Paris either. The university chair which had been promised to the author was withdrawn.

In the diagram on the next page, Gendarme shows how closely the great trading companies (Rochefort, Lyon, Marseille), the banks (Madagascar, BCNI), the sugar refineries and plantations, and the shipping companies are interconnected. He denounces the excessively high shipping charges, which effectively block econo-

[1] The CFA was formerly the *Colonies Françaises d'Afrique*, and is now the *Communauté Financière Africaine*. The CFA franc is worth two new centimes, two old francs.

2*

I. Diagram of Interrelationships between the Large Companies

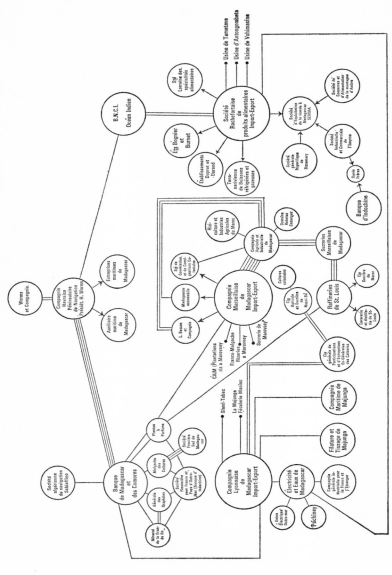

A line indicates a director shared by two companies, an arrow shows capital participation, a dot indicates a factory belonging to a company. Taken from *L'Économie de Madagascar*, Paris, 1960. Reproduced with the permission of the author, R. Gendarme.

mic expansion. These charges are maintained by a 'conference' between the shipping carriers (Messageries Maritimes, Havraise Peninsulaire, Scandinavian East Africa Line), 'which, from the economist's point of view, present all the characteristics of a monopoly. . . . The explanation for the prohibitive price of electricity, for the enormous trade margins (often 100 per cent), for the disorganization of local production – does it not reside in the action of the Companies, who thus do a grave disservice to France and to western civilization?' And he concludes that 'we find here, several centuries later, a virtually unchanged replica of the East India Company operations.'[1]

After my 1958 trip to Madagascar, I recommended a severe programme of technical modernization. In 1961 I was reproached, with reason, for not tying this to modernization of the trade structure. The peasant labour which had been freed for other work by modern methods was benefiting virtually no one but 'commercial adventurers' and their agents. There is little incentive for a worker to step up his efforts if business is the only beneficiary. In most African countries an efficient system to control trade and exports scarcely exists (except for the Marketing Boards in Ghana and Nigeria, which I will discuss later). Yet such a system is sorely needed, if modernization of agriculture is to take place.[2]

Chinese merchants on the east coast often buy coffee with a *kapoka*, or empty concentrated milk can. All they have to do is put a hand around the top of the can and bang it down to increase by a fifth the amount of coffee needed to fill it. Public scales were installed in one of the markets, which gave out tickets with the weight printed on them. For a week, the merchants in the market reweighed all the lots brought them and said to the suppliers: 'The scales of the *Fanja-kana* (administration) are wrong. They show 50 pounds, and you really have 55.' And thus, at the price of a few small

---

[1] The only aspect of the book I can find fault with is a trace of political paternalism. He writes 'Why not have a Christian democracy in Madagascar? We can see no other alternative, unless one cares to opt for force.' Gendarme is at the very least naive, if he expects a Christian democracy of the type known in Europe (even more apt to fail in Africa than at home) to bring into line the trading powers he is attacking.

[2] In the Northern Cameroons, where it has a monopoly on trade, the CFDT, or Compagnie Française pour le Développement des Textiles, is the only French counterpart to the Marketing Boards.

sacrifices, they made sure that no one wanted to use the 'suspect' scales the following week.

The next month the Chinese again cheated on weight, in the multiplication of weight by price, and by means of the mass of small tickets on the counter, which no one has the time to verify. Above and beyond this, they make extra profits by selling 'treaty' goods to their coffee suppliers. At Amboata Boeni, near the west coast, if a government group is paying 29 CFA francs for a kilo of peanuts, a *Karana* (Pakistani) group says it will buy at 32 francs, but in reality ends up paying 22. More and more the peasant is beginning to realize that he is being cheated, but he says nothing, because he cannot get along without the loans advanced against the coming harvest by the agent, at exorbitant rates. Normalization of trade will have to be accompanied by widespread use of modern credit and savings systems.

Europeans and Asians have not cornered the market on these swindles. Negro buyers cheat the peasants on the west coast on deliveries of palm oil. Even 'honest' trading cannot help but slow down development if it dominates the entire economy. It seeks exports, with a view to augmenting imports, which bring in even greater profits for it. But accelerated development requires a great deal more machinery and equipment, which means the reduction, if not the elimination of luxury imports, such as large private cars, wine and liquor, and the rapid substitution of local products for the great majority of imported foodstuffs and consumer goods, particularly cotton goods.

The dominance of commercial capital over industrial capital is a primary characteristic of underdevelopment. It is one of the evils held over from the days of treaty relations and economic exploitation, and constitutes the central obstacle to the development of the African economy. After the phase of 'exploitation', which dominated the beginning of colonialism, the Brazzaville Conference of 1944 thought it necessary to compensate for its opposition to all forms of 'decolonization',[1] by stepping up efforts to supply the colonies with

[1] An extract from the declaration drawn up at the Conference reads: 'The purposes of the civilizing work accomplished by France in her colonies obviate all possibility of autonomy or of evolution outside the French Empire. The eventual formation of self-governments in the colonies, even in the distant future, is to be avoided.'

equipment. They also bestowed on them the title of 'Overseas France'. By a change in terminology, France hoped to resolve problems that were more political than economic. Let us examine what has been accomplished by the *Fonds d'Investissements pour le Développement Économique et Social*, better known by its initials, FIDES.[1]

[1] The French, of course, have no monopoly on the evils of colonialism. The English grabbed the Kikuyu highlands in Kenya, which were undeveloped at the time, but the population increase stifled the Kikuyus on their reserve and led to the Mau Mau revolt. Portuguese policy has been the worst, leading to forced labour in Angola, starvation wages, and systematic colonization of the high plateaux (Nova Lisboa) with Portuguese settlers, in order to eliminate the Africans. This led to the concession of 'metropolitan' status, the last colonial hypocrisy. Workers originally from Spanish Guinea laboured on the cocoa plantations in Fernando Poó and São Tomé for appallingly low salaries, because the ocean prevented them from returning to their villages. Englishmen and Greeks took over enormous tracts of land in North-eastern Tanganyika for very extensive sisal plantations.

The Unilever trust developed some excellent plantations at Leverville, in the ex-Belgian Congo, but also owned other companies: *Compagnie du Niger Français* in Upper Volta, R. W. King Ltd in the Cameroons, United Africa Company in Nigeria, still another name in Dahomey. Its subsidiary in Chad, S C K N, controlled 70 per cent of that country's imports, with high trade margins, particularly in areas where it operated alone. For the ex-Belgian Congo read M. Merlier's article, 'La question agraire au Congo,' *Economie et Politique*, March, 1961.

CHAPTER THREE
The FIDES era, of aid often wasted

1. DANGEROUS EMPHASIS ON 'INFRASTRUCTURE'

Within the framework of F I D E S very large sums were granted to French-speaking Africa. In face of the immense needs, however, they seemed quite modest. The aid could in fact have been increased many times without a corresponding tax pressure, had France had the courage politically to decolonize more rapidly. Forty-six per cent of the F I D E S grants, particularly in the first four-year plan, were used to build roads, ports and airports. These were indispensable to open up the countries, but could have been achieved at less cost.

North of Bangui in Central Africa, the highway to Chad was more than doubled in width in January, 1950, although the traffic load in no way justified it. In Senegal roads are generally tarred, and just wide enough for one car. In order to pass, each car puts two wheels on the outside bank, which is made of stone or hard earth. So few cars pass that the necessary braking is justified by the money saved.

One sees far too many little ports in Madagascar. The Schneider pier in the port at Majunga was built (1938) in such a way that it blocked alluvial flow from the Betsiboka. Soon the site of the future port was totally enveloped in mud. Even though it was not one of the prestigious Public Works, a protective jetty could have been built to prevent silting, on the river side and not the inverse. The choice of a port other than the mouth of a river choked up with alluvium could have been examined. 'The port at Majunga is the prototype of the kind of development error not to commit in underdeveloped countries,' Gendarme concludes in *L'Economie de Madagascar*.

China and the U S S R are certainly not exempt from errors in agriculture. Nevertheless, the average return on Chinese agricultural projects is double that of India's, according to some estimates. The average economic interest on F I D E S investments is probably less than India's.

The basic error of F I D E S was the primacy it gave to the 'social' sector. Its aim was to bring French Africa up to France's level right away, without taking into consideration the vast difference in economic development and standard of living. This difference was often as much as 15 or 20 to 1. The Lycée at Tamatave, the Lomé hospital, and numbers of stadiums, town halls and schools at all levels display such luxury, in contrast to the average African building, that future African teachers are not willing to set up in a simple hut, after what they have been used to. The village primary school of the type built by F I D E S, which includes an apartment for the teacher, is such as to make the district head green with envy.[1] The furniture, imported at great cost, could have been made by local artisans out of woven palm from the lower Ivory Coast. This would also have helped cut down on rural unemployment.

In Guinea, Mali and Morocco there is a deep-rooted desire for education and public health. It would be easy to persuade African villagers to build their own schools and clinics. If they did so, the money saved could mean secondary routes, and, more important, land improvements and later on factories. Lodged more simply, the village teacher would be less apt to look down on the villagers, an attitude which only sharpens the social divisions in the villages. India[2] provides a glaring example of what happens when comfort and well-being are given priority over production increases: a tragic economic impasse, scarcity on the verge of famine, a slow-down in economic development. China has received a great deal less aid from the Soviet Union than has Africa from Europe, and it has been in credits, not outright grants. Emphasis was placed on factory equipment and raw materials, not school and highway construction. Tropical Africa can never catch up to China in this century if it continues to hold itself aloof from the economic imperatives of development.

[1] According to T. Balogh, the same situation prevails in the former British colonies. See 'Education in Africa' in his *The Economics of Poverty*. Weidenfeld and Nicolson, 1966.
[2] *Lands Alive*, Merlin Press, London, 1964.

Any policy which prides itself on its 'social' orientation in a backward country is sacrificing the hope of increasing production in order to gain immediate satisfactions. In the long run, it is anti-social. Monetary resources will soon dry up, since no local wealth is created to pay schoolteachers and nurses, buy equipment and medicines, and replace the youth taken from the fields. Improvements in social welfare could be financed by the beneficiaries themselves, who contribute their labour. In this way, schools and hospitals, and other 'social' benefits will be the result of development, and be considered in a sense as a reward.

2. THE SPREAD OF ALCOHOLISM

Before the arrival of the Europeans, Africans drank only fermented beverages with a very low alcoholic content. Palm and raffia wine contain Vitamin C and have about 4 per cent alcohol; millet or maize beer average around 3·5 per cent alcohol and also contain protids and Vitamin B12. It would be better, certainly, to eat boiled mashed millet, particularly in periods of want. In Chad, where a third of the harvested grains end up in the brewery, want is particularly severe in the period preceding the harvest. Palm wine can also be consumed before fermentation, as is done sometimes in the Ivory Coast during periods of intensive rice cultivation. Fermented fruit juices contain less than 1 per cent alcohol, and are a very 'healthy' drink.

Alcoholism was the first 'gift' presented to Africa by Europe. The situation became far more serious when stills were introduced in Dahomey in 1922 by Sodabi. Palm alcohol is still known by the name of its dangerous popularizer, who brought stills from France as yet another of the benefits of the First World War. From then on Africans distilled maize and manioc beer in the Cameroons, banana beer in Ruanda-Urundi, and even sugar water.

After 1949 increases in wine and liquor imports took on frightening proportions. In 1951 fifteen times more liquor was imported to French West Africa than in 1938, over three-quarters of a million gallons of pure alcohol. 1954 was a peak year for wine, the equivalent of 350,000 gallons of pure alcohol being imported. In 1953 8 per cent of the Ivory Coast imports and 9·6 per cent of Dahomey imports were alcoholic beverages. Wine and liquor monopolized 10 to 20 per cent of the urban budgets of the Ivory Coast in 1954. In French Equatorial Africa, the Cameroons and Madagascar, imports of alcoholic beverages continue to increase. In Madagascar they hold second place, to the disadvantage of needed machinery and equipment.

Since then heavy taxes and a fall in the price of coffee have at times reduced these imports, notably in the Ivory Coast. Local drinks profited thereby, also 'European' beers of high alcoholic content, which are being brewed locally to an increasing extent. A higher degree of intoxication has become the habit now, and only buying power limits consumption. It increases with every arrival of money; veterans' pensions play a big role. The buying season for peanuts, coffee or cocoa profits mostly the wine merchants and dealers.

Traditional fermented drinks were produced by the family and consumed mainly at traditional festivals and gatherings. Now they have become an object of trade, transported everywhere, and cabarets have made an appearance, particularly in richer areas. Every day of the year, depending on the region, they sell palm wine, millet beer or imported drinks. The effect on general health has been disquieting, and the economic effects even more important. Marriages and funerals cost considerable amounts of money, taken out of savings accounts and improvements, particularly in South Dahomey. The largest expense is for liquor.

In Chad, agricultural overseers are often incapable of any serious work after a not very advanced age, because they have become alcoholics. A good number of alcoholic civil servants draw their salaries for years before being dismissed.

The influence of Europeans living in the colonies was a determining factor in promoting alcoholism, as drinking was a mark of prestige. H. Bismith and C. Ménage (*op. cit.*, Chapter II) add: 'At the same time one must recognize the power of the wine merchants, and realize that big business in these countries has important interests involved (e.g., their relation to Bordeaux). . . . An officially sanctioned view points out the dangers of forcing the consumer to drink the "dangerous" local drinks if imported beverages are taxed (although taxing alcohol is the best way to counteract alcoholism). . . . Wine merchants and chambers of commerce are apt to encourage these arguments.' The same study discusses the particularly unfortunate effects of alcoholism in civil servants:

'Civil servants are exempt from the two factors that usually cut down alcoholism: buying power, and to a lesser extent, religion. Buying power applies to all, whatever post they may be holding; and if Islam is their religion, its teachings are watered down because they have chosen to live in a region usually far from their original home, and are detribalized, in a sense. This group pays a heavy toll for its alcoholism, proportionately to other levels of the population. At Fann 46 per cent of the African alcoholics are civil servants. Six per cent of the civil servants seen by the Board of Health in the Ivory Coast and Upper Volta are there for alcoholism.

'Aside from the obvious consequences, from the burden on the nation represented by these alcoholics (the large numbers on convalescent leave), their condition seriously affects the life of the nation, because along with those whose intoxication has caused behaviour incompatible with their work, are many others who are only mildly affected, but whose work suffers as a consequence. Yet they are responsible to the public. The consequences of alcoholism are increased when it impairs the leading class; even if it is only a minority, the crucial role it plays must be taken into consideration. Let us add, by the way, that the consumption of these drinks by civil servants in Moslem countries is largely responsible for the spread of alcohol into these regions.'

Areas most affected by alcoholism are southern Dahomey, mostly with palm alcohol; southern Ivory Coast, southern Cameroons, and Souanké in the Republic of the Congo (Brazzaville), thanks to income from coffee and cocoa; and the Bobo and Diola areas, where millet beer consumption is very high. The urban populations hold the record, though, being 'privileged' even from this point of view, and in urban areas civil servants head the list. Since their alcoholism is a serious obstacle to African development, their high salaries, which make it possible, appear in an even worse light.

The amount of money tied up in alcoholic beverages has never been estimated, but it is clearly enormous. Add to local breweries the tankers, 50,000 to 500,000 gallons each, the tank-cars, which replaced the old barrels, and all the distribution facilities. The flood of red wine pouring into the shanty towns is not an edifying sight either. Since the European is largely responsible for it, he has little to be proud of, particularly as he continues to set a bad example to African *élites* by having whisky and champagne parties. The growth of African resources through FIDES was in large measure sterilized by alcohol.

3. THE NEGLECT OF INDUSTRY

Until late 1961, FIDES and later FAC, the *Fonds d'Aide et de Coopération* which replaced it in 1959, granted money only for research, agricultural production and the 'infrastructure' of society. The absence of any department for industry[1] was very revealing, as the kind of aid involved could only prolong the 'raw material' economy of Africa.

I proposed in June, 1961, to the FAC directors that they consider revising the principles by which they granted credits. I felt that they should reduce aid to prop up tottering budgets and expenses for infrastructure, and increase grants for agricultural units, vocational training, and above all, industrialization. 'Before we can think in those terms, we must initiate exhaustive studies,' they replied. Granted, but a number of studies could have been made since 1947.

Their attitude reminded me of Jules Méline, who spoke before the annual meeting of the Association of Industry and Agriculture on March 8th 1899. He wanted 'to discourage in advance any signs of industrial development in our colonies, to oblige our overseas possessions to look exclusively to the mother country for manufactured products, and to fulfil, by force if necessary, their natural function, that of a market reserved by right to the mother country's industry'.[2] Today it should be clear to everyone that trade between a developed nation and a developing nation increases rapidly. The United States sells more to Canada, with its 15 million inhabitants, than to Latin America, which has 225 million. You cannot call a country a market when it is more like a counter over which certain goods are traded.

[1] I shall discuss later how difficult it is to get industry to develop spontaneously. Chapter VIII, 1 and 3.
[2] Quoted by H. Brunschwig, *Mythe et Réalités de L'Impérialisme colonial français.* Méline was a protectionist Minister of Agriculture.

The great commercial associations earn a great deal more, and more easily, from trade than from industry. In Madagascar's 1959–1962 Three Year Plan, only 2 per cent of the credits involved were designed to create industries. It will be indeed unfortunate if we must resign ourselves to watching the trading position of tropical countries become increasingly unfavourable. The buying power of their agricultural exports, spread thin for equipment and manufactured products, will continue to diminish if they remain vassalized producers of raw materials. The balkanization of western Africa and the current economic situation do not favour the growth of industries, yet they are the essential basis of economic independence. Somehow the situation must be modified, as it has no fixed or sacred character. First, let us examine several of the agricultural projects initiated by F I D E S.

4. HIGH COST OF THE LARGE IRRIGATION PROJECTS. NIGER OFFICE

The Niger Office was established in the pre-war period, before F I D E S, but F I D E S has always provided a good part of its funds. In March, 1961, total expenditures, re-evaluated in francs of that year, were estimated to be around 22,000 million C F A francs. This sum had produced 120,000 irrigated acres, villages for the settlers, roads, and an industrial complex (Markala, Niono). The basic constructions like the Sansanding dam and the large canals were not being utilized at anywhere near their capacity (the possibility of irrigating $2\frac{1}{2}$ million acres had been envisaged), so it was logical to try to extend the irrigated area.

It cost 275,000 C F A francs to irrigate $2\frac{1}{2}$ acres, not counting basic construction costs, for the dam and large canals. The average yield at the time was a little less than 4,000 pounds of raw rice, which sold for about 4 francs a pound, or 1,300 pounds of cottonseed, which sold at 30 francs. Let us say, then, that the gross profit was 3,600 francs per acre, 6·5 per cent of the investment. Businessmen estimate that if anticipated annual gross income is not more than a third of the investment, then the investment is not worthwhile. Europe, however, has capital to spare, and the $33\frac{1}{3}$ per cent figure, although it may be a useful index there, is too low for a young African country. Furthermore, some of the FIDES money was a straight subsidy, as maintenance costs were put under the heading of 'new works', because the credit-debit balance of the Niger Office was negative. The enterprise as a whole was typically bureaucratic, born of topographical considerations – water flows by itself – and lacked serious agronomic studies. More important, it was initiated without the desire or approval of the local population, which manifested decided hostility to it, like the Beni-Amir of Tadla in Morocco. As a result, it could be considered a failure by 1958, a good argument in favour of the capitalist thesis that 'the state is incapable of running an enterprise.'

The first settlers on the project were volunteers 'appointed' by village chiefs, who thus disposed of their enemies or difficult elements. As colonial authority weakened, peasants had to be induced to settle. On their arrival, they were given provisions to last until the next harvest, and a house. They had to pay an irrigation tax, but it was not sufficient to cover costs of maintaining the irrigation system. Work was done with tractors, with increasing difficulty, as the irrigation eventually hardened the soil. Harvests were shockingly low. Rice crops became invaded with varieties of wild rice and other weeds, and decreased rapidly. The deficit was even more striking in the section of mechanized rice cultivation at Molodo. The reaping and threshing machines cracked the over-ripe grains, and machine-finishing yielded mostly broken grains, much less valuable than whole rice.

A more intelligent solution would have been to furnish only provisions to the settlers in advance, and have them build their own houses during the dead season, which lasts for six months here. Such a vast enterprise should never have been undertaken until thorough experiments with crop techniques had been made,[1] as at Gezirah in the Sudan.

5. ADVANTAGES OF SMALL IRRIGATION PROJECTS

A complete irrigation network was thus installed on the dead delta of the Niger, aimed at total mastery of the water, at great expense.

[1] Appendix I is a discussion of the Richard Toll Project in Senegal.

Until recently the drainage was so defective that cotton output was kept at a very low level. Meanwhile, loans became smaller as wisdom penetrated, and the Agricultural Services began to study the shallow basins along both banks of the Niger, which are separated from the river by alluvial deposits forming almost continuous lines of 'padding'.

They had only to fill in the gaps between these natural embankments and install a few regulated sluice gates to control, partially, the annual flooding of the river. They thus greatly increased the areas under water, and the rice planted there had a much higher output; yields reached practically a ton of raw rice per 2½ acres. The cost of this project varied from 10,000 to 35,000 CFA francs per 2½ acres; return on investment was thus far higher than from the Niger Office project. It could have been raised still further if the local population, the ultimate beneficiary, had been induced to play an active role. Since the local peasants only cultivate on dry land, as opposed to land inundated by irrigation, they can only work during the six months of the rainy season. If they went to work during those six unemployed months, they could contribute a great deal.

FERDES (*Fonds d'Équipement Rural et de Développement Économique et Social*) asked future beneficiaries to furnish a third of the total expense of the planned irrigation projects, by providing free labour. The colony and France each provided a third also. But the Department of Agricultural Engineering, interested in fulfilling its part of the Plan, argued that unpaid work was very unpopular, particularly as the people did not understand its purpose. They evoked the spectre of forced labour for the whites, which had only been abolished ten or twelve years before.

Young engineers tried to reconcile these contradictory needs by 'interpreting' the FERDES regulations. North of Ferkessédougou, in the Ivory Coast near Upper Volta, they opened central drainage ditches in the small valleys, in order to accelerate evacuation of the heavy rains and reduce the duration of flooding. Dams were placed at regular intervals along the drainage ditches which supplied, at the end of the rainy season, a useful complement to irrigation works on rice-growing valleys. The cost was higher than along the Niger, but much less than the Niger Office project. And better water control enabled good farmers to attain a level of two tons of raw rice per 2½ acres.

In order to attract peasant labour to the project, they offered 100 CFA francs a day, a salary a third lower than that given by SMIG in the Ivory Coast. They got as many workers as they could desire. In the agricultural dead season, traditionally the time for government projects, there are very few offers of work for peasants, and these usually pay only sixty to eighty francs a day. But when the projects were finished, many of those who helped build them refused to settle on the reclaimed land, and the valleys, though irrigated, are nowhere near used to capacity. The peasants are not willing to help maintain the projects, which they consider the property of the State. They will not have the feeling of 'joint-ownership' unless they work long and hard on a project, without salary.

Western ideas regarding property do not exist in tropical Africa. It is still true, however, that a certain amount of 'finishing' is necessary to make irrigation works as productive as possible. After each rice field is levelled it must be surrounded with a small embankment. This retains a uniform level of water before and during the flowering of the rice; from seven to ten inches is the norm for good harvests. The African peasant is unwilling to make this effort, and this is understandable, since custom dictates that land be redistributed each time it is cleared again (this is for dry crops, the only traditional ones). He therefore has no guarantee of prolonged use of the land he has laboured to improve. I have heard that the situation is even worse in Upper Volta, where hundreds of acres of land have controlled irrigation systems, yet are still, years after the projects were finished, almost totally abandoned.

If the peasants can be induced to participate voluntarily in such projects, costs will be reduced, many more projects can be undertaken for the same amount of money, and rural development will be speeded up. This will also be the best guarantee of full utilization and optimum effectiveness. No peasant will contribute his labour if he is not anxious to benefit from it afterwards. However, 'labour investments' of this kind require a political environment different from that of 'dying' colonialism or independence deliberately favouring a privileged class.

CHAPTER FOUR
Too many tractors and coffee plants, not enough oil palms and food crops

I. THE PITFALLS OF EARLY MECHANIZATION

Right after the war the English were eager to put an end to rationing of cooking fats and oils, and started a 'Groundnuts Scheme' in the Tanganyika savannah; very poorly planned it was, too. Entrusted to a general, using in part material salvaged from Pacific beaches and too expensive to maintain, the scheme was undertaken in natural surroundings which were soon found to be very unsuitable for the crop. The climate was too dry, the soil quickly hardened, and the venture swallowed up 35 million pounds sterling. It was quickly abandoned.[1]

The French peanut project was decided on in 1947, and the Compagnie Générale des Oléagineux Tropicaux (C G O T) was installed in the centre of Casamance in Senegal, not far from the Casamance River, in a wooded savannah area depopulated by sleeping-sickness. The idea was to mechanize the entire process of cultivation, with the help of American equipment, and using methods originally developed for the fields and hills of Virginia, which have been under cultivation for a long time. In order to amortize the cost of a central repair shop, necessary in such barren country, it was proposed that an area of 75,000 acres be developed. The project was conducted with more concern for speed than for economy. The anchor chain of the defunct *Normandie* was purchased to fell the trees. Technicians, recruited in great numbers, soon made of Sefa the 'seventh white

---

[1] Extracting the roots of felled trees also proved terribly expensive. The Conservatives, on coming into power, liquidated the whole operation under the worst possible conditions.

city in Senegal'. The heads of C G O T boasted of this, although more than anything it betrayed the enormity of their expenses.

As early as December, 1947, alerted by the difficulties involved in mechanizing sections of Moroccan agriculture, which I had studied the previous summer, I in vain counselled prudence to these directors. Called back in November of 1950 to study the first results on the spot, I instantly recommended that they pull in their belts, stop the 'haemorrhage' of expenditure and proceed more slowly. It was relatively easy to demonstrate the cost of their haste. The soil, inadequately prepared, eroded quickly if the slope was more than 1·5 per cent. The scraping and hauling involved in felling trees, and too deep ploughing, brought up barren subsoil to the surface, which had to be improved with vast quantities of fertilizer.

In this wooded savannah, numbers of roots of trees remained in the ground, hampering the operation of delicate mechanized equipment. Fast-growing weeds spread quickly and smothered the crops. The uprooting brought on other disappointments, due to the irregularity of the October rains, which either hardened the dry ground or rotted the seeds in wet earth. In this same central Casamance, where no agronomic research has ever been done, a high level agricultural factory was established, before production techniques had been perfected. It was not put into the hands of agronomists, however, because it was a question of agriculture![1] Africans were turned away from the project, and only admitted as salaried employees.

Total expenses exceeded three billion old francs. The only positive results, the perfecting of several techniques, could have been obtained at an infinitely lower cost. Since then, C G O T has maintained a policy of using local peasants to cultivate peanuts, a more intelligent solution that cuts down the losses. The deficit could have been eliminated had ploughs been used instead of tractors, and draught animals used to pull them. Rice cultivation, which alternates with the peanut crop, still has the larger deficit, because it is still

---

[1] The *Institut d'Etudes Politiques*, the *Ecole Polytechnique*, and the *Ecole Navale* supplied the three top directors in 1950. The failure of the English scheme might have taught them something, because it was far more expensive. But contacts between colonial experts were rare and frowned on. They are not always encouraged by directors today. 'Each man looks only to himself, and is wrapped in a cocoon of vanity and error,' concludes J. Guillard.

entirely mechanized. Two tons per 2½ acres are needed to break even; from 1956 to 1961 the average yield was about a ton and a half.

The problem of mechanization is crucial, because African *élites* are seduced by the idea of modern machines. It is difficult to convince them that agricultural progress does not depend on immediate and complete mechanization. In Guinea, the Soviet experts have used this tendency to their advantage.[1] 'How can peasants make any progress with the *daba*? Why should we not relieve them of this hardship?' It is not that mechanization is impossible on African soil. Machines will be in wide use in the future. But there are still too many obstacles. I will discuss later ways to get around them.

Forests cleared for cultivation by peasants have roots left in the soil and large unburned tree trunks on the ground. 'They look more like a battlefield than a Belgian field,' a Belgian agronomist in the Congo told me. The savannah also has numerous bushes and shrubs. The fragile topsoil is quickly destroyed by machines, as has been the case in the tobacco plantations in the northern Republic of the Congo (Brazzaville). The price of buying modern equipment and transporting it into the bush is high. If the whole African countryside were mechanized at once, the governments would be completely without foreign exchange to equip factories.[2] Yet factories, safe under their roofs, operate year round, while tractors, particularly in the tropics, can often work only a few weeks out of the year. Highly qualified mechanics are needed to maintain them. These are still largely Europeans, and therefore expensive. Above all, tractors increase rural unemployment.

Use of tractors has been uneconomical everywhere: In Boulel-Kaffrine, the centre of mechanized peanut cultivation in Senegal, where they still scrape off the topsoil when they fell trees; at Loudima in the Congo; on the rice plantations in the Niger valley (Guinea, Mali, Niger) and the Logone valley (Chad, the Cameroons) and at the C R A M in Madagascar. From 1945–1950 the tractor was thought capable of solving all the agricultural problems of the Africans. In actual fact, it allows you to produce a peanut crop at a

[1] *Lands Alive*, Chapter XII.
[2] Cf. 'Réconversion Agricole de la Guinée', *Cahiers du Tiers-Monde*, 1961. And yet Ghana and Nigeria want to assemble their own tractors.

much higher cost in local currency than with the *daba* and manpower alone. The amount of foreign exchange necessary to mechanize an independent country, with an independent monetary system and a subsistence economy, which exports very little (Guinea), would be much more disastrous.

Current economic policy in Africa is unhealthy because it relies on foreign aid. 'This money didn't cost us anything, who cares if it doesn't bring in much.' Development demands that it bring in a great deal. A whole series of agricultural and general advances must be made before mechanization can logically be introduced. On the other hand, draught animals, wherever feasible, present only advantages, and can achieve the intermediate stage in agriculture, often the most useful and indispensable.

2. RESEARCH SUCCESSES: PEANUTS AND OIL PALMS

As a former 'colonial' agronomist, I know how difficult it is to achieve results on the spot. I also know how critical representatives from France can be who come down for a little overseas tour. The grand ideas behind these huge projects, and the men who spread them, are much more at fault than my colleagues in the technical services. The entirely specific nature of the laws that rule economies on the threshold of development is just beginning to become clear. In the 'pre-independent' phase, those that succeeded the best were those with open minds.

Their task was easier, because they didn't have to convince the peasants in those days, the element that Israel is fortunate not to have to cope with. As long as peasants remain uneducated, they often present the most frightening inertia to all forms of progress. It is true that they have sometimes been given advice proven wrong by experience. Nevertheless, the vocational training of the peasants will constitute the most effective lever for agricultural and thereby general progress in tropical Africa.

The Institutes specializing in types of crops which were set up during or after the war have come up with findings of the highest interest. The new varieties of cotton have both larger harvests and a higher yield after ginning, and better methods of dealing with their parasites have been found. Modern techniques of cultivating bananas and pineapples, and of eliminating cercosporalla have been perfected, notably at Kindia in Guinea, and at Martinique. The Ivory Coast is developing rubber, coffee and cocoa plantations, thanks largely to the Institutes.[1] O R S T O M and I R A T[2] have greatly contributed to a large number of problems also.

One of the most admirable achievements is perhaps that of the *Institut des Recherches pour les Huiles de Palme et les Oléagineux*, better known as I R H O.[3] On the coarse sand of Cayor de Louga, in northern Senegal, the soil was deprived of precious elements by the wind and produced only an adequate peanut harvest in years of very regular rain, perhaps one out of four or five.

By letting the land lie fallow for four to six years, applying 100 pounds of fertilizer per acre, and using a good variety of disinfected seeds, planted densely, they were able to achieve a regular yield of one ton per acre. In central Senegal, in the better watered Sine-Saloum area, they can surpass, with two years of fallow and three years of cultivation, their average of slightly under a ton per acre and attain almost two tons. Average current yields in these three regions generally run from 500 to 700 pounds per acre with traditional methods.

Even more spectacular is the progress that has been made with the oil palm, *elaeis guineensis*. The new hybrids developed from Asian and local varieties produce much more quickly, yielding a first crop after $3\frac{1}{2}$ years, and their shorter height greatly facilitates harvesting. Productivity is often ten or fifteen times that of wild oil palm groves; on cleared great forest areas in the southern Ivory Coast, almost four tons of oil from the pulp and over a ton of nuts per $2\frac{1}{2}$ acres are harvested. Gross annual profit can thus equal, under favourable circumstances, the total cost of planting and maintenance right up to the first harvest. It is therefore a much more profitable investment than those of the Niger Office. In the Dabou savannah west of

---

[1] Findings made by the *Instituts de Recherche pour le Coton et Fibres* (I R C T), *Fruits et Agrumes Tropicaux* (I F A T), *Caoutchouc en Afrique* (I R C A) and *Café-Cacao* (I F C C).

[2] *Office de la Recherche Scientifique et Technique Outre-Mer* and *Institut de Recherche d'Agronomie Tropical et des Cultures Vivrières*.

[3] Consult in particular its review *Oléagineux*, and the special issue of April, 1962, entitled *20 Ans d'Activité, 1942–1962*.

Abidjan, the application of potassium raised yields from 700 pounds to 2½ tons of palm oil per 2½ acres.

Progress has not been universal. Plantations in the Cameroons, at Dibomba, have reached a ceiling of somewhat over a ton of oil per 2½ acres, perhaps because of excessive rainfall (about 135 inches annually) and lack of sufficient sun (1,400 hours a year). However, if zones suitable to the oil palm are chosen, its yields easily surpass those of the best oleaginous plants in temperate climates. Colza yields have reached a ceiling of around a ton per 2½ acres. The question now is whether the peanut crop will always be able to equal the palm oil, should advances in peanut cultivation slow down. If not, the Senegalese economy, unless it takes the precaution to diversify, will be in a very difficult spot.

The steps being taken with coconut hybrids are also promising, though less well known. It is the only plant which can grow on very poor littoral sands. Here again, the new lines produce earlier, are shorter, and highly productive. With the application of potassium, and nitrogen for the young plant, copra harvests of three tons per 2½ acres, thus of two tons of coconut oil, are possible. Even on the very dry Dahomey coast 1,600 kilograms of copra have been harvested, with potassium and household garbage as the fertilizers, on an old plantation that formerly yielded only 465 kilograms.

3. YET MODERN PLANTATIONS ARE NOT BEING ESTABLISHED

The Ivory Coast was conquered to procure palm oil, at that time extracted from the fruits of wild trees by local methods. Yet the country is currently obliged to import palm oil, both to supply its soap works and in the form of soap, table oil and margarine. This is unfortunate, since good varieties of oil palm trees, as has been shown in Malaysia and Sumatra, adapt exceedingly well to industrial production, where strict crop discipline is applied, an imperative condition to produce these high yields. But French capitalists have preferred foreign investments for a long time, and have been hesitant about investing in 'French' territories much more than in Nigeria and the former Belgian Congo. Since independence, except in the Ivory Coast, their hesitation has hardened into extreme reserve.

One cannot, of course, depend on private capital to achieve satisfactory progress in Africa. South America has done this, and is paying heavily for its error. It would be sheer folly to put off the necessary reorganization of the economy in this vain hope. It is still true, however, that the African plantations have not taken up the job where the fleeing capitalists left off. In the Dabou savannah discussed a moment ago, the Agricultural Services have set up modern plantations, but they have been unable to turn administration of them over to neighbouring villages. As a result, the oil factory of the Plan took them over, so that they could finally harvest enough to operate at full capacity. This had not been possible since its construction in 1948.

Disaffection of the peasants with oil palms began in the natural palm groves, where men must climb very high to gather a relatively small harvest. In the lower Ivory Coast, the custom was for young people, nineteen to twenty-nine years old, to harvest the palms as a kind of 'community service'. The older members of the tribe, having gone through it themselves, refuse to exempt the young. They therefore rejected the proposal, a reasonable one, that the climbers receive at least half the profits, turning over the rest to the community. As a result, the fruits are rotting, and no one makes any profit.

I have seen fruits on young palm trees, carefully chosen varieties, which I literally had only to lean over to pick. They were rotting, and weeds were taking over the plantation. It is not a very promising sight for the future of Africa. The peasant has not grasped the difference in productivity of the new trees, which he too easily confuses with the wild groves, which spell hardship to him. However, peasant plantations are beginning to appear in the Ivory Coast, from the forest zone around Attingé and Alépé to the savannah at Dabou.

Between 1947 and 1960 about 900 million CFA francs, more than 2½ billion old 1961 francs, were spent by FIDES in Dahomey to distribute and plant, under technical conditions that were too often questionable, 7 million of the new varieties of oil palms. The result was that in 1960–1961 the country, 70 per cent of whose exports are provided by the oil palm, had just about reached the 1930 level. In the meantime the population had increased perhaps by 60 per cent, so there was a great decrease in foreign sales compared to per capita population.

All the formulas were tried. At Porto Novo new plants have been put in old plantations to replace dead trees. Under the trees corn is cultivated; but to provide more sun for the corn, which needs a great deal of light, the young palm plants are pitilessly pruned. Elsewhere weeds are burned, and the trees suffer terribly from the fires. After several years of cultivation, *Imperata*, a tropical weed that cannot be rooted out without damaging the superficial roots of the palms, invades everywhere.

Then, at public expense, plantations were established with large intervals reserved for food crops. 'Pure' plantations were set up also, of course, which left the growing of foodstuffs to neighbouring areas. But no matter how the plantations were organized, and no matter whose hands they fell into, all of them, by July 1961, were more or less totally invaded by the bush and totally neglected. Some, although already bearing well, were not even harvested. In the southern Cameroons the following October, where plantations were established and maintained for four years with F I D E S funds and then turned over at no cost to the owners of the land, the situation was no better.

South of Pobe a plantation of 200 acres of a good variety of oil palm was set up with F I D E S funds, and then handed back to a young African planter, the son of a chief, at the time studying agronomy in France. I saw the entire thing invaded by the bush; its proprietor has become a high government official. When political leaders set examples like this, you can give a country a substantial proportion of its current budget, 30 per cent not counting all the foreign invest-ments, and still there will be no progress, because progress demands that the country itself supply great efforts also. By persisting in such errors, the African countries will end one day in an insuperable impasse: economic ruin and therefore political ruin. Politicians, not always far-seeing, do not always grasp the connection between the two.

4. TOO 'COFFEE-MINDED'

The lack of interest in oil palms in the Ivory Coast is due mainly to the ease with which coffee is grown. Until 1930 France bought its coffee in Brazil and Central America. After that date, not only was colonial coffee exempt from import taxes, but the taxes levied on other coffees were in part transferred to it in the form of subsidies. An entirely artificial coffee production developed under the aegis of this double protection, since natural conditions for coffee were much more favourable in South America.

On the other hand, if African cocoa has largely surpassed South American since the beginning of the century, it has done so on equal terms. In effect Ghana, then the Gold Coast, depended on a free-exchange England, defender of world trade, which constituted the basis of its prosperity. Natural conditions for the cocoa bean in the forest appear to be comparable on the two sides of the Atlantic. With this crop, African peasants have been able to outstrip Brazilian landowners in Bahia.[1]

To return to coffee: by extending the 'imperial preference', as it was called in 1935, too long, with excessively high protective tariffs, France ended up with a surplus of coffee in the franc zone. This was despite the fact that in the beginning of 1962 world stockpiles were over twice the amount consumed in two years, and that in an average year production can surpass consumption, which is about three million tons, by over a million tons. Half the coffee exported in the world is consumed in the United States, which proves the theoretical existence of an enormous potential market. In order to expand it, however, price levels must be lowered. Although Brazilian Arabica coffee sells regularly for thirty cents a pound in New York because of an efficient reserve system organized by the Sales Office, one must remember that its market price was down to three cents a pound in 1933.

Although Robusta coffee is still, as I write these lines, at eighteen cents, planters in Uganda have maintained that they can sell at ten cents and still make a profit. Export duties and land taxes imposed in Brazil by the State and the landowners were such, at the time of my

[1] *Lands Alive*, Chapter III.

study there in the spring of 1958, that the small farmer, who bore all cultivation costs, only received in some cases 16 per cent of the world price,[1] yet he appeared to be doing fairly well. In a price war on coffee, Africa would not have a chance against South America. It is to its interest, therefore, to avoid such a war, and to this end the Association of African Coffee Producers was recently formed.

Robusta coffee makes up half of Ivory Coast exports, a third of Madagascar's. In southern Ivory Coast I saw rich forest land cleared to plant coffee which gave only four good harvests, 1,000 pounds of coffee per acre in all, before the land was exhausted. At the time of the fifth harvest, a few beans ended up ripening in the bush. Obviously such minimal yields waste the potential of the rich African forest soil. Over seventy-five tons of palm oil could have been harvested from the same area in twenty-five years, without leaving the land impoverished, if it had been well manured and maintained. But more labour would have had to be invested, and better techniques provided.

Up until 1960, at times even beyond that, Agricultural Services stressed coffee production. They attempted plantations too far in the north, in the dry forest where production is very marginal, like the Excelsa coffee of CAR, a very mediocre variety. Such technical errors would never have occurred without over-protection, and the zealous should now be prevented from taking advantage of it. The situation in the tea and cocoa industries is not nearly as bad, but it seems reasonable to expect that all these 'colonial' products will soon reach more reasonable, in other words, lower price levels, in comparison to other products. It will be hard on Africa, because a new fall in market rates will affect their buying power.

To slow down the fall of prices, I would support the proposal to create international regulatory organizations. These would require Africa to limit production of certain crops. The danger of such agreements is that they tend to seek high prices, while world-wide interest lies in expanding consumption first, in a stable market situation. If each country cut down production, the whole world, after all, would be the poorer for it.[2]

[1] ibid., Chapter IV.
[2] Cf. Chapter XIX, 7.
3

There must be a total reconversion of the agrarian economy of tropical Africa. It must break out of the perspective of the franc zone, the Common Market and industrial countries, and start thinking in terms of inter-African exchanges and exchanges with the Communist bloc, other developing areas and the world market. Africa must increase exports, but it must also develop its internal market, feed its population better, cut down on imports, and increase production of the raw materials of industry. Intensive cattle-raising and building up feed reserves will come a little later.

A true agricultural revolution of this type, which rests on an economic and technical base, is impeded by the artificial nature of the economy in the franc zone, although this will be improved by the Common Market. One cannot suggest crops to replace coffee without coming up against the protectionist measures thrown up for this over-abundant product, but not for products which are most lacking, like fats and oils. This kind of protectionism is all too similar to the outdated French viticultural statute protecting the wine growers. It obstructs every effort to convert plantations and renders all substitute crops much less profitable.

CHAPTER FIVE
Training peasant leaders an immediate priority

I. THE MALAGASY PEASANTRY

The achievements of F I D E S have not been brilliant on the whole. It stressed 'infrastructure' above industrialization, constructed expensive and poorly utilized irrigation networks, launched tractors without knowing whether it would pay off, produced excellent research without putting it into practice on a notable scale, and thought first of exports and the coffee crop. In my opinion, its fundamental flaw, which virtually negated the entire programme, was failure to educate the peasants, to give them vocational training and technical leadership. F I D E S failed because it had no real interest in the peasant, as a man as well as a producer.

There were plenty of indigenous Provident Societies, from Algiers down to Brazzaville. Particularly in Algeria and Senegal, these supplied seeds in bad years and prevented real hardships from occurring. They were run by administrators, and membership fees were deducted with the taxes (and therefore identified with them in the eyes of the peasants). The 'Commandants', openly scornful of the peasants, soon annexed the money, which alleviated the chronic inadequacy of their resources. None of this, of course, had much to do with agriculture.

In 1951, Madagascar wanted to import the famous Moroccan SMP, *Secteurs du Paysannat Marocain*, today called *Centres de Travaux*, on which I had made a fairly unfavourable report in 1947. The *Communes Autochtones Rurales* (CAR), soon modernized and called CRAM, were set up and received large credits. But in order to work, they would have had to show a profit immediately, even if basic structural costs were necessary, and this of course was impossible. In an effort to become profitable C R A M established administrative farms, somewhat like *sovkhozes*, still fully confident in the magic of tractors.

It is a pity that failure is not readily acknowledged, and therefore seldom serves as a lesson to others, the only way it can possibly be 'profitable'. The C R A M were under the jurisdiction of government administrators and not representatives of the technical services. They had a great deal of money, and therefore a lot of tractors, but no personnel to organize and train the peasants. Their policies were often technically incorrect. Heavy expenditures for unnecessary buildings and non-income-producing equipment precipitated their failure.

I cannot stress too heavily the dangers for a new country – and I include Cuba – of this infatuation with building and construction. Too many Europeans identify it with productive investments. Yet, like management, construction comes under 'general' production costs, and it should therefore be reduced to the bare minimum.

For centuries the Malagasy has built his tomb out of granite, and it is much more expensive than his house of reeds, because he believes that he will live there longer. The missionaries taught him to construct temples and churches, and on the high plateaux two or three-storey masonry houses are in current favour. The colonial administration lodged the 'commandant' in grand style, also its army and justice department, later the civil servants. C R A M advised peasants to shelter oxen and cattle in expensive – and subsidized – cattle sheds, which were sometimes better than their own houses. Tractors were put under large metal sheds. None of these buildings produced a grain of rice or a pound of meat, but cost a great deal.

The peasant organization that succeeded C R A M came under the aegis of the Agricultural Services and was far more sensible. It proposed to train a small group of farmers very thoroughly in all aspects of agricultural techniques. This was accomplished first with Europeans, some of whom were very dedicated. But because of this, the plan, although very expensive, only touched a tiny segment of the population. An effective political and activist force was not substituted for waning colonial authority, and without such a force no real enthusiasm for work can be instilled in the peasants.

The work of the peasant organization was also harassed by vengeful administrators. Under the pretext of egalitarianism, they were able to form associations of collective organizations at the district level, which they quickly took over. If the French administrators had been able to renounce their authority gradually from 1945 on, efface themselves behind technicians, teachers and economists, and favour early but gradual passage to internal and effective autonomy, the Africans and Malagasies would have been far better prepared for independence. In 1961 the new directors of these groups of collective organizations were ill-prepared for autonomy, and virtually all the groups went bankrupt. All the coastal groups in Tulear and Fianarantsoa provinces except two had to be dissolved.

The most regrettable experiment of all was that of the *'fermettes'*, or subsidized pilot farms. It became a disaster when veterans and urban unemployed (Congo) were installed on them. In Nigeria, £5,000 per family was spent in this way, not counting irrigation costs, as against £3,000 in Israel, a richer country, including planting and irrigation. Tractors used there caused very serious erosion.

2. AUTHORITARIAN BELGIAN METHODS

I studied Belgian methods of organizing the peasantry in 1949–50, from Yangambi near Stanleyville to Bambesa, in the cotton-producing north of the former Belgian Congo.[1] I returned in 1960, to Ruanda-Urundi, and went from the Ruzizi valley up to Mosso. The technical bases for peasant organization in these areas had been carefully elaborated by a serious research organization, INEAC.[2] The studies were drawn out for so long, however, that an element of rigidity crept into their conclusions. Sometimes the Belgians are apt to arrive at the 'absolute and only' solution, without realizing that agricultural modernization is a continuing and dynamic process. Their directors should have been better adapted to each stage of evolution of the population, and to each advance in research.

In the Ruzizi valley, too much emphasis was placed on the tractor, which once again produced only disappointments. Ten acres were given to each farmer, although a number of Ngozi peasants had only

[1] See *Economie Agricole dans le Monde.* Dalloz, 1954. Chapter II, pp. 46–62. (Out of print.) By the author.
[2] *Institut National pour l'Etude Agronomique du Congo Belge.*

a few hundred square yards, on nearby hills on the other side of the 'Congo-Nile' crest. Also, the Belgians followed methods developed for the under-populated Congo in over-populated Ruanda-Urundi. They did not go far enough in this valley to generalize irrigation, to intensify cultivation and use draught animals, although local animals were plentiful and under-utilized.

Authoritarianism was the basic vice of the system, as of all Belgian colonialism. It was based for too long on the monstrous slogan, 'no *élites*, no problems'. As an application of this principle, higher education was closed to the Congolese until 1955. They were forbidden to go elsewhere for study, and unable to do it at home. A Belgian colleague strongly reproached me in 1953 for having written in the book just cited that 'The peasant springs to attention before the agronomist; those not fulfilling the directives of the Plan run the risk of going to prison, eight days if they have not cleared the land, fifteen days if they have not harvested, up to a month if they have not burned the stalks after the harvest to prevent the spread of parasitic insects.' In the first version I had been harsher, and I later toned down the passage for his sake.

I am sorry I did so, for events have justified my warning only too well, although it probably would not have changed the course of events. In order to succeed, organization of the peasantry must have the full support of the majority of peasants under its jurisdiction. I am not condemning all forms of authority, only those that do not seek to the utmost to gain the enthusiastic adherence of the people, through education and persuasion. The role of these in China is largely underestimated in the West.

The appalling confusion reigning in the Congolese countryside now is above all due to lack of preparation for independence; more specifically to inadequate education of the peasants. They had been trained to obey rather than understand the purpose of their work. If authority crumbles, nothing is left of the constructions of paternalism. In this particular case, it is a sad sight for an agronomist.

3. COLONIALISM – A BALANCE SHEET

The number of settlers that came to French West Africa never equalled the large quantities that came to North Africa, to the Sous valley around Agadir, the olive groves at Sfax, the Meknes plateau and the Oran vineyards, the Mitidja orchards and the cereals in Northern Tunisia. A 'small' colonization, mostly from Reunion Island, arrived first on the eastern coast of Madagascar, on the rich alluvial land in the low-lying valleys. Coffee, cloves and vanilla were the main crops. It often seems 'small' from every point of view: level of intelligence, volume of capital invested, meanness and stinginess in paying salaries. Workers on the plantations were exempted from forced labour, which the abuses of canton chiefs made extremely harsh. Also, certain farmers gave worker's cards to those who consented to work for them without pay one day a week. It is easily understandable that the 'rebellion' of 1947 – its suppression caused great numbers of dead, particularly through starvation in the forest – sprang up in this area.

Settlers came in fairly large numbers to West Africa, where they planted the first coffee. There were a few good plantations, but the rest were far from being models. Best were the banana plantations, in Guinea, southern Cameroons and the Ivory Coast. The strict crop disciplines imposed by 'Cobafruit' on its planters resulted in Ivory Coast bananas attaining remarkable quality. Cobafruit is a co-operative organization, and profits are shared among members. It is in effect an '*élite*' of colonization, and the productivity of labour is very superior to that in traditional agriculture.

The great majority of traditionally run plantations were concerned only with producing for export and immediate profit. These included coffee and banana plantations in West Africa, rice and sugar in Madagascar. In Madagascar the large companies burn their rice straw after the harvest, although it could provide animal feed or humus. After the manioc harvest, over a ton of fragments are left on the ground per acre, that pigs could eat. In fallow years the wild grasses that grow up could feed a good amount of livestock; these are still ignored because concepts of modern livestock raising do not exist.

The companies operated in the seventeenth to nineteenth century framework of slave plantations, and scarcely progressed at all in the vital problem of relating agriculture and livestock-raising, although they had the means to do so. They might have found a way to solve the difficulties involved in it had they concerned themselves with two basic problems. One was that of improving their soils, of exploiting them with care to assure the increase and regularity of their crops. The other was that of producing the food crops necessary to improve the food intake of their workers. The heritage of slavery, and its modern version, colonialism, cannot be thrown off all at once, as can be seen in north-eastern Brazil. High productivity, which is sometimes to the credit of colonialism, is usually found in a few large plantations entirely devoted to the oil palm and, more recently, rubber. The success of these plantations is due above all to very strict control over cultivation and to the use of modern agronomic methods.

The last achievements of colonialism exhibit a kind of dissipation of its original dynamic. Since the large companies did not build modern oil-processing factories, these were constructed in the Ivory Coast, the Cameroons and Dahomey with FIDES funds. The management of these factories, constructed with public credits and part of the Plans, was turned over to private companies, a questionable step.

The last big private investments, Niari in the Congo and Sosumav in Madagascar, have been in sugar, one of the most protected crops. As a result, the Malagasy peasant, who in 1928 could procure crude sugar cheaply, has to pay 65 CFA francs, or 1·3 new francs per kilo. Often he buys it by the spoonful, and has to pay almost double. He cannot possibly buy enough to can any of his own fruits, most of which rot, as production is very seasonal.

4. POTENTIAL LIVESTOCK INDUSTRY, MILK, AND FEED

Archaic agricultural systems can be characterized by a separation of livestock raising and crop cultivation. Our systems in Europe are the more modern in that they combined the two earlier. Utilization of draught animals, the first stage in this evolution, was introduced to Europe very early, but the idea of building up reserves of animal feed, the second step, came much later. Real progress in the alimentation of animals is much more recent, and is analogous to progress made in feeding man around the Neolithic Age. It is a matter of going from simple gathering of wild feed to actually growing it. It became widespread in Flanders and England in the fifteenth and sixteenth centuries, not until the end of the eighteenth century in Western Europe. Eastern Europe did not reach this stage until the nineteenth and twentieth centuries.

Tropical Africa was unaware of the concept of draught animals even at the beginning of this century.[1] Research on feed crops made a timid beginning there after the last war. One of the principal causes of the delay was the absurd separation of the technical services in charge of research and education in agriculture on the one hand, and livestock on the other. For a long time agronomic research was concerned only with plants and not with livestock.

For historical reasons, the so-called livestock services were in the hands of veterinarians. Military veterinarians went out with the expeditionary corps to look after the horses and mules. They were confronted immediately with the health problems of local herds, and it was urgent that they be rid of cattle plague, peri-pneumonia, carbuncles and many other parasites. When the 'civil' technical services were established, they naturally called on their veterinary colleagues, who took charge of the livestock service.

During this early period the primacy of health problems justified such a position. But the veterinary spirit tends naturally – we all suffer from a certain vocational bias – to emphasize health problems excessively, even when, as is often the case now, the worst diseases have been practically wiped out. In a study I made on Madagascar in 1958, I pointed out the two weak points in the livestock service. It has somewhat overestimated the problems of converting to intensive livestock raising, with feed as the stumbling-block. As it was dealing with herders, it concentrated on developing better breeds without sufficiently attacking the feed problem. It is trying to perfect the herding system, in imitation of the private companies, by developing the 'improved ranch', which should be abandoned wherever there is even a modicum of population and the smallest potential for cultivation. This does not hold true for the Niari and north Chad.

[1] North American Indians in the post-Columbian period used horses as draught animals.

3*

In order to grasp the problems involved, the veterinarians should have had solid training in rural economy, which was not and still is not always the case. They received large credits for their research stations, and surrounded their pastures with expensive fences, something costing more than 600 CFA francs per metre! The mediocrity of the pasture land was such that the high expenditures could never pay off. Even more serious is the fact that they have advised spreading these ruinously costly fences to other areas. To this end, the livestock service of the Ivory Coast requested money at the end of 1959 from the European Fund, for the north of the country. If a high-yield feed is planted, enclosures are worth while. If not, a good watchman with sheep-dogs is more economical. Unfortunately no one is training dogs in Africa for this job. European peasant schoolchildren could never have gone to school so early unless their families had had sheep-dogs.

A further and equally serious error was exclusive preoccupation with meat production, and a consequent disregard of dairy products. One thought first of exports, then of feeding the local population with meat. Every year Madagascar's meat sales decrease, while its purchases of milk increase. Their trade balance of food products of animal origin may well become negative; this in a country that has more than 1·5 head of cattle per inhabitant!

Babel, a veterinary doctor whose career was jeopardized because he understood many of these problems better than his superiors, told me in 1961 that the average Malagasy consumes the equivalent of seven litres of milk a year, of which two are imported. A little more than one feed unit, or the equivalent of a kilo of barley, for a good dairy cow will enable one to obtain a litre of milk. Often twenty to forty of these units are necessary to obtain one kilo (live) of beef, depending on the varying conditions of traditional methods. Milk sells at 10 CFA francs in the middle of the bush, at 40 francs in the capital, as against 20 francs at Ankazoabe and 45 francs in the capital for a kilogram of beef. As can be seen, meat gives much less value per feed unit than milk.

Those Malagasies who were quick to adopt the dairy breeds brought from Europe as far back as the nineteenth century knew this. But they hesitate to use the cattle bred for beef offered them by the livestock service. Yet, by breeding the latter with dairy breeds, one could obtain enough milk to supply protein to the herders' and peasants' children (and their mothers), and have calves as well. These last would grow faster and produce more meat, as well as more milk. Here at last is a way to escape the double archaism of hand cultivation and 'hand-gathering' feed for the animals, which is both mediocre and unreliable.

It is harder to convince herders than cultivators to achieve intense cultivation of fertilized soil in combination with highly productive livestock raising. Cultivators are accustomed to regular work, grubbing in the soil with the *daba* and digging with the *angady*. Herders scorn farm work and prefer to wander with their herds, even for a very small profit and under difficult conditions. Also, adolescents take over care of the herds at a very early age.[1]

Evolution of a peasant deeply attached to his animals and his soil – the peasant willing to labour long and hard, who made the Industrial Revolution possible in the West, a fact we forget too easily – does not occur overnight. It took more than a thousand years in Europe, from the end of serfdom to the agricultural revolution in the eighteenth century. The task, as difficult as it is essential, was resolutely undertaken in the English East African colonies, but only lately in the French. I give two examples in Appendices I and II of continuous cultivation, pigs and milk in Madagascar and cotton in Mali, which have succeeded because the peasantry was fitted into an excellent organizational framework with sufficient well-trained cadres to run it.

5. A LAST LOOK AT COLONIALISM

These good results make one hopeful. The basic techniques of modern agronomy in Africa seemed to be very shaky at the time of my first trips to there in 1949–1950. In thirteen years we have come a long way, and precise formulas are being elaborated. This would not have occurred so soon, doubtless, had there not been such need for haste, nor would the mistakes have cost so much.

[1] It would be interesting to study the results obtained if one grouped together in cattle-raising co-operatives the herders of the two Mongolias, Chinese and Outer, to speed up their evolution.

Tubman, the President of Liberia, confided to Tunisian friends, 'We, who have not been lucky enough to be colonized . . .' He was thinking of the poverty of his country, apart from Monrovia and the Firestone empire. Let me insert here a last criticism of the FIDES era. Public funds flowed into these countries in a great stream, but the profits of the great trading companies, swelled by this influx, continued to flow back to the metropolitan country. In the last few years, the outflow of capital has taken on the aspect of a general 'disinvestment', but no effective measures are being taken to prevent it. FAC credits permit African governments to buy back European installations, usually at a high price because of hidden transactions. Some 'colons' refuse to integrate themselves in new systems of production and trade, so that they can complain bitterly that they are being robbed, and then sell, for a fat sum, an installation that never was profitable. The African country thus inherits worthless installations, but they want to utilize them, and efforts to put them into production bring on fresh losses.

To these sums flowing out of Africa must be added the savings 'repatriated' by Europeans, which now form a higher percentage of their salaries as their situation becomes more precarious. Many are more concerned about buying an apartment in France ('I'm buying this with colonial francs,' they admit freely), than with helping the African states. When France boasts that it is spending 1·4 or 1·7 per cent of its gross national income on tropical Africa and Madagascar, it does not take these facts into account. The English deduct them in their calculations.

Africans would be far better off if they tried to learn as much as possible from the colonial experience, instead of condemning it unilaterally. They might stop prolonging their errors and profit from their privileges. Prefects and politicians in the Somba country in Dahomey are regrouping isolated *tatas* in villages to 'facilitate contact' along the roads. The regroupment, achieved often by demolishing splendid houses, will hinder the transition to intensive cultivation, on small, individual farms manured with household wastes. In some areas co-operatives have become obligatory, with no explanation given; in others, *de luxe* highways are built for first-class tourism.

The African tendency to persist in these errors is frightening, and the essential reason for this book. Certain 'colonial' attitudes were very positive. There were Frenchmen among my colleagues who sacrificed comfort, health and sometimes their lives for Africa, although they could have lived out an easy life in France. Léon Blum once said that it would be possible to cite the good sides of colonialism once it had disappeared. Even Sékou Touré has remarked on some of them. The champions of colonialism, of course, refer only to these; from their point of view the Africans lived in a true paradise.

But it is a mistake to go too far in the other direction, and conclude that colonialism was an unmitigated evil. Its greatest failure was inability to adapt to the times, which, at its worst, produced the excesses of the O A S. Colonialism may have diverted evolution from its natural inclinations, but it also made positive contributions to development. A number of young Africans would benefit by devoting themselves to their countries as wholeheartedly as did certain colonials. Many of them are content to install themselves in power, in the place of the whites, and with the whites' former privileges, without always justifying them by their work and dedication to national interest. Because of Africa's general level of education, this is, of course, more difficult, and those that succeed in so doing are thereby much more deserving.[1]

However, what struck me most, during a study of community development in India I made in 1958–1959, was that the great majority of Indians still, eleven and a half years after independence, blame the English for most if not all of their problems. At times this attitude is a hypocritical way of concealing the appalling exploitation of the peasants by moneylending landowners, but often it appeared to be very sincere. Africans will make the same mistake if they continue to throw all the blame on colonialism.

The past cannot in any case be changed, and it is high time to analyse the present and seek ways to accelerate development, which is totally insufficient. Unfortunately, this preoccupation does not appear to be uppermost in most African countries. The most urgent 'decolonization' now is of the majority of African leaders.

[1] *L'Empire du Bakchich* by 'XXX'. Julliard, 1962. See also *Eloge du Colonialisme*, by Cheverny.

CHAPTER SIX
Independence is not always 'decolonization'

I. THE 'ELITES': A MODERN VERSION OF LOUIS XVI'S COURT

'One cannot develop a country by doubling the employees in administrative services or by distributing sinecures to one's friends, but only by mobilizing men and enthusiasm to work for an ideal based on the common good,' concludes R. Gendarme. The principal 'industry' of these countries at the moment is administration. It is not productive and simply adds to general costs. Such costs should be reduced, but in fact are being swollen to the point where personnel expenses alone absorb 60 per cent of the internal income in Dahomey. As presently conceived, administration will be the ruin of these countries.

The balkanization of Africa is one of the principal causes of it. Until more progress had been made, it would have been preferable to retain the former federal structure, French West Africa with Togo and French Equatorial Africa with the Cameroons, and be satisfied to grant each 'territory' a good deal of autonomy. By including Madagascar, three parliaments and three federal governments could have had only one diplomatic corps to represent their foreign interests.[1]

There should be a joint army, if forces other than the police are needed. At least African unity would not have made a step back-

---

[1] Iwiyé Kala-Labe proposes a system of one African representation in *Communauté-France-Eurafrique*, June, 1961. 'African diplomacies – why the plural? Because the young independent states of Africa have adopted a ruinous policy of diplomatic representation: ruinous for their fragile finances, which can never support, without immense and needless sacrifices, the enormous costs of installing and maintaining a diplomatic corps, whose direct importance to their countries is nebulous; ruinous also because the new states have other fish to fry, and more serious ones. They should concentrate on these, instead of joining the race for prestige which only serves to construct "Potemkin villages" and cover over the abysses in their budgets for non-existent equipment . . .'

ward. But we encouraged Houphouet-Boigny to reject the Federation and keep Guinea out of the group. This unfortunate beginning intentionally complicates the task of the new governments, and evokes the dictum 'divide and rule'.

A general reconsolidation of West Africa could do worse than follow the lines of former French territories. Colonial frontiers, a result of the more or less hasty occupations of this or that expeditionary force, did not take ethnic groups into account (e.g. Togo and Ghana) any more than so-called 'natural' frontiers. However, colonial history has thrown up barriers to a new division, such as diversity of language, administrative methods and monetary systems. Thus Cameroon admits of two languages, two monetary systems and three parliaments, none of which helps cut down administrative expenses. Certainly, the entry of England into the Common Market would facilitate these regroupings.

M. Apithy envisages a Benin union[1] of Ghana, Nigeria, Dahomey and Togo. Another recently proposed frontier is that of the Casablanca group, comprising Guinea, Ghana and Mali, plus Egypt, Morocco and Algeria on the one hand, and the Brazzaville 'twelve', together with Nigeria and Sierra Leone, on the other. The end of the Algerian war meant the diminution of many of the antagonisms that a union like the Benin would also have to surmount.

The former colonies confront one with fifteen governments, more than 150 ministers, several hundred cabinet members, and several thousand members of parliament. Yet as a unit, they have much less population and resources than France. Gabon alone, with 450,000 inhabitants, has sixty-five deputies, one for each 6,000 people, as against one per 100,000 in France. These countries have not quite understood their poverty yet, because they can 'touch' France so easily for money. In addition to providing the great majority of their investments (86 per cent in Upper Volta), France also balances their budgets, except for Senegal, the Ivory Coast, Mali and Togo.

Each cabinet member has an official car at his disposal, rarely a modest one, with chauffeur. The President of Dahomey cannot take a step without his motorcade, and many dream of equalling the ostentation of the Elysée Palace. This last costs us, for each reception

[1] *Jeune Afrique*, March 26, 1962.

given a visiting African head of state, a sum which could accomplish far more in African agriculture. President Youlou wanted his little Versailles, and went to Switzerland to borrow the money for it. Houphouet-Boigny has already built his, at a cost of six billion francs. Excellent buildings were demolished in order that his park might be enlarged. For its construction, hundreds of tons of malachite were imported from Russia . . . by air.

During the last phase of colonialism, the policy was to equalize salaries of Africans and Europeans in similar jobs, a defensible position only in the framework of 'assimilation'. The native civil servant, in addition to his regular salary, received a colonial supplement. This has been reduced in some cases, but not abolished. At independence, this pseudo-equality has led to flagrant disparity with the rest of the population, whose standard of living is often a fifteenth of the French.

Massive departure of the French resulted in a high rate of promotion of subordinate African civil servants, who thus earn even more now than before, for the same qualifications. The student returning from France is appointed director if he is the only African technician or graduate in his field. A labour leader who had been one of my students six months before at the *Institut des Hautes Études d'Outre-mer*,[1] was already returning for further training in France, by first-class aeroplane. He would no doubt have been astonished had I told him that the Cuban ministers cross the Atlantic in second. This tendency applies above all to the urban *élites*, and works to the detriment of the peasants. It could be postponed for a while.

The elements of the civil service, deputies and ministers constitute a highly privileged group whose members support each other. In England, a Member of Parliament draws the pay of a middle rank civil servant. In France he draws the salary of a top level civil servant. Because of the 'assimilation' policy, whereby the colonies were to be put on the same footing as France, a Gabonese deputy earns more than the British MP: 165,000 CFA francs, compared to about 100,000 CFA francs a month in England (£1,000 in salary and £750 for expenses per year). As for the cost of the Gabonese Presidency, Parliament and ministers, with all their supposedly

[1] A former colonial educational institution.

useful trips, it probably represents, in relation to the national income of the country, more than the cost of the court of Louis XVI in 1788, relative to French national income of that period. Certainly the latter supported parasites, and Libreville has less of them – but it too has its 'hangers-on', none of whom perform a useful function.[1]

2. LIFE'S WORK OF A PEASANT EQUALS $1\frac{1}{2}$ MONTHS' WORK OF A DEPUTY

A deputy works (?) three months out of the year, and receives 120,000 to 165,000 francs a month all the year round. In six months of salary, or $1\frac{1}{2}$ months of work, he earns as much as the average peasant in thirty-six years, a whole lifetime of hard labour. I brought out this fact in lectures in Porto Novo, Dakar, Tananarive, Douala and Yaoundé. There were always many civil servants, deputies, sometimes ministers, and in the last cities, the President of the Republic and the President of the Council as well. That time I permitted myself to add that 'This will not last thirty-six years'. They would appreciate my meaning in the Cameroons, where efforts to subdue rebels are still carried on, more easily than elsewhere.

Far-sighted Presidents and ministers build up savings accounts 'for their old age' in Swiss banks, and their wives buy villas on the Lake of Geneva. At that same gathering at Yaoundé in 1961 at the *École Camerounaise d'Administration*, I asked the group of two hundred civil servants and students if anyone there, out of patriotism, would be willing to give back to the government a substantial portion of his salary. One hand, a courageous one, was raised. I then remarked that this fact would be duly noted in my book. Four other hands went up. I appealed to their patriotism, but not one of the students present, which included the entire school, raised his hand.

The situation is largely a hold-over from colonial times, and is encouraged by the fact that France helps balance the budget in these countries. This relieves the African governments from facing up to their real difficulties, and thus holds off their economic maturity. A new type of bourgeoisie is forming in Africa, that Karl Marx would hardly have foreseen, a bourgeoisie of the civil service. One day we

[1] Reductions in salary are being made in most of these countries (Senegal, Mali, Guinea, Dahomey), but they are very insufficient.

may look back on the old bourgeoisie of Western Europe with nostalgia and affection, despite the criticisms we have levelled at it.

It often abused its privileges by exploiting peasants and workers, although they were the ones who built Europe. It often lived too luxuriously. But do not forget that in general it offered the two motivating forces of development, work and savings, and thus insured progress. Work was often pushed to excess. In order to save, Père Grandet imposed terrible privations on himself. In under-developed countries, laxity and profligacy are too often seen.

A typist for the Dakar government types an average of six to seven pages, double spaced, a day, less than a quarter of what an average French typist accomplishes, for a salary that is equal if not higher. At the Djebilor station in Casamance, the agricultural worker who is a *décisionnaire*[1] hoes an average of ten square metres a day, or scarcely 1 per cent of what his Californian counterpart accomplishes. As a *décisionnaire*, however, he earns almost 400 CFA francs a day, a sixth of the Californian's wages, which are about ten dollars. The hoed square metre ends up costing sixteen times more in Casamance than in California. Citrus plants cost twelve times more to raise than they do the Sicilian nurserymen. These *décisionnaires* consider themselves practically civil servants, and therefore do very little work, particularly as some of them are related to deputies.

Deputies, like the young students back from France and quickly promoted, can usually buy cars on hire-purchase with loans made available by the Treasury Department. In other words, public funds are being diverted for consumer loans. Even worse, the loans are used to pay for imported luxuries. The two or four horsepower Renaults are not considered good enough even for driving in town (the Mayor of Ouagadougou passed a law forbidding use of the small two horsepower cars as taxis). These loan concessions will make it more difficult to lower salaries, as too many civil servants are burdened with high monthly payments.

Any visit to a sub-prefect or prefect in the bush involves the inevitable glass of whisky, a solid colonial tradition. I have always refused it, asking instead for fruit juice or a local drink, adding that

---

[1] One so designated by a *décision*, who is given a paper stamped with a miraculous seal, which permits him to work less and earn more.

since I was going to propose that the government reduce my host's salary (among others) by 40 to 50 per cent, I didn't feel I should accept such an expensive drink from him! The governor at St Louis, an excellent man, offered me fruits imported from France by air. That evening I brought him six mangoes from the neighbouring market. He had insisted that local fruits were unavailable.

After having written this, I read *The Wretched of the Earth* by Frantz Fanon, from which I take these quotations at random. They attack particularly the business bourgeoisie. 'The national bourgeoisie, which takes power at the end of the colonial régime, is an under-developed bourgeoisie with practically no economic power . . . not oriented towards production, invention, construction, work . . . it enters, soul in peace, on the terrible anti-national path of a bourgeoisie flatly, stupidly, cynically bourgeois. Nationalization means the transfer to the peasants of injustices inherited from the colonial period . . . its enormous salaries are not reinvested, as it deposits them in foreign banks. Enormous sums are spent on displays of ostentation, cars, houses. . . . Despite declarations which are fine in form, but empty in content, it is proving its incapacity to make a minimum humanist ideal triumph.'

3. EXPENSIVE TOWNS AND NEPOTISM

The villas recently constructed in Dakar for Senegalese officials are widely spaced, as in the old colonial quarters, and form a striking contrast, seen from the air, with the 'native' town, which is extra-ordinarily densely populated. Aside from the high construction costs, there are enormous expenses for services: roads, water, gas, electricity and telephone. By spacing out the houses, the town is greatly enlarged, and transportation costs are raised accordingly. Highrise buildings, of twelve, fifteen or even more storeys, would be much more economical. Western aid favours this trend, both by helping to balance budgets, which make high salaries possible, and by financing investments in urban construction. If urbanization was dependent on local resources, Africans would be forced to build more modestly, mostly with local materials.

Africans rebel against the idea of a cut in their salaries, in inverse proportion to their degree of dedication and honesty. One Senegalese official told me that he could not possibly receive properly without his high salary. I have been received by Greek and Portuguese colleagues who earn far less than their African counterparts, and they live in countries where the general standard of living is much higher; their homes were extremely attractive.

Whether deputy or civil servant, the African who has 'arrived' feels obligated to take his large family in charge, sometimes his friends and village. The African tradition of hospitality is very laudable when it means, say, that a man supports his penniless nephew until he finishes his studies. In the old days, a visitor received in a Sudanese village took up the *daba* with the others in the season of planting, and hoed the millet, sorghum or peanut crops. In the city, a guest no longer does anything, and becomes totally parasitic. Africans are proud when they can 'maintain' young people in robust health, and enable them to be idle. This is a sad state of affairs for a developing country which needs all hands.

Agbessi, my Dahomean chauffeur at Bangui, had abandoned his wife and children in Porto Novo simply to get away from all his parasitic relations. One way of getting them off your hands is to find them a job, and too many positions are filled by nepotism, and not on the basis of competence. The top staff of a minister usually belongs to the same ethnic group as its chief. Officials, particularly ministers, lose precious time which could more usefully be spent studying their briefs or viewing problems on the spot, when they receive these parasites seeking favours.

Conditions in Cuba are in marked contrast. In August, 1960, the Hotel Habana Riviera, a luxury hotel built for rich American tourists, was suddenly invaded by ebullient *Maestros volontarios* and their families. These young men and women were mostly college graduates, and had come to teach literacy to peasants and agricultural workers, who came from the most distant parts of the country. They were highly indignant when several of them were offered jobs in Havana. Africa will be fortunate indeed if it can create a comparable spirit of service and dedication in its civil servants. When I talk about the 'general interest' in Yaoundé, people begin to laugh, much as they do in São Paulo.

4. TIE AND JACKET, THE NEW SYMBOLS

The Republic of the Congo (Brazzaville) had only eleven French-trained African doctors in May 1961. All of them were assigned to Brazzaville or Pointe Noire. 'Jobs in the bush are all right for the whites.' Too many young officials try to obtain a training period in France, often without caring whether or not it increases their usefulness. A stay in France is a mark of prestige, helpful to obtain positions in the capital. The Prefect of Education for the Northern Congo received just one such training period in France; now he no longer journeys into the bush, and never leaves his office, or takes off his jacket and tie.

Jackets and ties have become the new symbols of prestige. Ministers and cabinet members keep them on even when the heat makes them insufferable, which also justifies the expense of installing air-conditioning. Most of them require all officials, European or African, to wear jackets and ties when they appear for an appointment. People have been sent back to France for taking them off for a minute.

By insisting on these exterior forms of respect, Africans betray a fear of not being able to inspire it otherwise. As Bismarck said, every man has his own value, diminished by his vanity. I wonder by how much the construction of the Abidjan palace diminished the militant Houphouet-Boigny. Whoever dons a tie and jacket is eager to show his membership in the new *élite*. He does not realize, or perhaps he does not care, that he is drawing further and further away from the tieless, coatless peasant. For that reason I arrived without these 'attributes' to make my report to the Dahomey Council of Ministers, and to Presidents Ahidjo and Assalé.

At the Israeli Ministry of Agriculture one can quickly distinguish between subordinate civil servants, all wearing ties, and the service chiefs, top officials, the minister and his staff, none of whom wear one. Many of these are members of a *kibbutz*, and turn over all of their salaries to it, keeping back an amount so small that the purchase of a tie would mean sacrifices. I may seem to be stressing an insignificant detail, but if Africans followed the Israeli example their future would be much more hopeful.

5. CORRUPTION

Too many African *élites* have interpreted independence as simply
meaning that they could move into the jobs and enjoy the privileges
of the Europeans. Along with high salaries often go beautiful houses,
completely furnished, sometimes palaces for governors and a large
domestic staff, on the expense account, and cars usually with chauf-
feurs. After independence, the '403' car was succeeded by Chevrolets
in Abidjan and Mercedes in Yaoundé. These are often traded in
every six months, which of course enrages ordinary workers. When
some of these 'extras' were limited, some people were able to get
them back without being too particular about how they managed it.

Sudden accession to power affected certain leaders adversely and
corroded their moral sense. Corruption was certainly not unknown
in the colonial *milieu*, viz. the Indo-Chinese customs. Since independence, however, the increase in corruption has taken on alarming
proportions in certain countries, particularly the Central African
Republic, the Republic of the Congo (Brazzaville),[1] Gabon, the
Ivory Coast and Dahomey. Investigating committees were established in the Cameroons to ferret out corruption, and it has been
asserted that the embezzlements thus detected amount to a tenth of
the budget. This figure seems high, yet it is by no means certain that
the investigations reached very far up in the hierarchy.

Cocoa Purchasing Associations are entitled to allot premiums to
'superior' cocoas. During the 1960–1961 season, 25,000 tons were so
designated, but at the inspection service in the port at Douala, only
9,000 tons were found to merit the premium. Five or six thousand
tons of coffee beans had been mixed in with very mediocre lots.
Premiums on at least 1,000 tons, worth more than 200 million C F A
francs had been fraudulently allotted for lots which were either
fictitious or did not merit the classification. Equally bad, one lot of
high quality was sometimes given a premium two or three times.

A big effort to reduce salaries and promote honesty has been made
by Guinea, which has had the courage at least to point the way
towards complete political and economic independence. Mali has

---

[1] See the author's article in *France-Observateur*, June 15, 1961. After its appearance
one of my namesakes was coolly received in Brazzaville.

made great strides also. However, even there results have not always been satisfactory. The ardour for work among Guinean officials who accompanied me in 1959 was very moderate. I had hoped that independence would stimulate it; not at all. Corruption appears to be more developed along the African coast, perhaps because it has been longer in contact with the worst colonial influences, the exploiters, adventurers and prostitutes. Further inland, in the savannah, land is generally now owned individually. M. Mazoyer writes to me that 'the relationship between the degree of corruption in men and ownership of the means of production cannot be underestimated. It is here that man began to exploit his neighbour, here is the first robbery, the original sin which brings all the others in its wake.'[1]

[1] Conditions are worse in Liberia and Ethiopia than elsewhere. In Ethiopia the Civil Code provides that a landowner can claim up to three-quarters of the crop. This Code is the work of a French jurist, René David, and of a codification commission composed exclusively of landowners or representatives of the Church, a privileged and extensive landowner.

CHAPTER SEVEN
If your sister goes to school, you won't have anything to eat

1. PRESENT EDUCATION OBSTRUCTS PROGRESS

This statement may appear paradoxical to many readers, particularly coming from the pen of a professor, since education was the essential foundation of development in Europe, America, Japan, the Soviet Union and China. In Africa it has a certain utility, but this is greatly curtailed by the social *milieu* on to which the educational system was grafted. For most African children, in town and country alike, school represents above all a means of entering the *élite* class. Even in the most backward areas of the bush everyone has grasped the fact that the official with clean hands earns more and works much less.

Pushed by his parents, a peasant child quickly realizes that he can never go very far in agriculture; the only way to get ahead is to get out. He goes to school and works very hard, to this end, sometimes at the price of incredible sacrifices. I have heard of a child in Chad who walks twice a day the twenty kilometres separating his house from school.

Agriculture is only served very indirectly by this general education being given rural children. The number of children who spend more than three or four years in school, and return to the fields afterwards, is very small, particularly in the Republic of the Congo (Brazzaville).

The system worked when only 8 or 10 per cent of the children went to school. Today, the Republic of the Congo (Brazzaville), Gabon and Southern Cameroon boast of sending 60 to 80 per cent of the children to school; but they are thereby filling up the village, later the town streets with jobless and idle youths.

Before long, these young people end up in the shanty-towns of the capitals and become social parasites. Their days are spent writing requests for jobs, requests that pile up in all the administrations. Some of them, in Douala for example, join the underground.

The exorbitant advantages given to the *élite* class have, by comparison – standards of living are always relative – lowered all the other social groups. African peasants are becoming more and more conscious of being unfairly treated and looked down upon. Responsible Africans have not realized that the first step in peasant revolt is often refusal to pay the tax. From this standpoint, revolt has begun everywhere, if reports are correct that only 45 per cent of the head taxes are collected in Madagascar, 15 per cent in some districts. At Obala, north of Yaoundé, four million were collected out of thirty-six, a ninth of the total, in October of 1961. I grant you that M. M'Bida, the local deputy and a former President of the Council, campaigned against payment of the tax. With such leaders, Africa certainly has made 'a false start'. The peasant revolt could develop into a real peasant uprising, and result in a congolization; with effective leadership, it could easily lead to communism.

Current educational policy, I fear, can only hold up African economic development. In Japan in the 1880s, when the two sons of a peasant went to school, the most gifted became a teacher when he received his diploma. The other, who stopped after the equivalent of high school, returned to the fields. After hanging his certificate in the place of honour, he rolled up his sleeves and went to work. If he worked hard, as is usual in China and Japan, and owned enough land (about three acres), he could hope to earn as much as his brother, whose very modest wage equalled that of an average peasant. What did French teachers earn during that period? Eighty francs a month.

Apart from a few African 'planters' in southern Ivory Coast or the Cameroons, who drive around in cars, any hope of rivalling a civil servant is out of the question for virtually all African peasants. Even if they have been to school, the teaching offered them is much too abstract, being servilely copied from French manuals. Malagasy children on the north-eastern coast of the island currently practise artificial insemination of the vanilla plant, but their school books describe the reproductive organs of the chestnut, a tree unknown on the island.

It won't be enough to eliminate 'our ancestors the Gauls', nor to 'colour' the French school books in black or brown. They will have to be rewritten from scratch. This 'colonial' education in no way prepares students for the agricultural profession, but in fact turns them away from it. A primary school inspector complained that he was unable to admit all his former pupils into the administration. When it was pointed out to him that they constituted three-fifths of the children in his region, he replied that it was a great pity.

2. 'LOWER STANDARDS' VERSUS SLAVISH IMITATIONS

In 1958 I asked the Director of Primary School Education in Tananarive what modifications would follow from the fact that education in the villages was now concerned primarily with peasant children destined to become farmers themselves. Our meeting was brief: 'No lowering of standards, we'll give them exactly what they would get in France.' I cut short the appointment, realizing that we had nothing to say to each other.

For it is truly ridiculous to feel that everything that does not absolutely conform to the French educational norms can only be a 'lowering of standards'. Even in France the method is very vulnerable to criticism, in so far as it is detached from the real world and concrete examples, and does not seek to make the young peasant understand his village and his occupation. It is sheer stupidity to insist that the rice cultivator's child in Betsileo should be educated in exactly the same way as the worker's child in Paris. It was already a grave error to make the teaching of the French peasant in Lozère and the metallurgist in Lorraine absolutely uniform. 'We are perfect models, anything else would mean lower standards.' Africans are increasing expenditures in order to rid themselves of colonial schools, which only sought to educate Africans for subordinate jobs. The Republic of the Congo (Leopoldville) has done least in this area. It is high time for Africa to drop Western educational policy and evolve a more useful and imaginative system of its own.

Along with its bookish emphasis, totally detached from nature –
itself a book one must learn to 'read' – French education also develops
an antipathy towards manual labour, with which it is concerned little
if at all. France is training cripples as far as their ten fingers; no
entirely cerebral knowledge, which ignores manual dexterity and the
experience of the five senses, can be complete. African society is still
too wedded to the concept of the social hierarchy. In the Mali
Council of Ministers, a slave's descendant is not always as welcome
as the chief's son, who is Party Secretary. In such a framework a
child leaving school is contemptuous of his younger brother, still
hoeing the ground.

The colonial period had the rural school, with its garden – and its
abuses. Children often worked purely for the teacher's profit, and
were sent out to work in it as punishment. It was an effective way to
teach them to hate farming. For a long time in Chad school vacations
very wisely fell in the second half of the dry season, the hottest
period and the one most unpleasant to work in. The French teachers
insisted it be changed to July through September, 'the same as in
France', obviously. Aside from the fact that schoolrooms now are
unbearably hot from February to May, the former vacation period,
there is no longer the slightest possibility of cultivating even a tiny
garden, as the 'colonial' vacations cut the only season of growth in
two. Vacations as well need to be 'decolonialized'.

I had a great deal of difficulty in making African ministers admit
the irrelevance and faults of the French educational system, because
many of them are former teachers. How can they question in depth a
method of teaching that enabled them to do so well? The Senegalese
Minister of National Education has accumulated a good number of
doctorates. When the preparatory report of the CINAM Plan
proposed that rural teaching be overhauled, he rejected the idea
with horror.

The cost of the French system, which is based on the needs of a
more developed society, is far too high, particularly in relation to
results obtained with it. Upper Volta devoted 23 per cent of its
budget to education, with a result in 1960 that 8 per cent of the
school-age children could go to school. Three times their entire
current budget would be necessary to send all the children to

primary school alone.[1] Thus, in order not to 'lower' educational standards for African peasants, they do not give them any education at all. Europe was unable to provide free education for all children until it had reached a certain stage of economic development, which Africa has not reached. In the nineteenth century people had to pay to send their children to school, and schoolteachers lived in such poverty that they were in a sense proletarians, whose dedication was similar to that of lay missionaries.

The most distressing result, from the viewpoint of African development, is the almost total lack of educated peasant *élites*, despite the heavy expenditures. Seventy-five per cent of the children in Bamako go to school; only 3 per cent are enrolled in the bush in Mali. This is one of the worst kinds of 'anti-peasant' discrimination. As a result, efforts to spread agricultural knowledge, and set up self-help and agricultural co-operative organizations, have naturally failed. These latter organizations have been headed by non-peasants, some of whom (chiefs and businessmen) have exploited the peasants.

Schools do not pay enough attention to girls, although they are an essential element in agricultural work. In equatorial countries, they carry the heaviest burden of it, to the point where their entry into the school system (25 per cent of them are enrolled in the Congo basin already), disturbs me greatly, particularly as educational policy, here as elsewhere, has an anti-agricultural bias. I asked a pleasant schoolboy from Ouesso, in the aeroplane at Brazzaville, what he planned to be. 'I'm going to be a bureaucrat,' he answered. 'What will you eat?' 'Manioc and bananas.' 'No,' I replied, 'if your sister goes to school, you won't have anything to eat but your fountain pen.' I am certainly not a supporter of female servitude (I will discuss it later), nor of keeping the girls out of school; but the system must change first. 'We want a liberal arts education for our *élites*,' an African student told me, rejecting with distaste the idea of work at his school.[2] The

[1] The UNESCO Conference at Addis Ababa, May 15th–25th, 1961, on 'The Development of Education in Africa', predicted that expenditures for education would rise from 550 million dollars in 1960 to $2·6 billion in 1980, from 5 per cent to 12 per cent or even 15 per cent of national income. 'Africa is building an educational system on conventional twentieth-century bases, as it has been worked out in the rich, highly industrialized countries.' Thomas Balogh, *The Times Educational Supplement*, January 5th 1962; and the *New Statesman*, May 4th 1962.
[2] 'Education, work and guns' is the motto of the rebel Cuban youth.

education he calls 'liberal' is in reality middle-class, and is widening
the gap between the educated *élite* and the peasant mass.[1] He might
benefit from a trip to the Soviet Union or China to see how education
is allied with productive work.

3. THE DANGERS OF PREMATURE AFRICANIZATION

All jobs relating to authority and political decisions should rapidly be
taken over by Africans. African leaders have every right to make
mistakes, which is the only way to learn how to become a statesman.

As regards modern business enterprises, like factories, the problem appears in a different light. Both Dahomey and Cameroons
have 'Africanized' prematurely in this respect. The Dibombari oil
works north of Douala have never been able to function even at half
capacity because of inadequate oil palm harvests. Consequently,
Socfinol abandoned it. It was then turned over to the local administration, then to the Agricultural Provident Society, with disastrous
results. There was a twenty-five million franc deficit in the 1959–
1960 season, a third of the total turnover. A change in management
in April, 1960, reduced losses without solving the problems.

The main cause of the deficit was a rise in the price of oil palm
bunches, for political reasons. They went up to four francs a kilogram, and the factory could barely pay three francs for those coming
from groves of wild oil palms, much less rich in oil than the good
cultivated varieties. This basic economic fact did not bother the local
deputy, who in his political platform demanded a price of 6·5 francs.
A delivery strike resulted from his proposition, which ruined the
planters and seriously jeopardized the situation at the factory. But
the deputy, M. Belhé, was elected, became Minister of Labour, and
then Ambassador to Cairo. What did he care about what followed in
his wake?

Authority over personnel was taken away from the one remaining
European expert, as the factory was 'politically' oriented. Gas meant
for the trucks was sometimes resold, and the trucks themselves often

---

[1] The F A C gives large grants to a Vacation Association which allows African students
and trainees to have 'bourgeois' vacations for practically nothing on the Côte d'Azur.
This diverts them from a stay at Saint-Brieuc organized by the *Ligue d'Enseignement*,
which would put them in contact with radical groups.

used for personal errands. They were maintained so shoddily that when I visited the factory in October, 1961, practically all of them were out of commission. No one was bothering to estimate the amount of oil being stolen any longer.

In order to save the situation, I felt that three good European experts were necessary, until such time as Cameroon specialists could be trained who were honest, competent and dedicated to the factory and their country.[1] Next, all regional authorities, from the sub-prefect to the deputies, political leaders and agronomists, had to be mobilized to find ways to increase the quantity of oil palm bunches supplied to the factory as fast as possible. Thefts, which were common practice, had to be stopped; it is naturally more difficult to eliminate dishonesty when the example comes from above. To facilitate transportation of the bunches, the local population, which stood to gain by the success of the factory, would have to help maintain the roads built with FIDES money.

Years after it was established, the FIDES precedent of the 'political gift' continues to inhibit development in Africa. The peasant is accustomed to receiving everything free, and is encouraged in this attitude by the spectacle of innumerable privileged civil servants. It is hard to persuade him to make the great efforts necessary for agricultural development. His leaders have chosen the easy way out, preferring to make liberal promises, rather than get down to work. At a meeting of the local Committee on July 27th 1961, the Deputy, Nakota Ngalle, and the delegate of the planters, Labbe Mouangue, himself not a planter, demanded a 'grant to establish new oil palm plantations and to maintain the harvesting roads (which were practically all overgrown), like the grants we used to get.'

This statement is very revealing. Messrs Ngalle and Mouangue have not yet understood what independence means, and are still thinking in a colonial framework. It is enough that independence brought them to power, and gave them their privileges; for the rest, the manna of grants is there to solve everything. They have only to look out of their committee-room window to see a plantation started and maintained free for four years, up until the time it was ready for

---

[1] Navy mechanics were preferred in the oil plants operated under the Plan, as they were used to coping on board and were extremely competent.

production, with F I D E S grants. It is now overgrown by the bush, and tree growth damaged by the manioc crops that have been planted between the rows. The leaves of these precious trees, crucial for good harvests, are cut off under the most futile pretext. When the First Minister made a tour of the plantation, the trees unfortunate enough to be along his route were pruned and massacred.[1]

4. FRANCE BEARS THE BRUNT OF THE BLAME

To some extent the French have pushed the Africans into this unpromising situation. When French authority weakened, France sought to prolong it through African *élites*, to whom it gave these excessive privileges. My last book reproduced two pamphlets of the Councils of French Administrators in Madagascar. They had been widely distributed with the idea of making people vote '*oui*' in the Referendum of September 28th 1958, in a clear attempt to corrupt the native population.

The pamphlet made it seem as though a '*non*' vote condemned one to forced labour with an *angady* (a kind of Malagasy spade) and a muddy cart. No more problems for the faithful '*oui*' voter, who, through the magic of his vote would find himself perched on the seat of a tractor or truck, driving down a beautifully tarred road. This kind of falsification is criminal. Much in the same way, France implied that one had only to join the French Community (the Thousand Year Community that lasted two or three years), and economic development would automatically follow, with no effort on Africa's part at all.

Cruiziat said at the Jean Moulin Club that these problems are probably inescapable: one cannot after all reproach the Carolingians for having been what they were. In the same way, Africa cannot do better with its available cadres. Certainly, Africa is living through the 'childhood diseases' of independence, and they appear to be inevitable. But they will become far worse if the African leaders continue to ignore them, and make no efforts to remedy them.

I would be more than happy to see some true heroism among the African *élites*, but few of them have exhibited any talent for it.

[1] The Africanization of oil factories in Dahomey in the Plan is equally disquieting.

Community developments began in India on a small scale, with volunteers who were veritable saints. They achieved incontestable successes because they were wholly dedicated to their task. It was then decided to spread the movement to the entire subcontinent, and available people, Indian civil servants, were recruited. With these 'ordinary' men, the failures were resounding: no one seemed to realize that few men, whether leaders or followers, are saints.

European development speeded up considerably when a certain degree of honesty was reached among its administrators. Africans must find a hard, pure core among their leaders and younger administrators, which is strong enough to eliminate the corrupt elements, sufficiently dedicated to the general interest to devote itself wholeheartedly to it, and set an example of austerity and sacrifice. Except perhaps in Mali, Senegal and Guinea, one does not see a large enough core crystallizing. It will be important to discover what concept of man and society the core will have.

The need for such a core is great, because the current situation is on the verge of rapidly disintegrating, particularly in the Republic of the Congo (Brazzaville) and the Central African Republic. The best elements of French technical assistance, disgusted by their work conditions, which are becoming more and more difficult, and sometimes obliged to take on responsibilities which should not be theirs, are leaving one by one. Many of those who stay are doing so in order to put by some money, and these, clearly, are not the best ones. Road conditions get worse after each rainy season, much like general conditions. Governments are unable to expedite even current business. Development cannot proceed until they relinquish their nonchalant attitude and do something about their ignorance of economic problems.

'Until now we have been carefree and easy-going,' a solid middle-class citizen in Tananarive told me. Insouciance can only continue in a colony that has no population explosion. If Africa rejects colonialism, birth control and the big push needed to develop fast, it has only one way out: to send away all the doctors, and re-establish a high mortality rate.

The first part of the book has been long, but I cannot outline my modest proposals without clarifying the situation on which they rest. To sum up, the natural African *milieu*, which has fairly difficult soils and climate, is in no way hopeless, and good results have already been obtained (see Appendix II). The most difficult problem in releasing the 'hidden productive forces' of Africa is a human one. On the whole its people have been degraded by Western intervention, from slavery to colonialism and its aftermath, economic exploitation.

We imposed an administrative superstructure on a backward economy that could not support the weight; and a trade structure which benefits industrial countries but blocks African growth. Certainly, we are helping the new states to bear the weight, but this too holds back their economic maturity, on which real independence rests. Plans for African development cannot be made in the abstract any longer, in the framework of ideologies borrowed from Europe, Asia or America, ideologies that were worked out in completely different situations. The specific nature of Africa's problems must be taken into account with the greatest care, even if this involves hesitations and constantly changing and evolving formulas.

Underdevelopment is not limited to Africa. South-east Asia, the Middle East, Latin America and many other countries are also marking time, mostly because of unjust and outdated social and economic structures. The African situation falls in the more general framework of retarded economies.

Although geographers can sometimes remain within the comfortable limits of description, agronomists and economists must come up with concrete proposals. As regards Africa, these will be opinions, not directions. In order not to lose sight of this for a single moment (every technical expert is a bureaucrat at heart: beware), I will repeat several times that all decisions are and must remain in the hands of the Africans. My only aim, and it is a difficult one, is to seek to help them.

4

CHAPTER EIGHT
Economic planning

I. INDEPENDENT AFRICAN PLANNING

The African states, having decided to regulate economic development, are in the process of drawing up economic Plans. A planned economy allows one to allocate resources, which are always (more or less) inadequate, in the most efficient manner, and to attack the 'bottlenecks' of economic development. Ideally, the Plans should give priority to agricultural and industrial development, channelling the great majority of assets in their direction. This is far from the case at present. Once rapid growth is made a fundamental objective, the most urgent means to implement it are still to be chosen. All Plans are first of all classifications of priorities.

Such choices cannot be made on purely rational and scientific grounds, or by technical experts independently of political leaders; if they did so, they would become technocrats. They can, of course, bring together useful criteria for drawing up a Plan, as has been done by CINAM in Senegal and SOGEP in the Cameroons, and as France has done in several countries. But it is impossible to formulate an 'apolitical' plan.

A certain flexibility in planning, as we know it in France, can assure priority to the general axes of development, and at the same time maintain great disparity in wealth, and a role for capital gains and monopoly power. The objective involved is obviously both economic and social, because it has to reconcile present consumption with development for the future, individual expenditures and those that increase general economic activity.

Until recently too many plans have been virtually imposed on Africa by France. They should have been demanded by the African governments. Formulation of plans is given over to Frenchmen, foreigners to the country who have a difficult time establishing a give-and-take relationship with the political leaders. They have practically no way of discovering what the workers and peasants at the other end think. These plans are beautiful documents, full of pious vows, and outline projects involving millions of man-hours of work, but they remain on the drawing-board, as no one makes the slightest effort to translate them into reality. This is certainly the case in the Cameroons. A catalogue of projects is arrived at in the way that is designed to attract the maximum amount of foreign aid, as the Malagasy Minister of Agriculture explained to me.

The only plan capable of moving African economies (the economy in countries like the Ivory Coast, Senegal and the Cameroons is capable of a take-off right away) is one which requires the 'total involvement of government and people, the conscious choice of achievable goals and deliberate sacrifices', as J. Guillard has expressed it.

Certain African governments claim affinities with socialism as a way of achieving social justice and rapid development. However, they do not all conceive of it in the same way. Senegal and Mali interpret it very differently. For others it is a convenient alibi for many of their shortcomings. Nowhere in Africa is it a question of immediately socializing the economy under a strong central government, as in the Soviet type of socialism. Even Communist China, later in such a hurry, went at the first stages of socialism with great care for about eight years after its conquest of the mainland. And long experience with power, going back at least twenty years over large areas, preceded the conquest.

Let us imagine a hypothetical situation, in which a government desires, not to rush into socialism immediately, which would entail total upheaval, but to orient itself towards an 'African' socialism. It therefore seeks specifically African solutions for uniquely African problems and conditions, a praiseworthy effort, since the African point of departure is very different from that of the Soviet Union or China, and demands new structures. Such a search will be all the more necessary if this government is thinking in terms of a less 'tough' political climate than in communist countries. It will not, of course, be able to eliminate all restraints and controls; they are implied in the concept of society itself. Those imposed in capitalist states are not the most 'tender', but are more hypocritical because they are less clearly formulated.

Suppose, further, that this government affirms its socialist orientation and at the same time gives priority to satisfying the most urgent needs of the great majority of its people. Over massive imports of private cars, it will choose buses and trucks. Rejecting the idea of sumptuous palaces, it will build a great number of inexpensive schools and clinics. It will not sacrifice the primary education and vocational training of the peasant majority in order to provide higher education to a small group that will only swell the ranks of the privileged caste. It will seek to guard against protein deficiencies in the poor, instead of importing luxury foods for the rich. . . . Each of these proposals determines a series of orientations which are essential for development.

A 'pre-socialist' economy must, to merit the name, create an important public sector, as much in industry as in agriculture. The large plantations in the forest region lend themselves particularly well to this method of operation. But the great majority of the agricultural sector, practically all of it in the savannah, can remain quite individualized, for a period which experience alone will determine. However, agriculture will profit greatly by immediate integration with a co-operative network, which, in line with the provisions of the Plan, would supply it with the funds and equipment needed for rapid growth.

2. INVESTMENTS NEEDED FROM MANY SOURCES

Once the basic lines of development have been broadly defined, economic growth must be rapidly increased by securing more loans and investments. In 1962 foreign aid, mainly from F A C or the European Fund, was practically the only source of capital. A lender can impose political conditions, and his ulterior motives do not necessarily coincide with the development needs of the recipient. Neo-colonialism will not die by itself. There are interests, which the

great trading companies call 'French' interests, that are so incrimi-
nating that they should be quickly dropped.

Private investments continue to flow at a modest rate into Madagascar, Senegal, and particularly the Ivory Coast. The Blohorn oil
palm plantation at Cosrou could be enlarged a hundredfold, the
Dizangue rubber plantation in the Cameroons tenfold. But even if
laws were drawn up that were favourable to investments, these
countries cannot count on capitalists alone to build Africa. There are
first of all the investments for infrastructure, such as schools, roads
and hospitals, which, though essential, are non-income-producing,
and cannot attract investors seeking a profit.

In November 1959, when President Houphouet-Boigny explained
to Canadian investors that they could realize large profits from
investments made in his country, he implied that low salaries would
be maintained, and implicitly promised them freedom to export
profits. A not inconsiderable source of capital could be found right at
home if business profits were prevented from leaving the country.
Brazil is attempting to accomplish this. The profits could be chan-
nelled into development, which would justify maintaining private
capitalism at least for the time being. Development of native
capitalism is, of course, preferable from the African point of view to
ex-colonial foreign capitalism, as it avoids the danger of a kind of
North-Americanization by European capital.

Yet all these resources, lumped together, would still be inadequate
in the hypothesis, which I shall not abandon during the course of the
book, of *rapid* economic development. National savings must be
sharply increased, first of all by drastic and intelligent cutbacks in
government budgets. The greatest potential area of saving is salaries.[1]
It is at present very difficult to control the outflow of business profits,
unfortunately. However, if they are taxed more heavily, the additional income will compensate for the loss of customs duties on
luxury imports. These last absolutely must be eliminated and replaced by equipment and machinery, which should be duty free.
Many other sources of savings must be found, but one cannot
depend much in the foreseeable future on individual thrift.

[1] Many Africans have told me that they would accept a reduction in pay on condition
that the money saved went into investments and not into the pockets of the Ministers.

3. A PARALLEL INDUSTRIALIZATION AND AGRICULTURAL INTENSIFICATION

I have already spoken of the priority that must be given to industrialization. Without factories, an economy cannot get off the ground and effect rapid growth in labour productivity, nor can it provide for the massive demands of modern agriculture. Industrialization is also a symbol of economic progress, not a negligible factor in inspiring enthusiasm for development. Giving priority to agriculture alone is a typically reactionary position (which the Agrarian Party in Croatia adopted in 1930). During the last war the Germans ordered Charles Braibant to write a book called *La France, Nation Agricole*. Had its prescriptions been followed, France would have been led into a totally subordinate economic position. The Morgenthau Plan of 1945 wanted to make Germany a nation of farmers, which was completely unrealistic, fortunately, for Germany would have starved.

With this agreed, it is still true that industrialization will encounter tremendous obstacles in Africa, particularly in the beginning, which cannot be underestimated. The markets in each of these small countries are extremely narrow because the inhabitants have such low incomes. The average in Ruanda-Urundi is $45 per capita annually. Monetary resources are also exceedingly scarce, because the majority come from the domestic economy. The formation of economic unions, while extremely helpful, will not be enough to compensate for the balkanization of the area. As soon as national Plans are formulated, they should be related to each other, in order to eliminate duplication within a common market of large regional groups.[1]

One such regional group might stretch from Dakar to Elizabethville, including also Ghana and Nigeria. High transportation costs will be one road block to enlarging markets. In order to surmount

[1] In the *Economic Bulletin for Latin America*, March, 1961, Thomas Balogh underlines the obstacle of high urban salaries compared to those in the bush, and the easy profits made in business, which turn capital away from industry. The transportation network has been directed more towards the import-export trade than toward local industrialization. The free play of existing market forces cannot assure, may even prevent efficient distribution of scarce resources, he concludes. See also the articles by the same author in *Oxford Economic Papers*, particularly the issue of February, 1962, 'Equity and efficiency, the problem of optimal investment in a framework of under-development'.

national rivalries and achieve economic co-ordination, Africa will have to be possessed of a strong will for unity, and be ready to make great sacrifices when they are needed. Industrialization will not be effective if it depends on political pressures and not on basic facts of economic geography. Europe is just beginning to deal with the problems of internationalizing industries. Africa can and should do so right away, in order to avoid enormous wastage of investments in a better way than Europe has—an essential economy necessitated by her backwardness.

Any new industry in Africa will have a difficult enough time getting established, and it is almost bound to fail without vigilant and effective support from the government. Customs protection on a national level, and later on the creation of an African Common Market, itself protected, will be virtually essential in order to overcome a whole series of handicaps: weakness in infrastructure, lack of African technicians, high transportation costs, high cost of spare parts, and the inevitably small factories to begin with. Customs protection should not be exaggerated or continued too long, because the natural tendency of any businessman, even if it is the government, is to let up if he is behind a protective barrier. Other supports can be envisaged, such as the strong participation of government credits.

Accelerated agricultural development will be more of a corollary and aid than a preliminary to this necessary but difficult industrialization.[1] In order to buy more machinery and outfit more factories, exports must be increased, and they are still essentially agricultural and mineral. Purchases of food from abroad must be reduced. In order to demand more of an effort from workers, brutally torn from their fields, tiny gardens, or wild food gathered in the savannah and forest regions, they must be offered more and better food, with a higher protein content.

---

[1] In his *Problems of Capital Formation in Underdeveloped Countries,* Nurkse discussed over-populated countries, with disguised unemployment, where industrialization is immediately needed to absorb the unproductive labour force. For under-populated countries he estimates that improvement of agricultural productivity is a necessary preliminary for industrialization, in order to free the manpower. I do not agree: in under-populated and backward countries disguised unemployment also exists, often very pronounced. This is true of tropical Africa. The solutions thus differ only slightly in the two cases.

Industries during the change-over will have to be backed up by intensified agriculture if they are to develop. It will supply them with more of the raw materials of industry: cotton and sack fibres, like jute, and oleaginous plants, which play such an important role in western and central Africa. The increased demand for paper will soon call for the creation of pulp and paper factories and for the manufacture of other cellulose derivatives. To satisfy all these needs and at the same time increase the quantity and quality of foodstuffs, a sharp increase in agricultural productivity will be called for.

In order to accomplish all this, Africa will have to break out, if necessary a little roughly, of its infernal cycle of under-production, 'itinerant' crop cultivation, long fallow periods, lack of fertilizers, and reliance on manpower alone. By concentrating solely on industry one cannot solve the problems of rural unemployment for a good long time,[1] while agricultural jobs can more rapidly absorb the manpower and make good use of it. Only by increasing agricultural productivity can rural buying power be increased sufficiently to offer the new industries sufficient outlets. As in nineteenth-century France and present-day China, the savings of African peasants must contribute towards the financing of new industries, which could not finance themselves quickly enough at first otherwise.

Development needs in the two sectors are not always antagonistic, fortunately. To a large extent agriculture can develop on its own, starting with the 'hidden' productive forces in the countryside, by mobilizing the peasantry, their livestock, and utilizing the water for irrigation, the soils, and the cleared forest land. Industry will have to absorb the majority of the financial resources, largely provided by foreign aid at present. Competition between the two will, of course, exist for available credit and technical experts; arbitration, necessarily political, will have to intervene.

4. HEAVY INDUSTRY

In the Soviet Union and China an absolute priority was granted to

---

[1] Industry often employs only 5 to 10 per cent of the population in Africa at present, sometimes less than 5 per cent. Even with the maximum growth possible, it would only double this amount every eight years. Agriculture must therefore prepare, in any hypothesis, to absorb more people. (T. Balogh.)

4*

heavy industry on every level. This enabled them to develop rapidly, but at the price of enormous efforts and the sacrifice of a generation. Africa does not seem disposed to accept such a sacrifice at present, and we in the West are rather too comfortably off to be able to suggest a like mobilization of heroes. This blueprint for economic growth, which was applied dogmatically to the smaller countries in Eastern Europe, the 'popular democracies', has not always been very interesting from the economic point of view. It has brought on resounding failures, particularly in Hungary and Rumania, which the so-called revolutionary countries in Africa might think about, particularly in view of their small markets.

A different orientation would vassalize Africa, and it would become, like Latin America vis-à-vis the United States, the 'purveyor by appointment' of iron ore, or power for aluminium, to Europe. P. Kalck[1] points out that while African ore is necessary to Europe, European techniques are necessary to Africa. This does not, however, justify maintaining Africa in a state of economic dependency. (I shall discuss in Chapter Fourteen, 5, the possibilities of an African metallurgic industry.)

With the natural resources, inter-state agreements and the participation of Franco-European aid, it would be possible to produce in well-chosen areas in Africa hundreds of thousands of tons of aluminium, several million tons of cast iron, and tens of millions of tons of iron alloys.[2] The enormous sums this will necessitate may be completely wasted if each country, even the worst situated, with the smallest and most inaccessible deposits, insists on having its own 'heavy' industry to satisfy a desire for prestige.

Latin America has heavily emphasized the manufacture of consumer goods, and in so doing slowed down industrial development. Venezuela still exports its 'mountain of iron' at Ciudad Bolivar to the steel mills in the United States, in a raw state, like its oil. The blast furnaces and steel mills of tropical Africa will need fuel that is fairly

---

[1] *La Sidérurgie Atlantique et Son Evolution en Fonction de l'Afrique Noire, Industrie et Travaux d'Outre-Mer*, February, 1961. The author writes rather strangely of the 'neocolonialism of the East . . . which proceeds, as in the heyday of colonial exploitation, on the barter system, trading machines and experts for agricultural products.' Perhaps he is unaware that colonialism scarcely supplied machinery!

[2] A number of experts have cast doubt on whether foreign aid can result in really healthy projects in a 'neocolonialist' framework.

light,[1] an adequate market for their products, trained technicians, and reasonable transportation rates for the raw materials. Each case must be individually studied, leaving aside the question of prestige: as an income-producer, it has never been very satisfactory. Africa must have 'growth points', of course, but not at any price. Large industrial complexes have already been shown to be more profitable, like the alumina factory at Fria in Guinea (500,000 tons a year), which will be completed when aluminium is manufactured with the power provided by the Konkouré Falls. Because of the high cost of this second investment stage, which will be around 1·5 billion new francs, capitalist groups have held off, as they are not reassured by the political evolution of Guinea. Its new orientation may persuade them to change their minds. The Edéa factory in the Cameroons is already transforming alumina into aluminium; the very low cost of electricity has favoured the installations.

Together with uranium, the enormous hydro-electrical resources in tropical Africa can compensate for its coal deficiency and its recognizedly low quantity of oil deposits. Immense falls, like those at Inga on the lower Congo River, could theoretically provide 30 million kilowatts, or 225 billion kilowatt hours per year, three times the total of electricity produced in France annually. The rate of flow on the river's headwaters is 25,000 cubic metres a second. Add to this the already recognized potential of the Ikopa-Bestiboka in Madagascar (16 billion kilowatt hours a year), the Ogooué and the Nganga in Gabon (more than 10 billion) and the Kouilou in the Congo (7 billion on one site alone), and total hydro-electric production in France in 1959 is easily surpassed.

Natural resources cannot be divided up among various states, yet an industrial complex capable of utilizing fully the power provided by the Kouilou falls (iron-manganese, iron silicate, phosphorus, aluminium) would require an investment of around three billion new francs. President Youlou would like very much to procure this sum in France. But if a sum that high is invested in a country of 800,000 inhabitants, what amount should be allotted, to be meticulously fair, to Madagascar, which has seven times the population? Blinded by the drama of the Kouilou falls, the President of the Congo (Brazza-

[1] Nigerian oil and coal, perhaps natural gas from the Sahara.

ville) totally neglects agricultural and general development in his country. The worst aspect of these great complexes is that they create an illusion. The truth is that alone they can never create economic growth, particularly at the beginning.

Alucam, the *Compagnie Camerounaise d'Aluminium* of Edéa, forms a kind of foreign body in the Cameroon economy, as it contributes very little to development. It pays rents and salaries, which provide some outlets for local agriculture, but no aluminium industry derives from it. To avoid being nationalized the capitalists deliberately chose to manufacture alumina in Guinea and aluminium in the Cameroons. A great quantity of economic arguments have been advanced to show that it is impossible to exploit the bauxite deposits in the Adamaoua. I suggest that we remain sceptical for a while. Without denying the value of industrial complexes, one must also plan for an industrial development that is disseminated throughout the country, and integrated into the different sectors of the economy. This will contribute to progress in the economy as a whole, including agriculture. I will discuss ways of doing this in several areas which, if less prestigious, may be more effective.

5. SUGAR: VILLAGE INDUSTRY VERSUS THE LARGE REFINERY

Huge modern sugar refineries have recently been installed in the Niari valley in the Congo and on the Madagascar coasts. The largest is the Sosumav refinery at Ambilobe, in north-western Madagascar, which produces more than 45,000 tons of sugar a year. Yet the price of cane sugar there is higher than beet sugar in France, despite the fact that cane sugar is so much cheaper to produce that Java, Cuba *et al* would long ago have driven North American and European beet sugar out of the market, as it is an archaic survival of Napoleonic autarchy. But it is protected by powerful interests, at the expense of sugar producers in the poorer countries.

Interesting research could be done on the amount of profit made by the sugar companies and on the proportion reinvested locally.[1] Taxes established in 1929 have cut down on hand production of sugar in Madagascar, and it subsists only in smaller, scattered areas

[1] I would be grateful to anyone who can give me information.

on the high plateaux, around the capital, and south-east of Fianarantsoa. In these regions the altitude is too high for the canes, and its cultivation too marginal. The apparatus used to extract the juice is incredibly primitive, consisting of two wooden cylinders moved by hand and foot, between which pieces of sugar stalk are forced, having first been crushed with a mallet. Four people can extract eighty litres of juice a day, and a ton of cane cannot even produce 250 litres.

Somewhere between this archaic method, abandoned in the Antilles in the seventeenth century (read Père Labat), and the large modern refinery, a place can be found for a village sugar industry. Gradually modernized, it would be a useful stepping-stone. Stalks of sugar were sold around Fenerive on the eastern coast for 1·25 francs a kilogram. These are used to make *betsabetsa*, the 'wine' made from fermented cane sugar juice. Buying at that price, a well-equipped village 'factory' could certainly sell crude sugar on the premises for less than refinery sugar. On the central plateau it is sold for more, which indicates how highly it is regarded – on an equal level with luxury foods.

A three- or six-cylinder mill, capable of extracting 600 litres of juice per ton of cane, costs 130,000 CFA francs, and can process more than a ton of cane an hour. Including the motor, cauldrons, etc., the total price of installation should not go over a million CFA francs, and could produce more than a ton of sugar daily. In a season of four or five months, 150 tons of crude sugar can be produced without operating a night shift. A refinery producing 15,000 tons of sugar would perhaps cost, depending on its location, between 1·2 and 1·5 billion, or 1,200 to 1,500 times as much.

The economic superiority of a village factory which gradually introduces more modern techniques is incontestable in the case of sugar. Backward countries are low on capital, and we have seen how this dearth slows down agricultural progress in north-east Brazil. A hundred such small factories could produce as much sugar – far more if they operated at night – and tie up twelve to fifteen times less capital, as a large factory. This is certainly one way to speed up industrialization with limited resources. It also offers more jobs, and absorbs more of the rural unemployed, not only or even essentially in the factories themselves, but particularly in the fields. Cane fields can be spread out over a large area, almost half of the surface of the island.

Dispersion has many advantages. If you are only cultivating seventy-five acres in a given locality, you can choose good soils. Also, most peasants do not buy, or buy very little sugar, unable to afford it. Their children are totally unfamiliar with sweet drinks and preserved foods, and yet the peasants' fruit rots. The forty-five thousand tons of sugar consumed in 1960 'satisfied' Madagascar's needs, according to the experts. This is eight kilograms per capita, but less than two kilograms in poor rural zones, like certain districts in the south. One cannot decently talk of satisfaction at that rate.

Wherever he has good enough land, or a garden that can be irrigated, the Malagasy peasant, who is rarely overloaded with work, could produce enough cane for his own needs and take it to the village factory to be processed. He could pay for the cost by turning over a part of his canes. Thirty per cent seems a reasonable proportion, if the factory is well managed.

At present cane cultivation is concentrated around the large refineries, which waste almost all of the leafy tops of the stalks (called 'white ends' in the Antilles). This free by-product of sugar is good animal feed. The peasant who 'cultivates' his sugar could use it during the dry season when his animals most need it. Peasants would appreciate the advantages of a cultivated feed obtained without extra work. Once they have become used to this idea, it will eventually be easier to persuade them to grow crops solely to feed their animals. So far it has been almost impossible to convince them of the crucial necessity of this.

Suppose even that in regions only adequately suited to cane cultivation, crude sugar made in the factory is a little more expensive than refined sugar in the store of the large refinery. This is still not a strong enough argument to eliminate the village factories, because for the refined sugar you have to add transportation and distribution costs right up to the peasant, which are non-existent or negligible in the case of local crude sugar.

Although it is desirable to speed up the transformation into a buying and selling economy, distribution costs, swollen by poor yields and commercial profits, become excessive. Tools and sources of energy must be modernized also. Until this is accomplished, sales of refined sugar could be assimilated into the internal market, which would represent a great advance over importing sugar.

Most of the countries in French-speaking Africa, except the Congo and Madagascar, do not yet have a sugar refinery.[1] Many want to build one immediately. I have advised them to start with a series of small village factories. In order to find the optimum locale for a refinery, preliminary cultivation of more than five years' duration and on more than fifty acres is necessary in certain areas. The factories I have been discussing are exactly the kind that can handle the average harvest on such a surface.

By dispersing ten or twenty village factories on areas known to be favourable to cane cultivation, the best location can be determined at the same time that an edible foodstuff is produced from the experimental canes. Once the refinery is built, the small factories in its area can be moved to distant areas, to which distribution costs of refined sugar would be too high. Suppose that Senegal constructs in the near future its first sugar refinery, using cane sugar from irrigated fields, somewhere along the river of the same name. It would still not cover all the sugar needs of the country. The village factories will be justified for a longer time in upper Casamance and eastern Senegal, which is well watered but hard to get to.

Distilleries have been thought of as a way to get started. Although inferior to a refinery in terms of output, their maximum production would be much higher than the small village factory. However, the tendency of the African or Malagasy to extract alcohol from the canes is far enough advanced already, and there is no point in encouraging it. The danger of an alcoholic 'explosion' is indeed the reef on which my proposal may founder. The village factories will have to be under tight control, which is difficult to achieve, like all economic development, under present conditions.

The Research Institute at Lucknow in Uttar Pradesh, in the Ganges valley, has come up with a number of ways in which a small village factory can evolve into a large modern factory. One viewpoint has it that 20,000 tons of sugar a year is the most economical unit for

---

[1] The sugar surpluses in the Antilles, Cuba, Jamaica and Guadeloupe make one stop and reflect.

a sugar factory. It is an opinion usually held by those selling heavy machinery, who have stopped manufacturing smaller machines. It would be worth someone's while to make an economic study of factories turning out 1,000 to 2,000 tons a year, in the context of the world-wide economic situation, taking into account the arguments discussed above. Even supposing that manufacturing costs are 3 per cent to 5 per cent higher, the advantages of semi-dispersion would more than compensate for this.

The Senegalese leader to whom I outlined this programme was horrified at the thought of eating crude sugar, as if I had tried to make a savage out of him. It is better for the health, and widely used in India[1] and Nigeria, and is still to be found in South America. His attitude is characteristic of the new well-paid *élite*, who want the best of both worlds. He reminds me of the planters in the slave days, because he cannot conceive that Casamance peasants produced crude sugar for many years before they could afford to buy it. The future of these peasants means more to me than the preferences of the *élites*. The middle-class Malagasy is better advised: he is willing to pay a high price for it, as though it were sweets, but cheaper than imported sweets. In any case, it is unintelligent, at best, to import sugar into countries that lack protein so seriously. Moroccans drink too much tea and sugar already, and not enough milk.

6. AGRICULTURAL EQUIPMENT AND FERTILIZERS

Thousands of carts and ploughs are already in use in Mali and Madagascar; Chad is moving in this direction, and the others follow slowly. Many different types of farm equipment and machinery for draught animals, which up until now have been imported, are needed to work the soil better. Since they are not manufactured locally, few agricultural workers know how to repair them. At the Niger Office ploughs are replaced when they no longer cut adequately, instead of being sharpened or strengthened.[2] Imports of the iron and steel necessary to manufacture them locally would cost far less than importing the machines themselves.

---

[1] Where it is the food of the poor, and often cheaper than a cereal, particularly in the South. In Madagascar, sugar costs over twice as much as rice.

[2] Such wastage provokes a storm of protest from French farmers when they hear of it.

A concern manufacturing such equipment can start out on a fairly modest scale, with simple implements, and work up to more complex machines. In the beginning its products will probably cost more and be less well made than the imports. This in no way negates the idea, however. Aside from relieving the trade balance, it will be excellent training in metallurgy, and can gradually lead to the manufacture of more complex machines, eventually reaching the level of tractors, trucks and the most up-to-date machinery. Mali has already started in this direction.

Plans for industrialization must not neglect, right from the beginning, industries to supply modern agriculture with the means of production. Senegal and Togo are already producing enriched phosphates,[1] and Dakar is planning to manufacture phosphate fertilizers. Potassium deposits were found in the Congo while seeking oil. However, the potential Franco-German producers do not have the same impetus to exploit the mines as the Congolese. The present market for potassium in Africa is too small, so it would have to be exported. Also, each mine would have to reach a high minimum tonnage to make a profit.

The same holds true for nitrogen plants, an important element in productivity of African soils. Ruanda-Urundi could establish one on the shore of Lake Kivu, as it is possible to obtain methane in the water there, and hydro-electric energy is available at close hand. But the size of the factory is not easily reducible, as is the case with sugar. At least 35,000 tons a year of pure nitrogen must be produced. This could mean 175,000 tons of fertilizer with 20 per cent nitrogen. In 1958 the Congo used only 15,000 tons of all kinds of fertilizers, Ruanda-Urundi in 1960 only a thousand tons.

Government agreements will obviously be needed before such factories can be established. It should soon be possible to construct three or four of them from Guinea to Uganda, placed at reasonable distances. Increase in utilization must be energetically encouraged first, even if partial subsidies are necessary, wherever fertilizer is found to be economic, in order to enlarge the market. A factory can be built when consumption in the area to be served reaches even half

[1] 500,000 tons is forecast for 1961 at Taiba, Senegal, and 650,000 tons for Togo in 1962. Most of it will be sold outside Africa.

the projected output of the factory. The value of these fertilizers to the African economy is such that I would be happy to see, as in Japan after 1930, obligatory distribution to cultivators of good formulas payable after the next harvest. The IRHO did this with peanut growers in Senegal. When harvests are sold commercially by co-operatives and regional offices, like the Niger Office, this will be easier to achieve.

Studies on the use of fertilizers, particularly in food crops, could be financed by the proceeds of the French campaign against world hunger. French-speaking Africa would benefit greatly from such research, which should think in terms both of need and of the multiple effects of fertilizer application. At the same time it increases the size of harvests, the production of livestock, and the buying power of the peasants. Its manufacture deserves to be started before consumer goods such as textiles, bicycles, even household goods (J. Guillard). The development of education, cadres and activist movements in rural areas will be indispensable in encouraging its general use.

7. FOOD INDUSTRIES: CANNED FOODS AND FRUIT JUICES VERSUS BEER

Out of 200 million Belgian francs' worth of coffee sold in 1959 by the Africans in N'Gozi Province in Burundi, 120 million was used to purchase 'European' beer, brewed at Usumbura, and a good deal of the rest for banana beer. Breweries are considered 'one of the best' African industries in Senegal, the Ivory Coast, Guinea, Dahomey, Congo, Chad, Madagascar, Leopoldville, and Usumbura. If this tendency continues unchecked, the pure profit motive will dangerously increase alcoholism and slow down development even more.

A 'controlled' economy should intervene and put a ferociously high tax on imported liquor or outlaw it entirely. This would necessitate incorruptible customs officials. Next, it would cut down consumption of local alcoholic beverages, except those with very low alcoholic content, and favour fruit juices. In the general interest, government credit and other benefits should not support either harmful products or luxury goods like American cars.

Even more urgent is the establishment of food industries in order to cut down rapidly on imports of fruit juices and canned foods of all kinds. At the same time the necessary encouragement must be given to local fishing, truck gardening and livestock raising. Plants to process cooking oils are developing rapidly. Those that produce peanut oil can supply, if precautions are taken, a special oil cake, which can provide a meal with high protein content for the Africans. With the addition of manioc starch and wheat flour, it makes a dough richer in protein and less expensive in foreign exchange than that made of pure wheat flour.

Fish meal supplies amino-acids that are still lacking in the African diet. Palm oil factories should be established together with the new oil palm plantations, as well as cabbage-palm factories. These would manufacture soap, as well as oil cakes for hog farms. Peanut-oil cakes are also good feed for dairy cows in zones of high altitude.

The use to which African proteins are put today is a scandal. African peanut-oil cakes, which should be consumed by the Africans themselves, are mainly used to feed cows in north-western Europe. Their transformation into milk entails a high protein loss, compensated for by the higher quality of the proteins in milk. However, these 'superior proteins' contained in the skim milk left over after the butter is taken off are fed to the calves, pigs and chickens. They therefore end up on Western dinner tables, although we are already bloated with fats and over-burdened with cholesterol. This time the alimentary loss is massive both in quantity and quality. Right now, as an intermediary step, Europe should dry increasing amounts of the skim milk to provide powdered milk for African children, and others, until they have an adequate milk supply at home.

In a country as vast as Madagascar there is a great foreseeable demand for oil cakes in livestock raising. I suggest therefore that small oil factories be established throughout the country, in order to supply livestock raisers with local oil cakes at a cheaper rate, as the prohibitive transport costs would be eliminated.

Rice mills should follow the development of paddy, or raw rice, cultivation. Instead of whitening the rice too much, which removes nutritious elements and increases the incidence of beriberi, governments should launch a fashion in 'cargo' rice, which is simply hulled. If the grains are streaked with red as a result, such varieties can be called 'national' rice. Asia, from which rice originates, has in general rejected the ridiculous European preference for very long and white grains, which have a lower food value. The seventy-seven rice mills in Madagascar, which are too concentrated in the high plateaux, only operate at a quarter or a third of their capacity. In the rest of the island rice is pounded by hand, which entails heavy losses and over-work, work which could be better utilized in productive cultivation. In many cases parcelling out developed and improved land into individual pieces leads to great wastage.

From Dakar to Abidjan, soon in Tananarive, flour mills are rapidly being established, and consumption of factory-made bread is on the increase. Dakar is terribly over-equipped with mills. It would be far more advantageous to encourage rice consumption, as it is easier to produce locally. From Senegal to Chad, through Kano in Nigeria, tropical wheat can be cultivated. Looking ahead, the location of flour mills should be carefully planned, as they will some day be supplied with local wheat.

Ways should be constantly sought to get the highest possible value out of agricultural export products. For example, grated coconut can be produced in Dahomey, and cocoa butter in Douala, made from inferior quality beans. Nestlé is beginning to produce instant coffee in Abidjan. Until now all the coffee consumed locally, whether roasted, ground or instant, came from France.[1] The Cameroons have started to make soda water with a coffee base, much preferable from the standpoint of health and economy to coca-cola, manufacture of which is spreading all too rapidly in tropical Africa.

Chad already has a brewery and a flour mill, but no meat-canning factory, although it is a country of livestock raising. Even worse, although its cotton production is the highest in French-speaking Africa, it still has no spinning or weaving mills, unlike its neighbours of ex-French Equatorial Africa. It is still throwing away practically all the cottonseeds. Widely dispersed cotton gins, and the preference for quick and easy profits that a ginning monopoly can procure, has

[1] Ask for 'a good cup of coffee' in a Douala restaurant and the waiter will invariably say: 'This is French coffee, Monsieur.'

meant the neglect of cottonseed-oil factories.[1] Yet Chad could extract much more table oil, using the cottonseeds as Northern Cameroon is doing, than is already being manufactured at Moundou. One day modern livestock methods will make use of the valuable cottonseed cakes. At present they are ploughed back into the soil, in the agricultural zone; in herding regions more profound changes will be necessary to arrive at this stage.

8. TEXTILES AND WOOD, AFTER MECHANICS AND CHEMISTRY

I am not really qualified to discuss these two basic industries, but they should be among the top priorities wherever they are economically feasible. Assembling bicycles is next in line of importance after agricultural equipment, and should be started immediately, as is being done in Abidjan and Douala, and followed by motor-bicycles. In a few years, when the market has been enlarged through inter-African agreements, it will be possible to assemble and later construct trucks, scooters, buses and tractors. Assembly of private, therefore luxury cars, should be last, but has prematurely started in Abidjan, as a result of excessive salaries. High African officials, with a low average level of education, have many more luxuries than their Soviet colleagues, despite the fact that the economy of the USSR is far more advanced than that of Africa.

For most African countries, cotton goods are one of the largest items imported, and one which it would be easiest to manufacture locally. The most up-to-date factory is not essential everywhere at the beginning. Spinning factories can sometimes be equipped with fairly recent second-hand equipment no longer needed by large European factories. It might even be obtained free.[2] Hand weaving is still of economic value in regions of high unemployment, provided large looms are used, from 2½ feet to a yard and more, instead of six to eight inches wide, like the ones in common use in Mali and Chad.

A vocational school in Bamako undertook to train weavers on large

[1] A much higher price is obtained by exporting cotton directly from the research stations than by selling it locally to COTONFRAN. It pays 35 to 50 francs for a kilometric ton of raw cotton, as against the 20 francs paid by the CFDT in North Cameroon.
[2] Will Monsieur Boussac agree? It is not just a question of giving Africa second-hand equipment, but of adding this equipment to all that can be given already.

looms, recruiting high school graduates, as is done in France. Once they received their diplomas, they wanted jobs in the bureaucracy. Given Mali's present stage of development, use of new looms should be taught to the village weavers, even illiterate ones.

The textile industry is limited to Dakar, Bouaké in the Ivory Coast, Bangui and Antsirabé. Its development will have to be protected in some cases. In order to be profitable, each design will have to be run a certain number of times, which means that the local industry cannot offer the same variety as the imported fabrics. This will mean a certain austerity in dress, even and above all for the wives of the *élite*, who should set an example by creating a fashion in 'national' cloth.

Imports of second-hand clothes are large, especially in Madagascar, and slow down development of a national textile industry. In high altitudes the very poor cannot dress warmly except in this way. Some intelligent improvisation will be called for the day that restrictions on imports are imposed. Knitted fabrics made from hastily spun wools and animal furs could be substitutes. Rope and sack manufacture, with a hard fibre base of the sisal and jute type, can be developed to a great extent. At present the Cameroons import a thousand tons of empty sacks, Chad 500 tons of jute for cotton bales, the Central African Republic 300 tons.

Industries deriving from wood remain completely inadequate in the African economy. African countries continue to import Swedish matches and furniture, when they could export a great deal of these items, if they trained workers and equipped shops. The role of wood in the construction of furniture and houses is much smaller in Africa, even in forest zones, than in Central and Eastern Europe, Scandinavia and North America. Now, however, better protective measures have been found against termites and other wood-destroying insects. The sleepers of the Douala–Ngaoundéré railway are to be made of steel. If they were constructed of wood, a local timber industry could be founded, and branch out from there; but the French metal interests are protected by friends in the Department of Public Works. As for exports, despite the fact that sales of timber grew six-fold between 1938 and 1960, those of wood products are well behind the forecasts. Tax reductions would be of help in stimulating local industries. Plastics, perhaps with a castor oil base, such as Rilsan, could replace the worthless enamelled objects imported from Japan and Hong Kong.

Many industries are not mentioned here, as I am not conversant with all of the problems. But any new project must always be undertaken with specific African conditions in mind. For example, if it is established far from the coast and protected from competition by high transportation costs, the profitable unit of cement manufacture is much smaller than in Europe, and would be around 35,000 tons a year. One could be built in the northern Cameroons, if it supplied Chad also. Brick manufacture is neglected.

9. WAYS OF SPEEDING UP INDUSTRIALIZATION

The Ivory Coast, which with Senegal has the most developed industry, had an industrial turnover in 1961 of only eleven billion C F A francs. Madagascar, though larger and more *évolué*, 'civilized' for a longer time, only realized three billion in 1960, less than 3 per cent of national income, from industrial activity. The Cameroons announces that 10 per cent of its activity is industrial only by incorporating the large public works sector, and even then its estimate seems optimistic.

The inadequacy is even more marked in *quality*, because of incompetence, and the excessive priority given consumer goods. There is a marked lack, at times a total absence, of machinery, particularly the types needed to modernize agriculture. By continuing in this direction the Africans accentuate the gulf between the city, with its rich and industrial centre, and the countryside, which will stagnate, or even regress. The disparity, unless checked, will lead to a South American situation. New states must therefore reorient and speed up industrialization, taking particular care to put long-term interests first. The motto 'To govern is to look to the future' might be posted in the offices of African ministers.

As regards industry, grants from the European Fund have been totally inadequate. Of the 581 million dollars of aid in five years, ending in 1962, a higher proportion was invested in infrastructure even than of F A C grants A billion additional dollars a year is necessary to raise by 2 per cent the national income of the countries associated with the European Economic Community. At the present time the amount of investments, private and public, local and foreign rarely attains 10 per cent of this amount. As a result development is completely inadequate outside a few little privileged islands. Private investors, accustomed to the comfortable protection of the colonial era, have lost their taste for risk, which was the basis for the dynamic capitalism of the 'Manchester' era.

To resolve the problem, and remain in the neo-capitalist framework, J. M. de Lattre[1] proposes that Europe undertake to build the basic industrial structure: power stations, dams, railroad tracks, ports, and roads. Private enterprises could then be established taking advantage of these structures, which would have cost them nothing. In effect, the European contribution would assure European capitalists of profitable enterprises. I agree in general with the first proposition, but the second deserves a little thought. De Lattre points out that in no case can Africans themselves save enough to finance such industrial activity. This is true, if one thinks only in terms of monetary savings, but he neglects the potential savings in labour costs during the first phase of industrialization. Lattre then demands a whole series of guarantees for private investors, which are now being incorporated into the laws governing investments.

If it should develop in this way, industrialization runs the danger of perpetuating the errors I pointed out above, not giving priority to the long-term development needs, machinery and collectives. The lack of African technicians, both in quantity and quality, makes total and immediate socialization uneconomic, as has been shown in Guinea. The problem must be approached empirically, by paying the utmost attention to the particulars of African needs. Government decisions are crucial in this area. It is unfortunate that so far they have not all put the national interest above their own preoccupations.

In numerous areas a society with a mixed economy seems a way to reconcile the primacy of the economic Plan and national interests on the one hand, with a certain guarantee of expert managerial competence and honesty (until such time as sufficient and competent Africans are trained), on the other. The contribution of purely

[1] *Europe France Outre-Mer*, July–August, 1961.

African capital will be small for a long time. It can therefore be reinforced by the French *Fonds d'Aide et de Coopération* (F A C). To do so effectively, the F A C will have to change its policy, which has considered industrialization as the private preserve of the capitalists up till now. The current practice whereby all expenses are borne by the State and all profits go to the private sector, notably through their many affiliates, must be modified.

In the public interest, basic industries should be in the public sector, when these countries are in a position to establish and manage them economically. The experience of Mexico has shown that, in moving towards socialism, it is better to advance with care than to be forced to retreat after disastrous failures. The F A C could find the necessary resources to increase aid by cutting off its grants to balance budgets, which only perpetuate the weaknesses of demagogy, and prevent Africans from facing up to their problems and attaining maturity. Such a step would release enormous sums which are wasted at present, but could be highly productive if put into intelligent industrialization. Ultimately, when the Africans have achieved true economic independence, they will draw up economic plans solely on the basis of the national interest.

Industrialization must everywhere receive top priority, although the potential for it varies greatly across the African continent. Chad and Niger, which lack energy and minerals and are far from the coast, are evidently worse placed than Guinea or the Congo, with their ports, mines and waterfalls. Yet each country does have possibilities of economic interest, if they are regarded from the national and not the purely business point of view.

Take a difficult case, that of the Central African Republic, where President Dacko recently gave top priority to agriculture. Local sawmills, since markets are so far away, would mean a great reduction in transportation costs. The country still exported in 1961 6,000 cubic metres of logs, as against 4,000 of planks. Construction in wood is rare, despite the fact that all public buildings and schools would be far cheaper if constructed of local wood. Cottonseed, as in Chad, is usually thrown away. The brewery at Bangui is enlarging its installations while the cottonseed-oil factory is slowing up. The national interest is thus clearly subordinated to the profit motive.

The entire world is speeding up industrialization, from Asia even to South America. The latter, with its mineral deposits, could have begun to develop in the early seventeenth century. Its wealth alone has maintained the *dolce far niente* of Spain and gilded the statues in her churches. Southern Africa, from Katanga to the Cape, is advanced industrially in spite of its detestable racism. Egypt has begun to move, and the new Algerian government will accelerate the process in the Maghreb.

Will Black Africa always be left behind? Will it grasp the fact that industry, along with modern agriculture, is more efficient in the short run, and essential in the long run, for economic decolonization and true independence?

Perhaps it is a mistake to bring this to the attention of the African leaders, many of whom place too much hope in industry for the immediate future. Industry and agriculture are both indispensable. It is inadmissible, for example, that the extension of Gabonese industries should increase food imports instead of profiting the peasants, the primary producers. On the other hand, many years must pass before industry, installed at great cost, can achieve full employment, while agriculture, almost everywhere, is capable of putting the total available force to work right away. The productivity of the labour, of course, will vary greatly with the situation. Numerous traditional obstacles, which I shall examine, as well as poorly oriented aid programmes and the privileges of the new *élites*, help slow down modernization in agriculture.

CHAPTER NINE
Obstacles to agricultural development

1. 'DECOLONIZED' AGRICULTURAL DEVELOPMENT

While industry deserves high priority, numerous difficulties prevent its rapid growth. It will often be very slow, always very partial, and will leave vast remote areas untouched for a long time. In these areas production and income must be augmented by an immediate increase in employment. New and effective ways to utilize the available labour force must be found even if results are not extremely productive at first. Industry is incapable of assuring full employment anywhere in tropical Africa before many decades have passed. Agriculture, with a few rare exceptions, is in a position to assure it now. However, returns will be small in the beginning.

Agricultural development must go beyond its colonial framework. Until now the main emphasis, sometimes the exclusive one, has been on export crops. Efforts in this direction must, of course, be continued, as capital resources beyond those offered by foreign aid must be increased to buy equipment. But if all tropical countries produced only such crops, the total of this 'produce of the colonies', as the Germans still call them, would overtake demand in many instances.

The terms of trade have already fallen: from 1955 to 1959 export prices went down 15 per cent, entailing a loss to tropical Africa of 600 million dollars, twice the annual amount of foreign aid. If tropical Africa continues to orient itself towards exports, the collapse of the coffee market will undoubtedly be followed quite soon by that of cocoa, sisal and bananas, and then cotton and peanuts, tea and a good many other products. The Malthusian tendencies, already apparent in many farmers, would quickly come to the surface: 'What's the use of working and producing more, we'll just bring on our own ruin,' say the Africans. This is only true in the framework of commercial exploitation and big business interests, a framework carefully maintained by those who have a stake in it.

Let us look even further: expansion of African sales is already largely nullified by an increase in food and agricultural purchases. This increase is due first to the deficiencies and poor orientation of local agriculture, which cannot meet the increased demands that result from higher incomes, themselves largely a result of foreign aid. A large percentage of foreign purchases concern food which could be produced locally now, like rice, meat, fruits and vegetables. The village sugar factories could eliminate sugar imports and raise consumption faster than the large refineries. Meat, canned goods and dairy products will take longer: Madagascar has already started this development (in which Kenya is much more advanced). Cotton fabrics, clothes, shoes and other house and consumer goods will require – and inspire – a certain amount of industrialization.

Economically, from the point of view of the trade balance, eliminating a purchase is the equivalent of an additional export. But elimination of an import generally saves more, because costs of transporting, handling or distributing the product are also eliminated. In order add to an export product, on the other hand, you have to pay out a whole series of corresponding costs, from collecting to loading, which are extremely high because of anarchic trading conditions. Trade is justified for the export of goods when there are favourable natural conditions, and the import of those products difficult to make locally.

Replacing imports by local products is only a first step. Nutritional deficiencies are such at present that many more and more varied foods are urgently required. New countries, far more than their colonizers, should be concerned with the mental and physical potential of their citizens. Although peanut and fish meals could provide enough proteins cheaply and immediately, proteins in milk, leguminous plants and meat are better liked. Vegetable and fruit farming can supply foods that are both good to eat and rich in mineral salts and vitamins, with not much additional labour required to do so.

The development of industrial crops will provide further impetus to agricultural modernization, as they will supply new local industries with the raw materials they need. In favourable situations the cotton crop will be, as in communist countries, the standard-bearer of progress in this area, at least in its first stages. Rope and sack fibres, like jute and sisal, *dah* or *paka*, are still too neglected, and we have seen the need for them.

Oleaginous plants should not all be exported: a number of savannah areas lack them badly; increased exports will give them new buying power to purchase these oils. Their timber will provide paper, cellulose, lumber, furniture and many other by-products. Different types of canning factories will require farm produce, plus all the meats and meat products. The dairy industry, widely spread through tropical South America, has made a start in South-east Asia, and is already well implanted in East Africa.

These four areas of expansion – increased exports, reduction in imports, improvement of nutrition, and industrialized cultivation – are indispensable if African peasants are gradually to be brought out of a subsistence economy into a modern buying and selling economy. If they reach this level without increasing their production, as have the peanut producers in Senegal, they may see their standard of living go down. Only by expanding can you safely speed up the substitution of export goods, later industrial and feed crops, for food crops. Food crops should if possible grow in absolute value but always decrease in proportion to other crops. The development of feed crops will be more difficult to effect than in Western Europe, where natural and above all human factors were more favourable quite early on. Every possible way to accelerate it must be sought. Malthusian arguments fall apart before the multiple possibilities of development, but the defects of the commercial framework and the abusive privileges of the *élites* remain. A certain number of 'traditional' obstacles remain also, which I will now examine more closely.

2. LAND TENURE: DANGERS OF 'COLONIALIST' ROMAN LAW

A revolutionary agrarian reform which aims at a profound redistribution of land is not absolutely necessary to development in Africa. As

I pointed out in a previous work, this is not the case in South America, because of the abuses of large landowners. In Africa land tenure remains largely tribal, except in the coastal region and the high Madagascar plateaux. 'Land belongs to a large family, some of whose members are dead, some are living, and innumerable others have yet to be born', as a Nigerian chief explained it.

The chief of an area or village, or a council of elders, divides out the communal land among the families of the tribe. Each family then divides a part of its share between its members, the other part being cultivated in common. This is, of course, only a schematic version of what in fact is far more complex. If a man, after receiving authorization, clears a part of the savannah, he has full right to that land during a normal cultivation cycle. He cannot, however, use it beyond the time limit established by custom. This is in order that the fertility and perpetuity of the land inheritance can be maintained. When he stops cultivating, his rights over the land cease; he then receives another. Since clearing in forest regions is more difficult, his rights can be prolonged beyond the fallow period. Such a system thus assured a certain economic security to the African peasant, but only on a subsistence level, and he was not always fully assured of it.

The population explosion has meant that fallow periods cannot be respected in some places, around Kano and in the most over-populated Mossi districts for instance. And yet, preparations for rice cultivation require years of work before they pay off. The introduction of the plough in southern Chad means that tree stumps must be removed from forest areas that are cleared, a labour of several months per acre. Only peasants who are assured that they can have the land for a long time will consent to do the work. The same applies to scrub areas in the forest zone, the existence of which has already in actual fact resulted in individual property rights.

A revision of custom is therefore in order, to put it in line with the demands of modern agriculture. However, a change in traditional methods of tenure into modern co-operative methods is hampered by the repercussions of European intervention.

French law thought to modernize Africa by encouraging individual property. It was first introduced to facilitate European settling, as in North Africa. From this sprang the idea of land registration, more or less inspired by the Australian Torrens Act, which granted title to a property after proof of a certain degree of improvement. For those with good relations with the Land Conservation Services, titles were sometimes delivered before a sufficient effort had been made. The Tananarive middle class did quite nicely in this respect.

The French law of 1955 was more concerned with protecting customary laws, and restraining European settlers. It no longer recognized automatic reversion to the state of 'vacant' lands, which had allowed them to be turned over to European settlers, and gave rise to many abuses of the system, particularly in eastern, central and southern Africa. Under the new legislation, chiefs have been able to 'cede', more or less legally, their tribal rights over uninhabited forest land, which has never been exploited, like land in the southwest Ivory Coast or in the eastern Cameroons. This in turn has led to the second great danger of all land legislation, whereby people draw incomes without working, and thereby slow down development.

Laws such as this facilitated the creation of vast African plantations worked by salaried migrants, without much work on the part of the local inhabitants. The more deserving, more hard-working peasants from the savannah could have been established on the land as farmers working for themselves, if the public nature of these non-utilized lands had been preserved. By grabbing up immense stretches of land, which they neither exploit nor profit from, these scattered tribal groups prevent its being developed. Both the Mossis and the Bamilékés have been guilty of this. 'We have tied our own hands,' said the young Cameroonian Director of Agriculture. The cornering of available land in the lower Mungo region by the Bamilékés, more or less legally, in a somewhat anarchic fashion, was, however, a powerful factor in regional development, because of the inertia of the local, decadent tribes (Manehas, Bakakas, etc.). In spite of the current complexity of the problem, it is preferable to the wage-worker situation on the Mossi lands in the southern Ivory Coast (cf. J. Guillard).

The objective is to speed up modernization, and it is slowed down by a situation where incomes are received without work. Modernization requires vast land improvement projects: clearing and planting

,

erosion prevention, application of humus, reforestation and, above all, irrigation projects. Anyone who invests this much labour in land should be encouraged to do so by the guarantee that he will benefit from the results for a long time, and that his children will also. To a conservative or French law student, this encouragement is best given in the form of individual property law, in the Roman sense. Yet this law grants the right to use and abuse the land, *jus utendi et abutendi*.

Roman law was introduced to Africa with the slave society, where the *pater familias* had complete freedom to put his native slaves, sometimes even his children, to death if he so desired. Its continuation into the present is a dangerous anachronism, particularly if right to abuse the land is upheld. With the European and Asian peasant, whose instincts were to 'preserve the patrimony', damage was limited except on the Mediterranean. Sometimes, in China, say, or in Brittany, individual ownership often means the 'transformation of a rock into a garden', as Arthur Young has said. But the Betzimizarka people on the eastern coast of Madagascar, with an agrarian civilization not far removed from berry picking, already has a pronounced tendency to degrade their soil irretrievably with unfertilized crops. It is pointless to 'protect' their tendency to destroy and give them full licence to proceed full steam ahead by handing such people a title to a property.

According to the traditional tenure system, land cannot be ceded to 'foreigners', i.e. those not members of the tribe. When the chiefs do so, they are transgressing custom. 'Romanized' land, on the other hand, can be freely sold to the highest bidder; it is therefore quickly being concentrated in the hands of those with money, that is to say, the privileged class. I am not projecting into the future here; the phenomenon is already taking place. Businessmen and civil servants in the capitals, Tananarive, Abidjan, Dakar, Bamako and Freetown[1] are buying up surrounding acreage for weekend cottages. Above all, they are waiting for values on their land to soar, when it becomes good real estate, and the square foot sells for what the acre used to.

This is a dangerous process, helped along by F I D E S, which in

[1] The F A O study emphasizes the fact that 'in Sierra Leone it is to be feared that the inhabitants of Freetown and its environs (known as the "colony") are buying up agri-*cultural* lands throughout the country and dispossessing the existing tribes.'

its folly paid very high prices for urban real estate, distributing money in handfuls that had not been earned by the recipients.[1]

The rights of the nation as a whole, which must always strive to protect the land and assure best possible utilization of it, must be reconciled with the rights of the hard-working farmer, who must have sole rights to enjoy the fruits of his labours to develop land. This double requirement can be met by a collective form of land ownership, either tribal or national. Permanent and hereditary property rights can be granted to whoever develops and maintains his land in a responsible fashion. If, however, he degrades the soil and damages the land, which remains the collective inheritance confided by the nation to one of its members, his rights should be revoked.

Above all, this right should never be negotiable. A free real estate market, with the unrestricted right to sell, appears to me to be very dangerous. The seller, whether chief of an area, village or family, would unjustly dispossess the members of his clan or family, for his own personal profit. Land ownership would quickly become concentrated in the hands of the rich. Along with the government workers and businessmen, potential buyers would include the members of well-paid professions, priests and political leaders. This is an additional argument in favour of limiting business profits and government salaries, although that alone would not prevent land speculation.

Transfers of property rights will, of course, occur when the owner dies or changes professions. Therefore, a reimbursement for land improvements made by the titleholder should be offered to encourage improvements and innovations. But it is highly desirable that the land itself, apart from the improvements, should have no commercial value whatever, as is true in traditional tenure systems. Otherwise peasant groups, and then cultivators themselves, will enter into a violent struggle with the middle class for possession of the land, which happened in France for three hundred years. All the money sterilized in land purchases will be lacking for agricultural progress.

The property rights of the Mexican *ejidos* do not include the right to sell or mortgage. Although the *ejidos* have not progressed suffi-

---

[1] Land with no commercial value (the Douala airport) was paid for two or three times over, to the great profit of local politicians. Villages sell the land where their own school is to be built at very high prices.

5

ciently, it is because they received only the land itself and not the training or the means necessary to improve cultivation. The Israeli communities have preserved collective ownership of the land and been able to modernize at the same time. In the framework of its own ideology, each African government should seek a method of land tenure which does not fetter rural development.

In Madagascar, which is more Asiatic than African from this point of view, the situation is more serious, because large land concessions have already been granted, mostly to Europeans. A large proportion of this land remains unexploited, or under-exploited. A tax for 'non-development' of 700 francs per hectare annually has been effective in reducing these abuses. It should be proportioned to the potential fertility of the land, raising the tax on rich alluvial land, and to the locale, because the advantages accruing to landowners near towns from public expenditures can more than compensate for the tax.

The law of February 15th 1960 allows property titles to be given to anyone who puts land in good permanent working order 'according to local and current usages and the type of terrain'. This in effect means that the entire island can be appropriated very quickly with no real guarantee that land will be improved. 'Local and current usage' includes burning humus around Lake Alaotra, which leaves sandy sterile soil. It also includes brush fires in forest zones, designed to make the grass grow back in the dry season. Modern exploitation of the land will include in some areas protection of its rich organic matter and in others, collecting hay and silage reserve, by mowing grasses instead of burning them. Traditional usage on the east Coast is still *tavy* cultivation; no precautions to safeguard the fertility of the land are taken at all. Here anti-erosive measures should be introduced, either banking or terracing.

A member of the Tananarive middle class, if he comes from a good family and has connections, is likely to receive title to land. Titles thus simply become a way to earn an income without working for it, instead of a guarantee that land will be exploited. Registration will quickly aggravate the abuses of private ownership, already too widespread in this island, where individual property ownership is already more advanced than on the African continent. These abuses are tenant-farming and usury, which our report to the United Nations[1] signalled as the two fundamental, closely allied obstacles to agricultural advances in India. If Africa follows a similar course it can only lead to famine: the amount of grain available per capita in India fell from 270 kilograms in 1890 to around 180 kilograms in 1945 and to 175 kilograms in 1961.

3. TENANT FARMING – 360 PER CENT INTEREST

Our report on Madagascar in the summer of 1961 included two studies on tenant-farming in the appendix. M. Dufournet, who discussed the Lake Alaotra region, pointed out the variety of tenant farming contracts in current use. He outlined nine large categories, but the situation is far more complex.

The landowner's proportion of the harvest varied from a quarter to a half, which seems fairly reasonable. On delving a little more deeply, however, you discover that sometimes the land leased out is only a swamp, neither cleared nor prepared for planting. It has cost its owner virtually nothing, at the most 5,000 to 8,000 C F A francs per hectare, if he has purchased it recently. Given rent-free to the tenant-farmer for two years, its value becomes tripled for the owner as a result of the farmer's work. A land investment that brings in 200 per cent in two years is not run-of-the-mill in Europe. The owner then receives regularly, still at no cost to himself, at least a quarter of the harvests produced solely by the tenant farmer.

The seeds lent by the owner are paid for at harvest time for double their value. Rice is usually bought up by the landowner, who often owns the processing plant, for less than the going price; and free services are provided by the tenant farmer. Monsieur Molet of C I N A M has described a very precise case in the same region, in a report made in August 1961. The tenant farmer receives 2½ acres of land, ploughed by the landowner, who provides the seed. The farmer harvests 1,500 kilos of raw rice from it and the harvest is divided 'equally'. He thus turns over to the landowner 750 kilos of raw rice worth ten francs a kilo, which comes to 7,500 C F A francs. Having

[1] *Community Development Evaluation Mission in India*, by Coldwell, Dumont and Read. New Delhi, November, 1959.

borrowed 1,000 francs from him to live on while the rice grew, he pays it back with 280 kilos of raw rice, of which 100 kilos is the actual payment, and 180 kilos, worth 1,800 francs, is the interest in six months. The interest rate thus comes to 360 per cent a year. Beyond this, he has to tend the landowner's cattle without payment: the going wage for this in the region is at least 5,000 francs a year. Thus, on the basis of a total harvest worth 15,000 francs, the tenant farmer has paid out, in kind or in services, 5,000 plus 7,500 plus 1,800 francs, totalling 14,300 francs. He has not even received 5 per cent of the value of a harvest which he was totally responsible for producing. This is perhaps a world record for exploitation.

If this case seems exceptional, let us look at the landowner in the Marovoay region near Majunga. There, the combination of tenant-farming and moneylending, at the going rate of 100 per cent to 160 per cent for six months, or 200 per cent to 320 per cent per year, and payments for water and land, bring his share of the total harvest, in an average year, to between 64 per cent and 69 per cent. The share of the farmer actually working the earth can be further reduced if he is a sub-tenant farmer, which is quite frequent. How can one possibly ask this proletarian, who barely benefits from his own harvest, who hasn't got enough to eat until the next one, to invest his time and labour in land improvements? A government could only require it of him if he were not so shamelessly exploited, and profited directly from the improvements he made.

Well-meaning critics may call the kind of 'labour investments' I have been talking about coercion, but the tenant farmer is presently subjected to the worst kind of coercion, an inhumane exploitation. One can require him, through firm persuasion, to improve his land if he alone benefits. He will be raising his standard of living by his own labour, and he as well as his country will profit. Tenant-farming whereby landowners profit hugely without working or improving the land, is in a sense a crime against the nation, because of the population explosion,[1] and as such should be a punishable offence.

Fortunately, tenant-farming is not as widespread in western and central Africa. It is still the case in the Sahel region, where it

[1] An increase of more than thirty-two per thousand in Tananarive province, almost a world record.

seems to be a survival of the slavery in which herders maintained cultivators, although the actual conditions are, here also, extremely complex.

Usury is very common in the form of advances against the coming harvest, and is allied to corrupt trading practices, the evils of which it helps prolong. This is particularly true for cash crops, such as Senegalese peanuts or Ivory Coast coffee. Anyone needing an advance is forced into an extremely humiliating position, a fact which has not been sufficiently publicized.[1]

On the coastal plantations, the spread of the wage system has led to further social stratification, as peasants who become employers are freed from work. This trend is becoming more dangerous as increases of agricultural credit have recently furthered its expansion from Ghana, where it has existed longer, over into the Ivory Coast. Thus credits that are meant to increase production have simply meant that 'agriculturalists' do not work any longer, but hire others. It is difficult to see how relieving a substantial section of the Ivory Coast peasantry from work can be a positive factor in agricultural development.

4. DOWRIES AND GERONTOCRACY

In a large portion of the African continent, a future son-in-law must give his future parents-in-law a dowry. Originally, this meant doing a certain amount of work for them, in forest zones, and giving them cattle, in the savannah. With the advent of a money economy, the amount of the dowry has spiralled up, and become a real obstacle to development. In Central and Southern Cameroons and Senegal a dowry of 100,000 to 250,000 CFA francs has become customary. Government allowances for children – these are only given to the privileged class, which constitutes one more abuse – have made the amount even higher. In other words, the father-in-law often refuses to hand over the marriage certificate until the dowry has been fully paid. This effectively prevents the son-in-law, even if he is a father two or three times over, from drawing these benefits. A man lucky

---

[1] During the slack periods a man sells himself to the moneylender for a few pounds of grain. (A. Lemblé.)

enough to produce three or four girls has no need for an old-age pension: thanks to the instalment payments on their bride-price, he can stop working when he is thirty-five or forty.

All the savings of a farming son-in-law, which he could usefully spend on his land or rice fields, for fertilizer or insecticides, must be paid out to his exploiting father-in-law. The latter is not the only one to collect them, because whoever married his daughter often reserves the right to sell for his own profit the girls she may have. The consequences are not only economic – no one can freely choose a spouse. The young Christian women in the Cameroons, still sold like cattle, are beginning to rebel against the system.

In 1959 in Guinea dowries were limited, in certain circumstances, to a head of cattle or 10,000 CFA francs. It would be interesting to find out how far this excellent measure has been applied. The official who sponsored it, an African veterinarian, pointed out that livestock were poorly cared for, because they were generally acquired free as part of the dowry. For the same reason, peasants who knew that their heifers would go to their fathers-in-law the next season did not bother to feed them well either.

In some areas a matriarchy still exists, in which a man will see his heritage go to his sister's children, whom he scarcely knows. This hardly encourages him to increase his family's heritage. He therefore advises his children to start their own coffee plantation, which may well not be expertly looked after by them.

By giving the greatest economic power to the heads of extended families, African society is confiding the levers of progress to the oldest people, often least receptive to modern techniques. These last require a lot of work. They also represent, for a traditionalist, a risk that, as an older man, he is less willing to attempt. Without money, often deprived of the rich soils and sometimes of any land at all, the young people cannot hope to improve their standards of living through their own work and initiative. Even Guinea and Mali seem scarcely to have attacked this difficult but crucial problem. In the upper Niger valley in Mali, a BDPA inquiry showed that the average age of these heads of family was almost sixty years.

The village chiefs, whose powers remain enormous, are generally about seventy years old. The whole apparatus of chiefdom, with its long tradition of exploitation of the peasant, is a formidable brake on development. The Guinean government, realizing this, has replaced chiefs by party organizations, and does not hesitate to destroy certain social structures. In Mali the party cadres are either administrators or traditional chiefs, and changes have been more limited. It is not enough to socialize private investments; there were so few of them anyway. Independence must be accompanied by development. Young Africans still have a great deal to learn on this score.

5. EXPLOITATION BY MOSLEM PRIESTS

It is difficult to make a value judgment on the Mourides, a slightly heretical Moslem sect, but the cult does seem to 'erode' the resources of its adherents. It explains to them first of all that they have no need to worry about salvation, because the *marabout*, or priest, guarantees to his faithful, the *talibés*, that he will lead them to heaven. They therefore have no need to pray, unlike all other Moslems, to communicate with their God. While he prays for them, they labour for him.

The young *talibés* work in his service for many years without pay. What began as an exercise in religious education, for disciples who taught and begged in order to live, has become work camps, with a freely accepted atmosphere of quasi-slavery. The parents of the *talibés* clothe them, and the *marabout* graciously provides them with millet, or perhaps just the land on which they grow it. He and he alone decides at what age – sometimes it is forty – they are 'liberated' to start a family, and then gives them a wife and a home, 'lending' them a part of the money they earned in his service to get started.

In periods of famine the *marabout* aids them, but most of his money is spent on a luxurious life and the purchase of numerous wives, and also on contributions to the grand mosque at Touba. Its cement framework, not yet sheathed in marble, had alone cost almost two billion CFA francs by 1961, which makes it one of the biggest investments in Senegal.

The Mourides have fortitude and the spirit of enterprise: if their motto, 'Order, work, discipline' were effectively applied to everyone in tropical Africa, the chances of development would be much greater. Under their direction, the 'pioneer front' of peanut cultivation is quickly penetrating into the interior, particularly in the Ouoloff region. Wells are dug, roads opened, use of draught animals is spreading: but the toll is heavy.

We were invited to inspect the fields of the Grand Caliph of the brotherhood, El Hadj M'Backe, which were a little beyond Touba. After three years of repeated peanut cultivation without fertilizer, the earth was already greatly depleted and its capacity to retain water much diminished. After an early sowing, followed by a short dry season, the very small number of plants promised only a ridiculously small crop, 350 pounds an acre, despite the use of fertilizer for this third season. The Caliph would have preferred to plant his crop that year on his neighbour's land, whom he would simply have forced out. But the neighbour refused to give in, a sign that the times are changing, as formerly no one would have dared, and the Caliph had to fall back on his depleted field.

An image comes to mind, that of a mosque built by ruining the surrounding earth, a mosque that will ultimately look out over a man-made desert, from its 84-metre-high minaret. Yet an organization with such a hierarchy could play a very positive role. It is quite capable of rapidly spreading through the entire country the technical knowledge for modern peanut cultivation. I briefly sought to explain this to the Grand Caliph during my 1961 visit. But one of the faithful who preceded me – the waiting line stretched out interminably – had slipped three thousand franc bills into his left hand, and he was 'savouring' them between his fingers while we talked, as Molière's Harpagon fingered his gold pieces: a modern version of the joys of the miser. He was not as attentive as he might have been to my brief exposé.

A young *marabout* in the Caliph's family controls thirteen groups of ten to twelve *talibés* each, usually ageing from twenty-five to thirty-five years old. They get room, board and clothing. Each group cultivates sixty acres of a good variety of peanut, and is provided for that purpose with ploughs and seeders, drawn by three horses and a camel. By using modern methods and good seed varieties, they can sell a kilo of peanuts with a 3·50 franc bonus, for 24·50 francs.

As somewhat less than half a ton is produced per acre, gross income, on more than 350 tons, totals 875,000 francs. The net profit to the *marabout* is 500,000 CFA francs, because each of his groups separately cultivates twelve acres of millet for the next season. The 'Wednesday fields', cultivated on that day by the married faithful, are also cultivated for the *marabout*. According to the estimates, the Grand Caliph profits from 30,000 to 45,000 acres of cultivated fields, from which he has undisputed rights to the entire profit – he receives the entire gross receipts – and which are always the first in the village to be sown.

The land holdings of the various Mouride groups are well, aligned and have separating 'walls' of corrugated iron from which project a good number of 'sumptuary' mottoes.[1] A large part of their revenues is invested in urban business, to the detriment of agricultural and industrial progress in Senegal. They are firmly opposed to social progress: the Grand Caliph in Touba forbids a clinic and a primary school as well as co-operative organizations. The *marabouts* are very suspicious of the rural activist movement, so promising in this country, because it might awaken the slaves to the idea of progress. The movement proposes a 'Thursday field' to benefit the entire community, which would be concerned with projects useful to all. The 'Wednesday' field would no doubt compare poorly with it in the peasant's mind.

On August 2nd 1961, President Mamadou Dia gave the closing speech of the great *Magal*, the annual pilgrimage of the sect, and said that 'the principles of Mouridism are exactly those which the government has made its own for the harmonious development of the country'. If this is true, and Mouride principles are part of the 'African socialism' also preached by President Senghor, we will with some justification be anxious about the future of Senegal!

There are many other obstacles to progress that I have not studied, such as the repartition of land between families in the same village, and the social differentiation that results from it; or the caste systems, based on a craft, such as blacksmiths and weavers. By delving into these problems very carefully, young African students can make

---

[1] Trans.: Sumptuary law attempts to restrain luxury and extravagance on the part of the common people, as the sumptuary laws of Sparta.

an invaluable contribution to development in their countries. Unless a sociological *milieu* is extremely well understood, very little of worth can be done to change it, as efforts at rural organization have shown.

We still have to examine the best means of developing the enormous agricultural potential in the great forest zone, before looking at the problem of the savannah, which will be seen to be more and more difficult as one progresses further north.

CHAPTER TEN
Cultivation in the forest zone

1. CLOSE CROP SUPERVISION NEEDED

Here then is tropical Africa, with all its natural and human problems, its population explosion, tackling huge difficulties in order to industrialize, and for this very reason forced to modernize agriculture very rapidly, if it wants to 'take off'. With this goal, it is extremely doubtful if it will be content to follow the classic French path, very slow until 1945 (the growth was 1·73 per cent a year from 1788 to 1914). French agricultural professors started the campaign to modernize around 1875, but not until 1950 did it have a real effect throughout the French countryside. In countries where the population grows at a rate of 3 per cent a year, the total population multiplies by 18 in a century. France, where the population rate was stagnant, could afford to wait for progress and go slowly. This delay is absolutely impossible in Africa where the necessary haste makes everything more difficult.

China, however, in seeking to accelerate movement, has demanded too much from its peasants, and perhaps broken their resilience by stretching it too far. Its 'eight slogans' of agricultural progress are too dogmatic, and at times clearly erroneous (e.g., very closely packed rows), and they have been mechanically applied by incompetent cadres. China is now facing very profound agrarian problems. Everywhere in the world faster industrialization has proved easier to achieve than rapid agricultural progress, although the latter is indispensable, particularly at first, to get things going. Africa could seek to avoid the two dangers, European and Chinese, by proceeding quickly and well; but an enormous number of effective cadres will be needed, and the leaders will have to set the pace and the example. In this regard they need only observe their Chinese colleagues.

In its natural state the great forest zone produces virtually nothing. One can extract under the best conditions about one good tree per acre from it, once and for all. Its fertility is quickly damaged if it is planted with annual food crops without sufficient restitution of humus or fertilizers. Areas near the coast can utilize fertilizers economically on plantations. On the other hand, it seems difficult to make these pay with food crops alone. These are unsatisfactory as cash crops, and the market for them is unstable because they are difficult to conserve (corn), or very expensive to transport (macabos in Douala, yams from Abidjan and other cassavas). It has to be done somehow, however, and it will be easier near the coast and the railway, with national factories. It would be possible to feed a country, therefore, using less land, and to reserve more lands, and the best ones, for industrial plantations.

This same objective could be realized by purchasing a good percentage of the food needed in the forest zone from the savannah, where possibilities of growing export crops are not as good. In this way the savannah people would benefit from a reflection of forest zone 'prosperity'. The savannah already furnished the work force for the plantations, the Mossis from Mali and Upper Volta going to the Ivory Coast and Ghana. It could also feed these emigrants with the food of their own country, millet, peanuts or other leguminous plants which are richer in proteins than the tubers and plantains, of the forest.

Developed regional specialization like this will require a great increase in labour productivity, cheap transportation, and an efficient distribution network. Meanwhile, corn and peanuts, the latter where rainfall is not too heavy and there is some dry season, with a well-drained soil, can provide forest zone inhabitants with less deficient foods.

Vegetable and fruit farms can also be a good source of supply, and later goat's milk, when the taboo forbidding it has disappeared.

2. LOCAL PEASANT PLANTATIONS – SEMI-COMPETITIVE COFFEE

I have already discussed the economic difficulties in raising coffee and advised against relying too heavily on it. But the African and

Malagasy economies cannot, of course, be deprived of this resource overnight. African coffee should be made more competitive, first of all by excluding it from areas which are too dry. M. Loué, of the *Institute de Café de Bingerville* in the Ivory Coast, has defined the boundaries of zones well suited to coffee, based on climatic conditions. Long after publication of his map in 1960, the Agricultural Services at Tiebissou, situated outside even the zone categorized by Loué as marginal, were still principally concerned with coffee seedbeds.

Agronomists in the Cameroons advised it even in the savannah in 1961, in the area south of Adamaoua, under the pretext of being unable to propose other good cash crops. The adoption of crops to replace coffee has until now been held back by the excessive protection accorded it. In the appropriate climatic areas, soils suited to coffee should be reserved for it; however, the best soils should be given to cocoa, oil palm or rubber. Intensive coffee cultivation will require mulching. To reduce transportation, plants for mulch should be grown very near the plants they are to protect, since it will be more difficult to utilize draught animals in this area. The obvious solution is to plant rows of a large plant like Tithonia between the rows of coffee.

Here again, fertilizer will not pay until most of the other, less expensive, modern techniques have been put into effect. Producing multicauline trees will facilitate periodic regeneration of the fruit-bearing branches without lowering production. Clearing the under-brush will prevent the forest from encroaching, and plant health treatments will be in general indispensable.

The next stage is improved handling of the coffee bean. Commercial coffee beans are still prepared by the 'dry method', with mediocre results. If the bean is put to dry where it has direct contact with humid earth, it blackens. A few black grains suffice to depreciate a whole batch, or else they have to be picked over by hand, bean by bean. The first step is to dry them on flat cement surfaces, or better yet, on framed mats or screens. In case of rain, or for the night, they can easily be put in a series of 'drawers' open to the wind and sheltered by palm roofing.

The second step will be to prepare the beans by the 'wet method'. This involves more complicated equipment, and preferably a co-operative organization. Such a co-operative, however, must be careful not to involve itself in hasty investments, as one in Ruanda-Urundi has done. Collecting the beans, as well as harvesting and maintenance, may be excessively expensive if numerous small plantations are dispersed in the bush on the small cleared areas. This scattering is a result of tradition, when coffee was planted on forest land originally cleared for food crops. Often, as around Gagnoa in the Ivory Coast, there is no more available forest land, if one wants to control the future and avoid turning the entire forest zone into savannah.

I would therefore recommend a partial dissociation of food crops and large cash crop plantations; the latter should cease being subordinate to the first. Food crops can be cultivated on the large spaces between rows of coffee, which would benefit from the manure and care given the food crops. Next, permanent rice fields should be installed in the low-lying areas, with irrigation works. By replacing traditional food crops, rice will contribute to the permanent un-coupling of the two types of production. This will necessitate the rational development of the small dispersed fields; cash crops will be planted on the soils which best suit them, and food crops will be put in second place. Animal husbandry should be reserved a place in the very near future.

3. INTENSIVE COCOA PRODUCTION

Even the best African coffees can never compare with those that grow from Mexico down to Colombia, particularly those from southern Brazil. The maximum yield in Africa is a ton of Robusta coffee per hectare, as compared to South America's five or six tons of Arabica. The difference between the two known records is too great to en-visage open competition. In the case of cocoa, however, Africa has already proven that it can defy South America; it already supplies more than half the world's cocoa, as against a fifth at the beginning of the century. This is despite the fact that the average yield in Nigeria is 110 kilograms of cocoa beans per hectare, in Ghana not quite 300 kilograms, in the Cameroons 350 kilograms, compared to 600 kilograms in the State of Bahia, the principal source in Brazil.

African competition is made possible by the absence of large land-owners. The peasant often retains the entire profit from his work, and employers, when there are any, are less corrupt than those in Ilheus, Brazil. Furthermore, the remarkable organization of the market in Ghana has eliminated the abuses of the trading system. Africa's cocoa-producing potential appears to me to be at least equal to that of South America. From Ghana to the western Cameroons (ex-British), the best cultivated plantations, receiving regular treatments against capsids and brown rot, where organic materials and fertilizers are applied, and trees shading the cocoa plants cut back, have surpassed $3\frac{1}{2}$ tons of beans per hectare. Urucuca in Brazil has obtained the same results at research stations, but the large absentee landlords of the big estates are seldom concerned with modernizing their plantations.

With good leadership and crop control the African peasants can easily surpass South American planters, and thus raise even higher the African proportion of the world market. If the Eastern bloc countries simply satisfy their children's desire for chocolate a little more, the over-production, or rather under-consumption of cocoa, which is far less than that of coffee, would disappear overnight. Unfortunately they have only agreed to purchase 60,000 tons a year, all of it in Ghana, which is well placed politically. This represents a fifth of Ghana's cocoa production.

More efforts to improve quality must also be made. Conditions of fermentation are essential, but beans entirely attacked by brown rot, like some I saw near Yaoundé, cannot furnish a good product. As with the 'wet method' of handling coffee, it would seem useful to envisage fermentation of the beans in fairly large shops. They would be brought there fresh from the fields as soon as the pods open. The pods themselves should be returned to the fields and ploughed in. It is already being done by the traders in the lower Mungo; an organization of farmers could also profit by it.[1]

However, concentrating operations will only be worth while if peasants use the time thus freed on other crops. Otherwise there will be an increase in rural unemployment, which is already visible in the cocoa plantations. A well-run plantation is almost self-sufficient,

[1] This technique is widespread in Jamaica.

demanding almost no maintenance except treatments and harvesting. The standard of living of African peasants cannot be raised without a rise in the amount of labour they supply, because increases in productivity will remain small for a long time without new equipment and new sources of energy.

The equipment for co-operatives involves heavy investments; unfortunately, peasants are more often in debt than not. A large part of the capital could be furnished by 'self-financing', easiest to accomplish in the form of free labour. One would simply have to set up a co-operative plantation maintained at no cost by the members, and the crop would feed the joint capital of the co-operative preparing coffee or cocoa beans. Supervised by the agricultural inspector, it would constitute, like Yugoslav communal farms, a progressive model initiating its members into the most modern techniques. A dozen well-cultivated acres would be sufficient, each producing a half to one ton of coffee or one to two tons of cocoa, to enable the co-operatives to equip themselves rapidly and make their annual loan payments easily. We thus propose that public credit be reserved for co-operatives whose members supply an important part of the financing, both in money and in labour.

4. OIL PALM: MORE CROP CONTROL NECESSARY

Coffee and cocoa can be produced with current techniques, which are still adequate, by peasants with good leadership. But the extent and authority of the leadership must be increased with good varieties of oil palms. The oil palm will not produce profitably unless it is carefully and expertly maintained. The absence of such care explains the repeated failures at Dabou in the Ivory Coast and in all southern Dahomey and the ex-French Cameroons.

We asked peasants in Dahomey, who refused to take proper care of the oil palms, although they had received them free, how one should go about developing oil palm production in their country. 'Don't bother us with these special varieties,' they answered. 'We just want to be sure of our 100 francs in salary every day.' They were aware that the minimum guaranteed salary for agricultural workers in Dahomey[1] is in the neighbourhood of 200 C F A francs,

---

[1] Another 'social' measure too far ahead of economic development.

the equivalent of four new francs; but they willingly admit that it is too high, and peasants hiring other peasants do not offer that much.

In short, many peasants seem to prefer being a salaried worker – which, to their minds, is closer to being a civil servant, however modest the pay – to being a farmer on his own, running risks. This search for security, which some would call proletarization, makes large plantations advisable. Where public morality is lacking, which would interfere with state farms, privately owned plantations should be encouraged. On the condition, of course, that the status of the salaried employees is protected, and that reinvestment of the major part of the profits is insured and controlled.

If carried to its logical conclusion, this last clause would, of course, remove the very criterion of capitalism, since it is nothing if not in control of its profits. I have already stressed the dearth of private investments, and it is absolutely essential that they be increased. Meanwhile, some of the burden can be carried by state companies, which I would define in Dahomey as intermediaries between authoritarian co-operatives and state farms. The expert must have complete authority over all aspects of cultivation: methods of planting, ways of handling the seedbeds and young trees, cover plants to protect the soil, planting food crops between rows, the different fertilizers; these all constitute strict requirements, without which the plantations lose most or even all their economic value.

Decisions cannot therefore be submitted to a vote of the assembled members of the co-operative, at present too ill-informed on these problems. If the co-operative is adopted, the technical director must be able to obtain immediate and full execution of the necessary regulations from the members. This will be easier to achieve if the members receive a status, at least in the beginning, approximating that of salaried employees. It would be demagoguery to promise them high pay or big profits in the near future, because almost all of the profits should be invested in further developments.

Soviet agrarian structure tends to approximate production co-operatives and state farms, the *kolkhoz* and the *sovkhoz*. Dahomey plans to allow the co-operatives to relax their authority once plantations begin production, and divide the land among the member families. Given the evolution of agriculture towards large units, and the need of the nation to accumulate resources, this atomization does not seem advisable. It could be useful as a provisional stage, if the beneficiaries turned back all the profits realized, but this would be improbable and difficult to ask. Naturally, this will be up to the African governments; the essential remains to have modern forms of production develop rapidly.

Coconut palm plantations can achieve the maximum harvests possible on the infertile sands along the coast, with fertilizer. This tree is hardy, and can do with less care than the oil palm, and would thus be adaptable, if necessary, to a less rigid form of co-operative. The recent fall in the price of oleaginous plants should not, in my opinion, discourage West Africa. The constantly increasing world needs for fatty materials would guarantee larger markets in the long run. I cannot think of any oils that would be more economical than those from well-run plantations, using good seed varieties, in a well-chosen location. The future of the peanut, which will have difficulty competing with these oil trees, is far more uncertain.

5. RUBBER – EVEN TIGHTER CONTROL NECESSARY

A certain hesitation is justified about the future of natural rubber, increasingly threatened by synthetic rubber. The prices of the latter are themselves synthetic, as governments have generally had a hand in financing the factories. World demand for rubber has increased so rapidly that one hoped for a respite recently in the competition, but synthetics are also moving ahead quickly. I advised some extension of rubber plantations in 1960, from the Ivory Coast to the Congo, but I would be more hesitant about it today.

The rubber tree can stand a much poorer location than the palm, and in particular can adapt to excess humidity and insufficient sunlight, as in the (French) Cameroons, from Edéa to Douala. But it demands far stricter and more constant care as regards cultivation, during the entire period it is being exploited. The incision of the bark to let the sap run out is quite an art, in which Africans are as skilled as Asians. As soon as latex is gathered in pots it must be immediately transported and treated in the processing plant. If it coagulates it loses two-thirds of its value.

For this reason, the factory should be in the centre of the plantation, under the same management. But, around this plantation and processing plant complex, whether an industrial type or a closely controlled co-operative, it would be possible to set up individual farms, delivering fresh latex to the same factory or processing plant. Only the very latest and most productive varieties should be cultivated. The new African states want to manufacture tyres some day, but to be profitable such a factory should have a market beyond national boundaries. It would be unfortunate if they were reduced to buying their raw material in Europe.

In Madagascar all of these equatorial products adapt best not to the whole eastern coast, as has often been said, but to the northern part of it. The southern portion spills over into the tropics; although Robusta coffee is still planted there, it is a mistake. Conditions for oil palm, cocoa and rubber around the Gulf of Maroantsetra are often very acceptable and sometimes excellent. Logically, the few flat areas should be reserved for the palm, with rubber and cocoa, which are less demanding in terms of transportation, planted on the hills.

6. BANANAS: CONTROL NEEDED THROUGH THE RIPENING STAGE

The volcanic lands at the foot of Mount Cameroun are among the richest in Africa. European banana plantations were established on the plains there before the war. African planters followed in 1946 but they were forced to plant on the hills also. They cultivate the Gros-Michel banana, generally along with coffee, cocoa and many other annual crops, particularly *macabo* (*taro*), a tuber which the women plant. Such a mixture naturally produced poor results for each crop: coffee harvests are laughable, and the cocoa is attacked by parasites. But the banana, heavily protected in the French market, did very well for a long time without requiring much effort.

Since 1958 everything has changed with the appearance of cercosporalla, which requires expensive treatments. Only plantations with large harvests, hence those which are well run, can afford them. The insecurity created by the guerrilla movement has resulted in many plantations being invaded by the bush. Only one-crop banana plantations really pay now. The government has taken charge of the treatments and covers half the cost. This subsidy, granted to a crop which is already privileged because of the tariff protection, has cut down on the possibility of productive investments in the Cameroons for other products. Current harvests of about a ton per acre have become much less acceptable, because a good number of the bunches do not attain the minimum weight of twelve kilograms required for export. Many of the heavy bunches are also rejected by the inspectors at the banana port at Bonabéri across from Douala. This occurs most frequently with fruit that is already turning, and has cream-coloured flesh before it has even attained the necessary volume per banana, called 'three-quarters full'. Rejected on the docks, the bunches have already cost the planters a great deal for transportation, by truck from plantation to station, then by rail. These trucks and freight wagons are rarely full, which raises the cost per kilometric ton still higher, mostly because of the multiplicity of sales co-operatives, which number sixty-eight. Seven or eight would be sufficient, one for each embarkation station.

The appearance of the 'Panama sickness', fatal to the Gros-Michel banana, and spreading at a dangerous rate, is an additional argument for reconsidering in its entirety the banana industry in the Cameroons. You cannot mend a suit torn on all sides; it is cheaper to order another for which the tailor could come down from Abidjan. Certainly Cobafruit, the sole banana co-operative of Ivory Coast planters, includes an excessive proportion of European planters. This is technically advantageous, but politically undesirable, especially in the present Cameroons atmosphere. The land, held by local tribes, was turned over by them to the Bamilékés, hard-working peasants and aggressive businessmen, with loosely drawn-up contracts. Here again the land tenure method whereby the peasant receives the security to enjoy the 'fruits of his labour', but does not own the land, should be put into effect.

The new plantations should include an increasing number of 'Poyo' bananas, which are resistant to the 'Panama sickness' and can produce very high yields. Planters could then afford not only fungicide treatments, but also chemical fertilizers, particularly nitrate and potassium. Certainly customers for the two varieties differ. The Germans still prefer the Gros-Michel. But north-eastern France, which also buys it, can be won over like the other provinces to the Poyo. Business interests, by opposing the changes made necessary by technical conditions, take on a heavy responsibility. They may pay dearly for it, and the planters with them.

The Poyo banana will naturally require unmixed cultivation, and the land thus freed – the banana market cannot be rapidly extended – by the quota system of exports, as well as rapid growth of yields, can be devoted to other crops. In the nearby ex-British Cameroons, the state company harvested 3,800 kilograms per hectare of cocoa. Aside from palms, rubber and sugar cane, it would be possible to develop fruits and vegetables, first of all to supply Douala better. Fresh pineapples, very sweet grapefruit and limes could become exports; and summer lemons especially, which are scarce when most in demand.

The banana industry should then be subjected to the most strict supervision, from the planting stage right to the ripening sheds in Marseille, as in the Ivory Coast. Each planter would count and date his blossoms, and notify his co-operative, which on the basis of these facts would give him the order on when to cut and deliver his crop. A small scales could eliminate bunches of less than twelve kilograms, and thus prevent them from being sent to the port. Along with the leaves and trunks of old banana trees, *macabos* that are too small and palm-oil cakes (an extension of the Dibombari oil factory), these rejected bunches could provide for extensive pig farming, on cement yards, as in the Sakay in Madagascar.

'Pre-inspection' of the bunches would be organized by one co-operative at each station, which would fill goods trains full almost entirely with acceptable bunches. Inspectors at Bonabéri would simply verify the quality of the work. A co-operative federation could fill the boats, or almost, and thereby obtain better cargo rates. It would retain ownership of its 'floating' fruit and could thus direct it towards Genoa, for example, if it discovered that prices were higher there than in Marseilles. If a Banana Office took over the wholesale trade in France, the situation would be even better. Denis Bergmann proposed this measure after analysing production in the Antilles, where the anarchy of trading conditions is much worse than in the ex-French Cameroons, and prevents the producer from receiving as much as he should.

7. THE INTERNAL MARKET: TRUCK FARMING AND ANIMAL PROTEINS

So far I have primarily been discussing exports. In the lower Mungo I stressed the market-gardening possibilities; as far as vegetables are concerned, Africa has always thought in terms of European and *évolué* tastes. European vegetables are cultivated for this *élite* group, sometimes at great expense, without streamlining either production or distribution. This is because they command very high prices, often on a level with imported vegetables. In this respect, the Europeans' prejudices do 'cost' them a good deal.

In Douala, very cheap oranges and more particularly bananas are available, those rejected for export. But in Yaoundé rejects are sold at a very high price, because the distribution system is very poorly organized; vegetables, apart from native varieties, are often impossibly expensive. The situation is even worse in the rainy season, when plants introduced from Europe grow poorly. Why not therefore develop production of properly 'tropical' vegetables, which have originated in Africa or been introduced from South China? It is a pity that Cantonese gardeners do not come along with their seeds: the best techniques of cultivation would spread more quickly. Only Madagascar, which has a large Chinese colony, is familiar with Chinese cabbage, a variety of *Brassica*; but China has a far wider variety of vegetables.

Pig raising, using banana rejects, sweet potatoes and oil and other cakes as feed, would quickly increase meat consumption if pork prices fell. Dairy farming with cows bred in the savannah has been found to be difficult in the forest zone. It is possible, however, with trypanotolerant breeds, on condition that they are better nourished, particularly in proteins and mineral salts, and correctly milked. Goats (see Chapter Twelve, 7) resistant to trypanosoma would, of course, allow milk production to be developed more quickly. But there is a taboo on goat's milk at present and many Africans still refuse to drink it. Consequently, they are never milked, and only the meat is consumed.

It is, of course, true that the very small black goats raised at present have a very limited production capacity. Research should be initiated on breeding them for high milk production, while maintaining resistance to trypanosoma, using animals free from brucellosis and Maltese fever. It will be no mean feat to accomplish, but the stakes are important enough to justify the effort. So far nothing has been done in this area. I shall return to these questions of animal husbandry, on which depends the entire agricultural future of Africa. Let me first try to outline the fearsome obstacles blocking agricultural progress in the savannah, in the Sudanese and Sahelian zones.

CHAPTER ELEVEN
The difficult savannah

I. THE SAHELIAN ZONE

In the forest region, except among certain Gabonese tribes, where males are particularly averse to work, famine is infrequent. There is always a bunch of bananas about to ripen, or edible tubers like manioc and yams in reserve in the ground. But since it became rapidly populated, because of new plantations and waves of immigration from the savannah, game has become very rare in many areas. Game formerly provided most of the proteins, but it has become even scarcer with the advent of guns, used by the Pygmy hunters who are maintained in a state of servitude by the Bantus.[1]

As one enters the savannah region tubers become less and less available, although yams are found deep in the Senoufo and Minianka areas in the Sudanese zone, and manioc even further to the north. Agronomists have propagated it from Dakar to Ruanda-Urundi in order to have food at hand, even if mediocre in nutritive value, when locusts ravage the cereals, formerly the only food crop. The basic foods were sorghums in the south and millets in the north, where the drought is more severe. In eastern Africa corn is dominant. There is only one harvest a year here, and it is subject to many hazards, first of all the rains. The gap between harvests is particularly difficult for the peasants to bridge. However, a better organization of society is slowly being established, with the foresight to store and save harvests.

Although the centre of the agricultural zone in Niger receives fifty-five centimetres of rain a year, the same amount as in Beauce, France, it falls in thirty days of the year, and eight months of total

[1] This has seemed to redouble since independence.

dryness are aggravated by the desiccating desert wind, the *harmattan*, which brings the hygrometer down almost to zero. Furthermore, the sorghums and millets yield only two to five quintals per hectare, as against twenty to eighty of corn in Beauce.[1] From there on towards the north, the Sahelian zone, its thorny bushes a symptom of even greater drought, is the most difficult area in all tropical Africa in which to intensify agriculture. Where its population was dense, it was often classed as a famine zone by geographers; although the efficacy of the anti-acridian battle has greatly reduced this scourge, and crops grow better now.

The fact remains that outside zones which can be irrigated, efforts to intensify agriculture will be of very limited value in the Sahelian zone. It seems reasonable therefore to concentrate efforts during the first phase at least in the southern Sudanese zone and the Sudano-Guinean zone, where the water supply, the absolute essential for vegetal growth, is less limited. The army is no longer recruiting there, and industrialization so far from the coast will remain at a disadvantage. Therefore stepping up of massive agricultural migrations appears necessary in the beginning at least to 'decongest' the Sahel and move the population towards the plantations in the forest zone. Later perhaps they can be moved towards the southern savannah. The latter is more populated and has a better water supply. It will thus be easier, once techniques have been perfected and become really paying, to effect the necessary agricultural revolution there. This will consist of continuous and fertilized cultivation. It will be helpful to start by associating food crops and industrial crops, already done to some extent, which will bring a higher profit on the first modernization efforts.

2. FIRST STAGE OF INTENSIFICATION: COTTON IN CHAD

In 1960–1961, Chad harvested 98,000 tons of cotton seed for the first time in its history, and put out the flag a little too soon. The efforts of the authorities to get the peasants 'back' to work, as they had slacked off a great deal the previous year during Independence

---

[1] A large part of this discrepancy is due to fertilization and the better varieties used in Beauce, but not all.

celebrations, largely contributed to it. Also, rains were well spaced, and continued through the whole month of October. If the 1961–1962 total is back to the region of 45,000 tons, it is mostly because efforts slackened again and sowing was started too late.

The average date of sowing is about July 1st. If this date is simply moved up fifteen or twenty days, 30,000 to 60,000 tons of cotton are gained, depending on the year (see Chart II and Appendix IV). The peasant in Chad sows his millet first, and it is hard to criticize this instinctive priority accorded to his 'daily bread'. An essential reason for his lateness with sowing cotton is that at the time when he should leave to prepare the fields he has just barely sold the cotton of the previous season. The work required to sow, in great heat, is psychologically far more difficult if one's pockets are full of money. The date of cotton sales should therefore be moved forward as much as possible, and purchases of equipment and draught animals encouraged.

Peasants should also be encouraged to save money, to tide them over the difficult period between harvests. If necessary they should be forced to do so, by having the payments for cotton given to them in instalments. The last payment would be made after verification that the peasant has planted before the deadline, the date being advanced to the end of June. Those who have done so would receive a bonus, whereas the last planters would not receive their last payment until later. There is no need for highly qualified engineers in each cotton zone village to sound reveille at five-thirty in the morning, from the first of May on, the date of the 'agricultural mobilization', to call all villagers to the fields.

Only the first steps are hard, because once work has started the peasants continue willingly on their way. Educational campaigns among the peasants will play an essential role in this basic advance, early sowing, on which all the others depend. It is not a matter of regimenting the peasants, or of militarizing them as it is done in the Chinese communes, particularly at first. Each peasant will remain master of his fields. One could, however, suggest in this framework the need for a transitory period of enlightened despotism, which, as long as it cannot be realized 'by the people', should at least be 'for the people'. All this presupposes, as an absolute necessity, an African

II. COTTON: EARLY SOWING BRINGS HIGH YIELDS

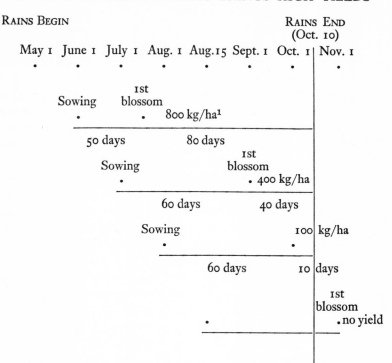

RAINS BEGIN   RAINS END
                                                (Oct. 10)

May 1 June 1 July 1 Aug. 1 Aug.15 Sept. 1 Oct. 1| Nov. 1

                 1st
Sowing   blossom
   .   .   800 kg/ha¹

      50 days   80 days
                               1st
          Sowing   blossom
             .   . 400 kg/ha

            60 days   40 days

               Sowing   100| kg/ha
                  .   .

                  60 days   10 |days

                                    1st
                                    blossom
                        .   .no yield

The first blossom appears 50 days after the June sowing, in earth that is still warm; but only after 60 days for the July 1 and August sowings, in earth cooled by the rains (*Institut de Recherche pour le Coton et Fibres*).

Yields, roughly speaking, are proportionate to the number of days which remain between the first blossom and the end of the rainy season. The Tikem Station has shown that while sowing in the beginning of June, assuring 80 days for this key interval, can yield 800 kilograms per hectare of cottonseed, the mid-August planting, which requires the same amount of labour, may have no harvest all and is not even worth attempting.

'Night of August 4th',[2] achieving the abolition of the new privileged class. It is useless to set fire first to a few 'great houses': they can be put to better use. In Appendix III I have made an attempt to class

---

[1] Kilogram per hectare.
[2] This was the night in 1789 on which the privileged class in France 'voluntarily' and because their châteaux were burning down surrendered their privileges.

by priority the four successive stages of modernization in the cotton industry, each of which is dependent on the others.

If the steps discussed in the appendix, which demand a great deal of work, are effectively followed, tractors can be brought into use, which will mean their widespread use in twenty years. I can see my African friends jump at the idea of such a long delay. If it is unacceptable to them, the preceding stages can be done in double time, in an African great 'Leap Forward', hopefully a more reasonable one than China's. Otherwise, there will be heavy losses, and a slowdown in the 'take-off' of the economy. The acceleration of the rhythm of progress is here, as elsewhere, a matter of the immediate dissemination of agricultural skills. However, the tractor of 1975, very different from today's, will be easier to introduce through the area; cheaper, more durable and manageable, sometimes electric, perhaps operated with solar energy, all of which can shorten the delay by a good deal. The economic failure of tractors was often related to the gigantic size and bad management of the public or co-operative enterprises which utilized them. Smaller units, placed under the effective responsibility of their managers, offer a better economic potential.

3. PEANUTS IN SENEGAL

The I R H O has obtained satisfactory results in Senegal by alternating, with the rotation of peanuts-millet-peanuts, two to six years of fallow (Chapter Four). The *Centre de Recherches Agronomiques de Bambey* is still advocating millet cultivation with a view to ploughing it back in the earth as fertilizer, but has not proven the advantages of this system. It seems in any case foolish, if not worse, to advise peasants who fear they cannot last until the next harvest to destroy their food crop in its full growth.

In order to bury this mass of growth you need a plough working the soil quite deeply, which may bring on or increase erosion. On these sands, a harrow with four or five teeth would suffice. The pair of oxen needed for the plough cost 25,000 to 30,000 CFA francs, take a long time to train, and are difficult to feed in the dry season. A donkey is more energetic and easier to handle, costs 3,000 to 5,000, is easily trained in ten to fifteen days, and is content with dried-out feed, only supplemented with a little grain during the season of hard work. The light equipment for the donkey, which will pull the harrow with four to five teeth, serving also as a plough, and the seeder, is within the reach of the peasants now.

Heavy equipment pulled by oxen often costs as much, with the pair, as 150,000 CFA francs. Paying it off is too much of a burden for the peasant.[1] Most of the mutual credit societies in the Upper Volta who have similarly equipped their members have gone bankrupt, as a report by Mariotti and Gillain shows. Each farmer could be equipped with a donkey – even a horse, where available (mules are too difficult to breed) – and several teams of oxen with their equipment would belong to each village co-operative. Or, perhaps better, a voluntarily formed group of four to six families could share a pair of oxen and its heavy equipment.

Senegal, where animal traction is already more widespread, should give top priority to introducing it everywhere in its most economical form. Note that donkeys and horses cannot be utilized, for the moment at least, where there is much more than a metre of annual rainfall, because they adapt badly to wet regions and demand more care there. However, farm horses are already in use in the Sakay in Madagascar. Oxen will thus take first place in wet savannah areas, as around Bouaké in the Ivory Coast, where feed will be less of a problem. All the equipment should be very simple and of local manufacture, whence the interest of the Diourbel factory in Senegal. But the expense of the animals and their equipment will mean that the strictest agricultural disciplines will have to be observed, in order to repay the loans easily.[2]

[1] In northern Cameroon the CFDT grants a pair of oxen for 13,000 francs, ploughs for 5,000 and wagons for 20,000 CFA francs. This is far cheaper than in Senegal, yet it is far away from anywhere – why such a discrepancy?

[2] Good seed varieties, treated with fungicides, will have to be sown densely: 11 to 20 grains per square metre, depending on whether they are slow or fast growing varieties. Dressing, or weeding, of the cultivated area must be done early, often and carefully. This will produce yields high enough to pay for mineral fertilizers of 70 kilograms of ammonium sulphate and 30 kilograms of bicalcium phosphate per hectare in the north of Senegal, with molybdenum, boron, copper, zinc, iron and manganese. Around Thies, 50 kilos of ammonium sulphate with 50 kilos of potassium chloride should be used. The rest of Senegal should employ as usual 100 kilos of fertilizer, this time with 6 per cent nitrogen, 20 per cent phosphoric acid and 10 per cent potassium.

4. THE DAILY MILLET

Peanuts and cotton are industrial as well as food crops. Ground peanuts used in peasant cooking provide both oil and protein: thus it is undesirable to replace them with commercial oils. Aside from the cost of extraction and particularly of distribution, the substitution increases the lack of proteins.

The peanut 'blossom' eliminates such deficiencies economically and rapidly. Cottonseeds provide oil, and cottonseed-oil cakes can supply animal feed. The toxicity of the gossypol they contain has been greatly exaggerated; they are widely used to feed Danish cows without the least ill effect, and African cows consume large quantities of the seeds.

However, seeds without gossypol are available in equally productive varieties, and cakes made from these seeds can be used for human consumption as well. But, besides all these, the time has come to pay more attention to millet as a food crop. By cultivating sorghum or the smaller varieties of millet with peanuts every year – one row of sorghum to three of peanuts, or one row of millet to five of peanuts – one could obtain a total harvest, of both peanuts and cereals, much superior to what is produced by alternating these crops by seasons.

Grain cultivation can profit from the technical advances made on these industrial crops, and make the most of donkeys as draught animals. Father Chaix, of the Manga mission in Upper Volta, has been able to convince some of his catechism pupils of its advantages. Thus Michel Doamba 'scratches' the soil before sowing with a hand plough fitted with three teeth, and pulled by two donkeys. Since he owns three of them, he can work every day at the beginning of the rainy season, from midnight to midday, by using the donkeys in shifts, before the worst of the heat begins.

This method of cultivation slows down weed growths, and two, instead of three, weedings are sufficient. This is a great help, since weeding is the worst of the stumbling blocks to progress, as it is extremely arduous work. It can be done with the same plough, fitted with four teeth, if the sowing is done in lines, which makes it easier to carry out with a small, donkey-drawn seeder; or done by hand with a string line, as the Japanese do when transplanting rice. The combination of careful cultivating and animal energy has allowed some families in Upper Volta to triple the amount of land sown with great speed.

It is not a simple matter, however. The introduction of draught animals poses a number of problems: first of all the method of harnessing. The shoulder yoke used with French oxen is superior to a head or horn yoke, because the effort of pulling is not held back by a painful compression of the neck vertebrae. Individual collars, like those used until recently on Rhenish cows, would be far superior, but they require a higher grade of tanned leather. Until this is available (it will be needed for a national shoe industry also), Father Chaix employs straps braided from imported twine.

If sisal were cultivated, straps could be braided locally, with the fibres removed by hand for local needs; rope manufacture is a simple matter. In humid zones *dah* (*Hibiscus cannabinus*), particularly in regions of unemployment or out-of-the-way areas, could serve to make sacks for local needs, even if old-fashioned craft methods are used. An up-to-date factory would require too much capital, and entail excessive transportation and distribution costs. Certainly, Africa need not relive the entire history of European industry. However, to copy our present stage despite very dissimilar economic conditions is not necessarily the best solution either.

From the northern Ivory Coast to Upper Volta a series of millet mills run on a motor have been set up. They all operate at a loss. Smaller, slower models, activated by wind or water-mills, if not treadmills like the irrigation *noria*, with oxen or donkeys walking in a circle, would have been more intelligent. The treadmills are no longer made in Europe, and should be manufactured locally, provided a certain amount are turned out. A Polish prototype can be imported and tried out before they are put into general use. Old rear axles from cars can serve as the axes.

These time-saving devices can mean a great extension of cultivation. The women will no longer have to stamp on the millet and other grains, a very arduous task, and the men will be freed from the labour of digging. This will, however, present certain dangers in already over-populated areas, where it will shorten, perhaps dangerously, the length of the fallow period. P. Sarlin calculated on Michel Doamba's plantation that the time freed by the donkey-drawn plough could be used to spread five tons of dung per hectare per year. In other words, continuous cultivation could be adopted without ruining the land. Next, fertilizers will be needed: so far from the coast, they are too expensive at present. In order to pay for them, agriculture must significantly increase its exports; everything points to the need to manufacture them in Africa.

Other advances seem possible immediately, as research done on new cereals has shown. *Ragi*,[1] cultivated in the south of India and southern Africa, has produced thirty quintals of grain per hectare near Mysore with 800 millimetres of rain. A moderate application of manure and a dose of fertilizer similar to that applied to the Senegalese peanut crop was sufficient. With such yields in cereals, one could cultivate more cotton and peanuts, which will provide the necessary funds to buy fertilizers.

Classical sorghum is a cross-fertilizer plant like corn. Other hybrids adapted to the terrain can be easily and rapidly created, and their higher yields will make progress in cultivation, as do fertilizers, more feasible. Much more attention should be paid to this than is being done at present.[2] The agronomic research station at Clermont-Ferrand in France can supply vital information to African countries in this area.

If the development of crops cultivated on dry land, such as peanuts and cotton, perhaps some day *ricin*, the castor oil plant, is added to that of cereals in already over-populated areas, too frequent planting of soils may continue for too long before there is sufficient use of organic and mineral fertilizers. Consequently, other sources of foods and useful works must be envisaged, such as developing irrigation systems, to occupy the 'long winter' of the dry season.

5. IRRIGATION, SCHOOLS FOR DONKEYS AND SHEEP-DOGS

Vegetable and fruit farming exists already in tropical Africa, but in the rudimentary form of little household plots, and these only grow

---

[1] English finger millet, *Eleusine Coracana*.
[2] No research station for food crops exists in all of English-speaking West Africa.

in the rainy season. Livestock has been allowed to wander freely for too long in Africa, and they avidly graze on the young seedlings. This, of course, slows down the growth of these food crops. They no longer ripen in time to feed the family during the long dry season and only yield small harvests, despite fertilization with dung, because the length of vegetation on soil that is still wet is very much reduced. The wandering of the livestock necessitated the enclosure of Western and Corsican fields. It is a survival of the enslaving of settled peoples by the nomads. The smallest plot of garden or orchard has to be enclosed at great expense in labour and wood. The deforestation of Fouta-Djalon has increased dangerously because the *tapades*, the cottage gardens in upper Guinea, had to be fenced in.

Father Burtz has formed groups of young peasants at Dissin in the Upper Volta. They have realized that wandering livestock obliged them to sow the furthest fields first: this involved a great loss of time, the last sowings were late and too spread out, and weeding the land was neglected. They have therefore decided to pasture their sheep and goats on stakes, each attached by a cord, and to be pitiless about using bow and arrow on any loose animals. Two vagabond sows were thus 'executed' without protest from their owner. The common good can triumph.

The cows are watched by children ten to fourteen years old. If they are sent to school, this work must be done by several older children, fourteen or fifteen years old, aided by sheep-dogs. The livestock services have not realized the importance of training dogs for the 'agricultural revolution'.

The children water the crops, but donkeys wander in the streets of a village in Mali: I therefore suggested schools for these donkeys, who have all the time in the world to go, unless of course they take over the work now done by the over-burdened children. To do this, all that is needed is fifteen days of training, pulling a log. Between Segou and Markala a field of 200 square metres of tobacco is situated fifty metres from the river, thus at the extremity of the irrigable strip that runs down the Niger. It is watered with containers carried by hand. This field requires roughly two or three hours of labour per day for two waterings, morning and evening, during the sixty or seventy days of vegetation which follow the thinning. If this

6

figure is exact, 120 to 200 hours on 200 square metres correspond to 6,000 to 10,000 hours per hectare of tobacco.

A donkey led by a child, pulling water from the river or from a well (with a pulley and goatskin jug that automatically discharges the water) in a raised trench made of a half-circle of cane bringing the water right to the field, could accomplish the work of four men. Thus the cost of the donkey, say 3,000 francs, would be recovered in five to eight days. And in two or three months, adding the cost of the necessary equipment (once the well is dug): what industrial capital attains such a rate of amortization?

Cultivation of asiatic bamboo with large stalks should also be developed further; it can furnish the basis for a paper pulp industry and for an artisan industry with unlimited markets. When rainfall is more than 1·50 metres, the central part of raffia plants can replace bamboo. A rural community of the Japanese type can be developed in this way, without excessive imports of raw materials.[1] One wonders why pre-colonial Africa has remained so far behind South-East Asia in the progress of its artisan labour?

6. TRUCK FARMS AND VERY SMALL IRRIGATION SCHEMES

Temporary rivers, or *wadis*, run through numerous villages in the Sudanese and Sahelian zones. Digging down into the dry river-bed one finds a subterranean current which used to water some of the river-bank crops. Windmills (as far as the 20th parallel; below it the wind is insufficient) could be equally well substituted for containers on a rope; not our expensive steel models, but the simple durable ones like the Rhodes, or even better, the Shanghai models, with a bamboo frame and cotton sails, easy to dismantle before a bad storm. By simply importing an axis on ball-bearings, until they can be manufactured locally, results much superior to those of Middle Ages windmills can be obtained.

The crops can be protected by a fence along the *wadi*, if the idea of guarding the livestock is slow to come into effect – let us hope that this is not true, however. The same can apply to mango orchards and other fruit trees resistant to drought. If a part of these cultivated

[1] The spiky North Vietnamese bamboo can make good hedges for enclosures.

surfaces is devoted to feed crops, the combined stable and manure shed should be situated close by. The village itself, if far away, would do well to move closer to the irrigable zone.

This type of small irrigation scheme can be done by the peasants themselves, and is thus a priority whenever the cost is reasonable, the phreatic surface not too deep, and the land near the source of water valuable. Generally, recent alluvial land is the best. But what can be grown there? If a town is near, market-garden farms can be developed, not only to replace imports, but also to feed poorer classes in the town and later in the country with fruits and vegetables at modest prices.

To reduce costs, in other words the time spent on cultivation, methods of ploughing and dressing the land must be modernized, as well as irrigation systems and transportation (with wagons with tyres or trucks). Carrying three cabbages on one's head for ten kilometres to the market in Bamako takes more than one hour per cabbage, going and coming, two hours counting the waiting and bargaining. Selling collectively (wholesale selling) would cut out these time losses. When vegetables and fruits go down in price because the market is overloaded, the producers can eat them. Let us hope that they will develop a taste for them and encourage their consumption among peasants, along with the local school canteen.

These improvements in truck farming, by lowering production costs, can lead to the manufacture of canned goods, juices and preserved foods, thereby replacing imports. Factories have been built for the export trade (pineapple juice and slices), which have had great difficulty with the foreign competition because of the excessive cost of equipment, particularly tin, and the freight charges.[1] Customs protection will be justified in the beginning, so that fruit juices can combat alcoholism by eliminating almost all imports of alcoholic beverages. Canned tomatoes and tomato juice from tomatoes grown on the *baibohos* in Madagascar at Amboato Boéni can be competitive because production conditions there appear to be very advantageous. It will be more difficult to achieve in Senegal on the less fertile *niayes* in the back-country.

[1] A tin can imported from France, and filled with water in Martinique, costs more back in Paris than the same can full of pineapple juice coming from Singapore.

The villages should plant more varieties of fruit trees in order to supply the markets and the villages during a longer period. The mango tree, often preferred because it is hardy, only bears fruit two or three months of the year; guava trees are also hardy, if the drought is less severe.[1] If they are watered, papayas, pineapples, citrus fruits, bananas *et al* can be in supply the whole year, remedy the lack of mineral salts and vitamins and thereby provide the peasants with more energy for work.

Market gardening cannot, of course, be developed too far from towns and canning factories. Local tobacco, when its quality is improved and its manufacturing costs diminished, can supplant most imported tobacco; there is scarcely another crop capable of supplying as many hours of employment per hectare in the dead season. Corn, in the Sudanese zone, and wheat and barley in the Sahelian zone, grow well in winter, there the dry season. These grains would benefit greatly from better organization and particularly from the use of draught animals. The grains of leguminous plants are precious for their protein content. As well as *voandzou*, cultivated in the rainy season (its husks are ploughed back in the earth like those of the peanut), and *niébés*, many varieties of beans and peas can be grown in the dry season as catch-crops.

7. RICE AND LARGE IRRIGATION SCHEMES

Rice is a very precious food if it has not been blanched too much and if the external and most nutritive layers of the grain are preserved. I have discussed some of the more or less successful attempts at large irrigation projects using government credits. Such schemes can be realized far more effectively with more participation on the part of the future beneficiaries, provided they are guaranteed that they alone will benefit from their work.

Along the valleys of the Niger, Chari, Logone, Senegal and Volta Rivers, projects to regulate flooding should be undertaken, to progressively increase control of the waters. At present the basins are filled by only one opening, beginning with the lowest ditch. The

---

[1] In Cuba and Madagascar they have become self-propagating. Guava jelly is easily preserved and transported.

depth of submersion therefore varies a great deal, from a few centimetres to two and at times three metres. One method of adapting to this situation is to use different varieties of rice, depending on the depth of the water, 'floating' rices being sown in low areas. They can rise with the water, provided it does not rise more than five centimetres a day. But yields progressively diminish wherever the height of 1·2 metres is reached.

I have discussed projects which adapt sluice gates to 'natural' dams. The next stage of progress can utilize tributaries emptying into these basins, if they flow at least for part of the dry season, for a second irrigated crop: vegetable, cereal, tobacco or livestock feed. Simply watering rice fields after harvesting starts the young rice plants growing again, and these young leafy growths are excellent animal feed, rich in protein. It is a good complement to the savannah grasses which during that season dry up on the stalk, particularly for lactating animals, whether cows, goats or ewes.

The Niger River could accumulate seven billion cubic metres of water behind the Niandam Dam in upper Guinea. This would reduce flooding and put in reserve an enormous mass of irrigation water, available during the dry season. It would also facilitate navigation the entire year, and produce huge quantities of energy. Though an expensive one, the project is not the equivalent of the Aswan Dam, and could be undertaken by the two principal beneficiaries, Guinea and Mali, or even better, by all the riparian states of this great river of Western Africa.

The first step in this enterprise to control the water should consist of reforestation measures to prevent erosion and protect the reservoir, and prevent it from being as quickly silted up at the Cheliff River in Algeria. At that point the basins could be irrigated with precision and not more or less brutally submerged as at present. To this end they would be defined by small embankments thirty centimetres high, laid out along contour lines. Each 'floor' of the rice plantation, isolated in this way, would be fed by its own regulator, so that if desired the highest stretch could be irrigated without thereby having to drown all the rest.

Each strip would then be contoured in small lots, to cut down on terracing, and reduce the banking and scraping that brings unfertile subsoil up to the surface. With the establishment of these horizontal gradations, the rice at all times and everywhere will have its optimum water level. Transplanting the rice will then become necessary, to derive maximum yields from the project. The double annual harvest, wherever water is available in the dry season, will mean that these African valleys can at last produce yields close to those of southern China.

Since rivers flow in the dry season, the next stage can install oil pumps, then pumps run on electricity provided by the dam, which by then will be supplying the entire region with electricity. Later, solar energy will be used. Lastly, wherever water is rare, and when agricultural knowledge is much more developed, research can be done on the economic possibilities of irrigation by sprinkling. In the end the expense per hectare will be about equal to the projects of the Niger Office type – which I have already criticized for their hugeness. My outline does not include any provision for consumer goods and houses. Spacing out the improvements will facilitate the financing by the local inhabitants, since harvests obtained from the first improvements will help finance the next stages, through savings and through the labour provided.

These expenditures to control water supplies, a prime factor in agricultural progress, will bring a return in proportion to the value of the peasants using them. Projects as expensive as this should not be turned over to ignorant and lazy African peasants, but should be preceded by massive education campaigns among the peasants, who should also be given sound leadership. Elimination of the undesirable elements among European settlers, which the Niger Office for a long time refused to do, is as indispensable as the political education of the African peasants. The Niger Office made an interesting attempt to remedy their mistakes in 1961.

8. POLITICAL EDUCATION AND THE NIGER OFFICE

I advised in 1961 against extending irrigation projects for rice cultivation, since the gross returns were derisory and the net returns negative (Chapter Three). A large part of the land already irrigated is too clayey, but is, however, suitable only for rice. The yields come up quickly, thanks to transplanting, which leaves plenty of time to destroy the wild rices and other weeds which spring up after irrigation. Transplanting is demanding work, but it means one less weeding, and greatly increases the yields; up to 2·5 to 3 tons of rice per hectare can be harvested. The use of fertilizers later will double the yields again.

The amount of land allotted to settlers here, a hectare per inhabitant, demands less work days per unit of rice field than in southern China. It will therefore be more sensible to introduce transplanters pulled by draught animals, than tractors. Use of the transplanters will further the education of peasants in the use of machines, and facilitate eventual mechanization. The Chinese model which has arrived in Mali is very satisfactory, and appears to be easier to construct than the delicate Italian machines.

The current 'demechanization' of the State mechanized units at Molodo, as tractors wear out and are replaced by oxen, will allow them to cut down on their deficit, the chronic plague of the Niger Office. To increase its receipts, cotton production must be intensified and its proportion increased, as an industrial high yield crop. Scrupulous and careful levelling should be introduced (the Arrighi de Casanova method), as it eliminates all stagnation of water, so harmful to the young plant.

It costs 50,000 CFA francs a hectare, using very large machines, D8 caterpillars and scrapers, to transform all the rice fields with suitable soil into levelled earth for cotton. Given the small amount of earth to move, it is like using a pile-driver to crack a nut. De Cazo thinks that he can level it 40 to 50 per cent less expensively with sixty-centimetre rails and Decauville tip-wagons (which Europe is discarding), loaded by shovels. Often simply men and shovels would suffice to do the job. Once drainage is perfect, the other factors in cultivation start to pay off, fertilizers as well as insecticides. A yield of more than two tons per hectare is within reach of hard-working settlers, those who prepare the fields well, and early enough; but it is not possible for the others.

The educational campaigns after independence seemed to have greatly improved the atmosphere that reigned at the Niger Office. The Mossi or Bambara farmers, up at arms until the end of 1958 against colonial power, were invited after independence to contribute their utmost to the effort of putting the country back on its feet. The village that fell behind in harvesting its rice was quickly called to order by the others, and a small village of drunkards, where no one worked, was simply evacuated. Until that time levelling land had paid 200 C F A francs a day and workers manipulated with little enthusiasm or effect their two cubic metres of soil. For the construction of embankments for seedbeds in March, 1961, the workers were made to understand that since they were working for themselves they should be less demanding and more hard-working. As a result they levelled five cubic metres a day for 100 francs. Each cubic metre levelled was therefore five times cheaper, and almost everything which had been running on a deficit began to pay its way immediately.

In such conditions, levelling at a cost of 25,000 to 30,000 francs a hectare would mean gross yields could be raised from 600 kilograms to two tons of cotton, from 19,000 to 66,000 francs a hectare, which is very promising.

This result led me to propose for the first Mali Plan (1962–1965) levelling 10,000 to 12,000 hectares of land suitable for cotton, and already irrigated (2,000 had been levelled in 1961); and an extension of irrigation on 4,000 hectares of new lands suitable to cotton. The slight decrease of land planted with rice could be mostly compensated for by an increase in yields, resulting from transplantation. And the rice needed for the country would be obtained at less cost in the irrigated basins.

9. AN ADVANCE ALREADY IN JEOPARDY

The enormous investments made by the Niger Office have always resulted in deficits. Once independent, Mali could have brought the projects out of the red, if more efforts and sacrifices had been demanded of the settlers: contributions of labour at reduced wages, sacrifices in money, whereby irrigation taxes would be raised to a level where they covered both costs of maintaining the existing network and a large part of future expansion.

But until now the settlers on the projects have been of the privileged class, whose standard of living has been high, mainly due to their investments in France. The time may have come to impose some basic social justice and eliminate privileges by relating volume of revenue to volume of work. In applying this proposition I proposed an outline for gradual financial recovery in 1961, which started by eliminating the deficit. Next, the Office was to take over an increasing percentage, eventually all of its agricultural projects, later the industrial complexes. According to the plan, the Office would have been able to deposit increasing sums every year in the Mali Treasury, starting in 1971–1972, to add to the necessary accumulations for general development in the country.

The plan required first reorganization of industrial crops, utilizing those with a higher return even than cotton (many soils are not suitable for it). Attempts at cultivating sugar cane are essential, and they are being undertaken. If they succeed it will be interesting to plant the sugar on already irrigated areas, and install a large sugar refinery in the centre. Its success and regular provisionment with sugar will demand very great care in cultivating the canes, which will fail if given inadequate treatment. Cutting must be done according to a schedule set in advance each day of the season, which cannot allow time off for traditional festivals and taboos. Sugar is a 'lay' crop.

In the spring of 1962 the situation at the Niger Office deteriorated and the deficit increased: in the region of 260 million C F A francs in 1961. Refused elsewhere, broken grains of rice, formerly bought by Senegal, were not purchased anywhere, and accumulated in the storehouses of the Office. It was difficult to get the rice transplanted as the workers thought it too difficult. Intensive cultivation of cotton, involving as it does watering, ploughing, fertilizer, aeroplane spraying, means that each settler has to pay taxes, the equivalent of 900 kilograms of cottonseed per hectare. While the yield from carefully tended fields is over two tons, that of the inefficient settler falls at times below the 900 kilograms. Thus, after a season of work, they find themselves still in debt. The weeding or dressing of the cotton fields coincides with that of their non-irrigated millets outside the plantation, to which they are still too attached. They are not psychologically converted to a money economy.

6*

Sanctions against defaulting settlers seem to have quickly taken on racial overtones. The Mossis, originally from Upper Volta, have felt particularly persecuted and are beginning to leave. On the other hand, the too rapid Africanization of technical leadership gives rise to serious anxieties about the future of what could become the real 'axis' of development in Mali agriculture. As in Dahomey, this situation brings into question the social structure of the Office; whether or not African settlers, even with leadership, are capable of accepting the cultivation disciplines required for intensive cultivation, which the high costs of irrigation projects necessitate. More authoritarian formulas for settling the land, which have in general succeeded (Sudan)[1] or state-controlled projects or co-operatives could be tried; particularly if the authority employs persuasion more than coercion. It is advisable to hold off on the establishment of the sugar factory until cultivation and the new organizational structures have really proved themselves.

Aeroplanes spraying the cotton are under the aegis of a different service from that of agricultural development. This means that the decision to spray, which should be done the same day, is slowed down by bureaucratic inertia. It has been proved in the Soviet Union that the separation of responsibility between the *kolkhoz* and the machine-tractor station does not give good results.

10. WHAT NEXT?

Sugar cane grows both in the forest zone, where rains are sufficient, and in the savannah, if it is irrigated. I prefer the second solution, which brings a big source of income to a very deprived area, and where it is often possible to find better soil. Sugar cane requires irrigation water for the entire year; in order to cultivate it over large areas, the big Niandam Dam must be built.

A number of ways to intensify production seem difficult to effect: sowing animal feed in rice fields, before or just after the harvest, on heavy gaseous soil, without organic matter, has failed; if one has to wait to plough it, the soil hardens. However, the large roots of sugar

---

[1] Where the settlers have meticulously carried out the weedings and insecticide treatments. Technical leadership is proportionately considerable.

cane or of tall grasses, like elephant grass, 'remake' the structure of the soil, so that a larger variety of crops can be grown. Wheat and barley have been successful in large fields with rapid irrigation, but the cost of growing them is still high. *Dah* seems more profitable, notably for its grain. By irrigating in the cool season, very intensive production is possible. On the *polders* of Lake Chad near Bol there are three harvests a year, with watering: one of wheat, twenty quintals a hectare, and two of corn, fifteen quintals a hectare each, which is already fifty quintals. With intercalation of food crops and the application of fertilizers, each cereal harvest could go over forty quintals.

In the dry savannah, intensification seems dangerous to me in the long run if it remains on a basis of peanuts and cotton. Competition with the oil palm will become more and more formidable for peanuts. Using its proteins in foods will increase its value and its financial and therefore competitive possibilities, but only within certain limits. Even if cotton by-products are utilized better, its future will be quickly open to discussion once cellulose fibres (Chapter Thirteen) or synthetics become more economic.

The vast Sahelian-Sudanese area must seek new forms of production, therefore, related to other sources of wealth. More thought must be given to cattle-raising, and not just as an adjunct of agriculture providing draught animals and dung. An ox which works six days per year, the average in northern Cameroon, or even fifteen days, the maximum, has to be fed during 365 days. It can only be economical if it is a young growing steer destined ultimately for the butcher's shop, or a pair of cows giving both milk and calves. Animal energy, the basis of progress, is not economically interesting unless it is also a source of foods precious for their quality proteins, milk and meat. The smaller agricultural revolution in industrial crops could thus be succeeded by the greater revolution of cultivated animal feed and intensive cattle-raising. This is the change-over that can mean the complete modernization of tropical agriculture. To understand the possibilities and particularly the difficulties involved, let us take a look at traditional methods of cattle-raising.

CHAPTER TWELVE
'Sentimental' versus Modern Livestock Raising

I. TRADITIONAL OBSTACLES

When motives for raising cattle are not economic, they can be called 'sentimental'. This occurs when prestige is measured by the number of cattle (not including smaller livestock) owned rather than the revenue obtained therefrom. The word capital derives from *caput*, head of cattle, originally the real wealth. Great attachment to these animals, which are considered part of the family, has been observed from Fouta-Djalon down to south-western Madagascar. The herder will only consent to sell one if absolutely forced to do so.

The *Peuhl* women have been instrumental in making livestock a commercial venture and changing over to the 'economic' stage because they want gold ornaments. On the other hand, the poor conditions of sale hold back this desirable evolution. In the Senegal river valley livestock traders still owe herders enormous sums, the real value of which is rapidly diminishing. Some of the debts go back a long time. Sales are easier and more frequent when a co-operative pays out the entire established price, but it is a practice virtually unknown at present. Our 'sentimental' herders thus remain very receptive to the economic argument of hard and immediate cash.

Hova cattle traders exploit the herder in western Madagascar, often giving him a down payment of a third or even a quarter of the agreed price. They then leave with the animals, to sell them in the slaughterhouses of the capital. After several weeks, uneasy that he has seen no more money, the herder goes to join him. 'My poor friend,' says the trader, 'the butcher hasn't paid me,' or, 'the sale was a disaster. I cannot give you anything, wait a little while.' Soon our peasant, tired of waiting in an expensive town, accepts a bad compromise. He knows he has been badly cheated, which does not encourage him to 'go commercial'. He therefore waits until the big chief dies and honours him with huge animal sacrifices of cattle. Transportation conditions for the animals is also slowing down development of the industry. To stand up well under long journeys on foot from Ngaoundéré to Douala in the Cameroons, or even further, from Mopti in Mali to Accra, the cattle must be seven or eight years old. Sent by truck, rail or plane, the steer would have been saleable at four years; this would put twice as many cattle on the market using the same amount of feed and the slaughter animals would be only half as old.

The growth rate of cattle herds in Africa remains too slow (often 11 per cent or 12 per cent as against 25 per cent in developed countries) to procure a satisfactory revenue. The slow rate of expansion, in sharp contrast with the human population explosion, is due to many reasons. The very composition of the herd, which has an excess of males and over-age animals, means an insufficient proportion of reproducing cows. The reproduction rate of the cows remains very mediocre, often less than 50 calves per 100 cows a year, as against 85 to 90 in Europe. This is due to poor sanitary conditions, and above all to feed deficiencies, especially in proteins and mineral salts (phosphates).

The general mortality rate of the herd, 4 per cent to 8 per cent in Rhodesia, becomes catastrophic if it hits the calves, because in the same country, according to the F A O Africa report, 'the proportion of calves which succumb to disease, malnutrition or attacks by animals is as high, according to some estimates, as 50 per cent.' Malnutrition at weaning is of capital importance. When the calf no longer receives its mother's milk and goes abruptly to a diet of dried grasses, which are woody and full of cellulose, the physiological effects, due to the two essential lacks, proteins and mineral salts, are similar to those of kwashiorkor in the infant child.

2. ECONOMIC OBSTACLES TO INTENSIFICATION

The productivity of the African and Malagasy herd is thus very feeble, since their 93 million cattle produce on the average only twelve kilograms of meat per head per year, as against seventy kilograms in Western Europe. The difference is much greater for milk production. However, Africa can derive much more from its herds, as we shall see in the case of Madagascar. The basic obstacle is current economic regulations and the general disorder in trading conditions, which offer sale prices which are not attractive enough to stimulate the new industry.

Conditions of life for the herder are very primitive, to such a degree that he turns over the herd to his children at a very early age, under the burning Sahelian sun. He is satisfied with a very small profit, because this type of 'noble' life is compensated for by his sense of prestige, which lets him exploit the agriculturalists still, or even maintain them in slavery, as in the oases of the southern Sahara. The tall Tutsi herders of Ruanda-Urundi, who came with their herds towards the fifteenth century, dominated the small Bantu cultivators, the Hutus, until our times. The latter adopted a curious form of 'pastoral servitude'.

In exchange for a feudal type of protection and renting a cow, the Hutus gave a disproportionate amount of labour and supplies. The revolt of the Hutus against the incredible exploitation that they suffered under the Tutsi only dates back to 1957 and only became violent in 1959–1960. At that time the Belgians, who until then had supported the dominant class like all good colonial powers, realized that it was to their interest to take the side of the Hutus.

A herder charges a stiff price for the services of his oxen: in Chad, 10 per cent of the millet harvest is given him just to transport the harvest several kilometres from the field to the village. On the other hand, prices of meat and milk are still too low, particularly in the countryside, to make certain that the expenses required to modernize cattle-raising will ensure good incomes. Milk is still bartered at Yelimané in northern Mali, two jugs for one jug of grain. At the Niger Office, where recent extension of cereal crops has upset this milk-grain relationship, the exchange is now for equal amounts; and the same jug is used, the grain dust being mixed in with the milk.

Meat is sold very cheaply, because of the low average buying power of the African population. However, the coast and the towns are rich and pay quite a lot for it. But transportation on foot is burdensome, less because of the cost of leading the herd than because of the loss of weight *en route*. Air transport is being used more and more. From Ngaoundéré in the Cameroons to Pointe-Noire in the Congo the freight charge is seventy CFA francs a kilogram, and ninety francs to Leopoldville. At this price whole carcasses are loaded, including bones.

It would be more economical to bone them, shipping only the good cuts and leaving the second-rate cuts to supply a local canning factory. The failure of Malagasy companies has shown that this industry cannot compete with Europe (which cans only the second-rate cuts, which are worth less and less), by canning the entire animal, even if it is sold cheaply to the factory. The Diego-Suarez factory, in northern Madagascar, only operated half of the year in 1958, and only 50 per cent of the available hours for that six months. Capital is lacking in poor countries, yet often they under-employ it.

3. THE DAIRY INDUSTRY

It is difficult to expand cattle-raising and make it pay on the basis of cultivating feed, which is expensive. This is, however, the only way to raise African animal production to the level of its alimentary needs. Grazing and steppe lands produce very little and their feed resources are irregular and seasonal. The animal loses in the dry season almost everything he gained eating grass in the rainy season. The great lack of proteins and mineral salts cuts down the rate of reproduction and increases the mortality rate, and also results in a late calving season.

It is difficult to break out of this vicious circle. In many cases the only solution will be continuous production on the soil, rotating food and industrial crops with grazing meadows. If humus is applied and the soil structure 'remade' with large rooted plants, intensification will be facilitated and the soil can produce a double crop per year in irrigated zones.

But it will cost a great deal. Why not modernize the most lucrative sector first, production of fresh milk for the large towns and capitals? When milk is sold for twenty-five CFA francs a litre, cultivating feed rich in protein is a worthwhile proposition. Right now, 10,000 feed units per hectare are produced in the Sakay (Madagascar. See Appendix II). By also using fertilizers and irrigating, the Niger Office can harvest much more. It would be a good idea first to set up a small 'milk basin' for the capital in the area irrigated by the Niger Office at Baguineda near Bamako. The experience acquired there, as around Tananarive where the cooler climate will favour progress, will help to reduce costs. The dairy farmers will have to be efficient, feed the cows well every day, provide them with water, and milk them thoroughly. If this is done, a factory for concentrated or powdered milk could be supplied economically, to replace imports.

At first a subsidy can enlarge the market for milk, and is here preferable to Customs protection. The economic potential of this 'pivot' of agricultural development more than justifies it. The first dairy factory in Mali should be situated, if the Niger Office recovers financially, near Niono, or in any case not far from the future sugar cane factory, because the by-products of the latter are excellent feed. In Madagascar the first dairy factories will be in the Sakay, doubtless, around Fianarantsoa and Antsirabe, on the high plateaux where altitude favours dairy cows. The Bamiléké country in the Cameroons, particularly towards Douala, would be better than the Adamaoua mountains, where the 'sentimental' attitude is liable to persist longer.

There is a good chance of success on the condition that economic feed is obtained. In Burundi the stations of the former INEAC still produced cultivated feed units in 1960 for fifteen CFA francs, which is two or three times too expensive. New and still more economic methods of producing feed must be actively sought. By watering the sides of the valleys in Ruanda, which have steep slopes, with small drains running along the flanks of the hillsides, the Rubona Station has already obtained cheap feed on these wild irrigated areas.

In the 'Belgian' areas of the Ruzizi valley in Ruanda, after two years of cotton and two years of manioc, fairly rich lands will spontaneously produce wild but good grasses, particularly *Brachiaria ruzizensis*. If they are systematically grazed while the grass is new, by cows attached to stakes set out at intervals and periodically moved, the grass will come up again in the dry season. This eliminates the brush fires, a feat no law has been able to do, because the cattle have eaten all the dry grasses, and the fire cannot spread. This 'wild' meadow takes the place of unproductive fallow land, remakes the soil structure at no cost, and at the same time provides continuous production.

The cessation of cultivation does not result in valuable 'wild' meadows everywhere. One should therefore begin where results are certain. The best breeds of dairy cows were not raised on the Khazakhstan steppes in Eurasia but in Great Britain and the Low Countries, which are more favourable to grass. In the same way Africa should start in the wet savannah area bordering the great forest, on sufficiently rich soils.

In the Ivory Coast I advised intensification of feed production in the Bouaké savannah, where the rainfall is 1·30 metres between March and November. Wild growth of elephant grass or Sissongo (*Pennisetum purpureum*) are promising in this area. Nearer the forest, precautions against sleeping-sickness must be redoubled. But if fallow lands there, after a not too prolonged cultivation, suddenly sprout *Digitaria umpholozi*,[1] they are well worth it.

4. MEAT PRODUCTION: THE NECESSITY FOR RICH PASTURELANDS

A steer raised all its life on planted grazing land would be too expensive, at current prices. But if the mother is a good dairy cow, the value of her milk would pay for a large part of the feed. However, the steppe must continue to furnish most of the feed at a low price. A feed crop will be justified if it eliminates the worst deficiencies in the beginning. Young grass and proteins fed to the calf at the time of weaning will be worth it if the animals can be slaughtered one or two years earlier. When the cows are properly fed, their rate of reproduction as well as their milk supply will increase. Supplementing their diet during periods of great want at the end of the rainy season will prevent the losses of weight and ruinous mortality rate.

If the Diego-Suarez factory had received enough animals in good condition twelve months of the year to operate at full capacity, and

[1] Closely related to *Digitaria decumbens*, this Pangola is completely changing cattle-raising conditions in the Caribbean. See *Lands Alive*, Chapter VI.

if it had trained Malagasy experts, its director told me in September 1958, he would be in a position to pay fifty C F A francs per kilo of live meat during the entire dead season. This amount was double the current rate at that time. Profitable extension of the industry should rest, as in South America, on a pronounced division of labour. The Ankaizina Mountains, traditionally an area of herding, supply the factory with a good part of its needs, but the long 400 kilometre journey on foot entails great weight loss. These mountains, being too far from the factory, could produce and raise the calves, supplying the thin animals for another area closer to the factory, where they could be fattened up.

Between the Ankaizina and Diego-Suarez is the large irrigated Sosumav area, with 8,000 hectares of sugar cane. Fifteen to twenty tons of leafy stalk-tops from the canes would constitute 1,500 to 2,000 feed units, available in the depth of the dry season, to fatten up the thin cattle which had been driven down from the mountains. In the middle and end of the rainy season, and in the beginning of the dry season, the Ankaizina can provide cattle in good condition, if planted grazing land along the way is available where the cattle can rest and be brought up to strength.

The road to the Namakia sugar factory west of Majunga is deliciously perfumed with molasses, used to hold down the dust. This food, which is of great value, is wasted due to a lack of intelligent management.[1] Often up to 3,000 feed units per hectare of stalk-tops and molasses can be obtained, enough to make five cattle gain sixty kilograms in four or five months, a total of 300 kilos per hectare. This is perhaps more than a Normandy meadow provides. If you calculate on the basis of the 8,000 hectares of cane sugar in the Sosumav area, it would mean a gain of 2,400 tons of meat, live weight.

In this tiny valley corner, only 0·12 per cent of Madagascar, the use of currently wasted by-products can produce an increase equal to 1·5 per cent of current meat production on the entire island. Actually the created wealth would be greater because it would enable the factory, as well as the natural pasturelands on the mountain, to operate at full capacity. Freed from the present excess of animals in relation to its resources in the dry season, the Ankaizina

---

[1] Its use in the manufacture of rum is still to be feared.

area could feed its cows and calves adequately after weaning, increase their rate of reproduction, and sell the steer after three years instead of five.

5. IMPROVING FEED PRODUCTION: ADVANTAGES OF TROPICAL CATTLE-RAISING

By following the above steps an ascending spiral of progress in cattle-raising can be initiated. Exported in the form of bones and frozen quarters of beef, by a trade office similar to the Kenya Marketing Board, the meat of well-fattened cattle, later of better quality breeds, will command much higher prices. At this point cultivation of feed on good pastureland can be economic. In cool or irrigated climates, elephant grass has topped world records of feed production, at the testing-station in Puerto Rico, with 63,000 feed units (F U) a hectare annually, the equivalent of sixty-three tons of barley.

Western Europe has barely reached 25,000 F U with the Jerusalem artichoke. The average meadow in Normandy only produces 2,000 to 3,000 F U. This has exploded the myth of the inferiority of tropical cattle-raising in relation to temperate countries. Certain meadows planted with Pangola in Cuba have provided enough food for a 1,300 kilogram cattle-weight increase per hectare annually. This is more than twice what the best cultivated grazing lands in France provide. But although the ultimate success of cattle-raising is a certainty in Africa, its debut is difficult in many situations. Not all areas are as favourable as the high plateaux in Mexico and Madagascar, or the rich plains of the Caribbean islands, Camaguey in Cuba, Beauport in Guadeloupe and Grove Place in Jamaica.

Developing existing grazing land where vegetation is suitable, as in the Adamaoua in the northern Cameroons, will facilitate this difficult beginning. Foresters can find thorny species adaptable for 'live hedges' difficult for animals to cross. Plants like *Euphorbia Firucalli* are sufficiently hardy, also the thorny euphorbias or Avelloz of north-eastern Brazil, or the thorny bamboos of North Vietnam, for wetter zones. Pasturelands thus enclosed at small cost can be grazed in rotation, the herds only remaining three or four days in each field. The grass would be left to grow again, according to the season, for twenty to forty days; at times even fifteen and sixty days, in periods of very rapid or very slow growth. Large collective parcels of land should be enclosed to avoid the error of too dense woodland in western France, demolition of which is costing a great deal today.[1]

Regular mowing of these grasslands once or twice a year, eliminating the new shrub growth and cutting back clumps of the tallest grasses, will constitute the second step in modernization. The third will be storing the wild feed in silos in the rainy season. To reduce transportation, it should be piled up and consumed where it grows, on the edge of the field. Hay, without its water content, is four times lighter. It can be dried at the end of the rainy season or during brief rifts in the clouds when the sun breaks through. If you wait too long to cut it, the hardened grass has lost practically all its value.

Hay and silage still cost quite a lot; mowing them is more economical with animal traction, if done on fairly flat land, cleared of tree-stumps, new shrub growth, rocks, ant-hills and other obstacles. To do this the fields must be ploughed, which encourages the idea of passing to the fourth stage of development directly, profiting from this necessary ploughing to actually plant a meadow with a highly productive species. This will make the mowing and storing of the feed more worthwhile. From this stage on, as Cuba has demonstrated,[2] chemical fertilizers, and then irrigation in the dry season, very quickly become economically productive. This order of priorities, here very schematic, should be modified according to varying conditions, whether natural or economic and human.

In the north Sudanese or Sahelian zones, in East Africa and South Madagascar, the Indian fig (*Opuntia ficus indica*) can revolutionize feed production, in a similar way to what has been done in the Brazilian *Nordeste*. With equal rainfall, the African *milieu* is more arid than the *Agreste* of Pernambuco. The Brazilian *Palma* thrives if it receives between seventy centimetres and one metre of rainfall; the Indian fig can manage on less in Africa. It has already done well west of Antsirabé with 1·50 metres of rainfall, planted on

[1] M. Mazoyer proposes semi-enclosures under watch, with just a rope, watchmen and dogs; this absorbs some of the unemployment.
[2] *Cahiers du Tiers-Monde*, 1962. 'Réforme Agraire à Cuba'. (P U F). See also 'Elevage' by J. Coléou in the same issue.

very filterable volcanic soils. Stagnant water is very harmful to it, even for very short periods during the rainy season.

It could be attempted, on light soils and well-drained slopes, as far north as Korhogo in the Ivory Coast, and in central Dahomey and Togo. It would undoubtedly run over towards the south into Chad, Niger, Upper Volta and Mali. A four-year crop rotation in the Senoufo country would use the land more fully if Indian figs are planted at the same time as the third-year crop. Planted between the rows, they would profit from the tending and cleaning up after the third and fourth crops, making the fallow year very productive. This cactus can be consumed when one needs it, and thus forms an 'on the stalk' feed, always available and very economical.

This feed crop, relatively easy to plant in semi-arid zones, will provide the decisive food complement necessary to herders, and cut down the current high weight losses and mortality rate. It can completely revolutionize the livestock industry in semi-arid regions, as Pangola has already done in cooler tropical zones. One day it will be elevated to the status of a key plant in feed and agricultural advances, along with clover; always provided that the nitrogenous supplement for lactating or young animals is not forgotten.

This cactus leads us to think also in terms of 'feed trees'; some, like the acacias and the mesquites[1] can grow right along the edges of the desert. *Faidherbia* or *cadd*, whose leaves grow in the dry season, feed the livestock of the Serer tribe in Senegal, and form the basis of a semi-intensive agriculture. The Fulani tribe in northern Dahomey feeds its animals by trimming Senegal mahogany, *Khaya senegalensis*. It is only recently that tradition has reserved the word feed for herbaceous plants. The early inhabitants south of the *Massif Central* and the Alps in France prepared bunches from the leafy branches of elms and ashes, which enabled their sheep and goats to survive the longest winters. Although these leaf feeds were expensive and not very nutritive, beechnuts and acorns fattened the pigs, whose smoked hams participated in the crusades. Carob trees and honey-locusts, with clover, constitute the pivots of increased feed consumption in North Africa.

[1] The inermous varieties of honey mesquite (*Prosopis juliflora*) developed in the Sudan produce abundant pods with a sweet pulp.

6. ZEBUS AS DAIRY ANIMALS

Once correct feeding procedures,[1] absolutely essential, are established, the large expenditures for feed improvements will not pay off until modern methods of livestock-raising have been put into effect. Selecting good breeds of cattle will be one of the first steps. In Mexico, Venezuela, Hong Kong and Alagoas in the Brazilian *Nordeste*, it has been shown that Frisian cows can prosper in the tropics, if they are very well fed and sanitary conditions are carefully supervised.[2] This breed has just been selected for the high plateaux in Madagascar; it would also succeed in the Bamiléké country and on the highlands around Fouta-Djalon, wherever pasturelands have been improved.

In the plains of tropical Africa and Madagascar, zebus, a small humped cattle from Pakistan and India, are worth considering as dairy animals. If the dry season is long the Sahiwal breed, which is doing well in Kenya, can be advised. In wetter climates, the Red-Sindhi and particularly Kankreg breeds seem preferable. Our veterinarians have introduced mostly the Texas Brahma, bred for meat. Lacking milk, the calves do not grow quickly, and the herders' children, like those in neighbouring towns, suffer from lack of proteins.[3]

The exclusive concern with exports over the years has meant that the pressing needs of the native population have been ignored. It is high time to 'decolonize' the technicians. Near the towns, stock should be bred for milk production. In the bush it should be bred for three functions: work, milk and meat. If the animals provide nothing but work, their maintenance will be ruinously expensive. Africa should aim for milk with a high protein content, and avoid repeating the errors of Europe, which for the last century has bred only richness in fatty materials. Vegetable oils are much more economical and probably better for the health than butter. Amateur

[1] There is a saying in Dahomey that 'the cows of the lagoons keep pace with sleeping sickness,' implying that neither milk nor work can be obtained from them. Rather, they keep pace with under-nourishment.

[2] The total eradication of ticks has facilitated their progress in Puerto Rico. It took nineteen years.

[3] The nomadic tribes of Mauritania lack protein more than the sedentary cultivators, because their flocks are distant and they do not drink milk. Feed cultivation will allow them to become sedentary.

methods of breeding, based for example on the colour of the hide, have to be stopped. Performance is more important than aesthetics. The choice of animals for reproduction must therefore be based on inspections of their milk and meat production. This will not be effective unless animals that are equally fed are inspected. Otherwise, the diverse performances observed will simply reflect the differences in their diets. Correct milking procedures must be closely supervised. Calves cannot be depended on to extract all the milk, as their appetites vary considerably, and production will suffer if the cows are not completely milked.

7. NATIONAL PARKS – IMPORTANCE OF GOATS

An English school of thought, more sentimental[1] than not when it is a question of protecting nature, has struck a responsive chord in UNESCO publications. It would like to see national parks proliferate across Africa, to protect the natural flora and fauna. Some of its members go so far as to say that more meat can be obtained from organized hunting than from cattle-raising. If you take the very worst cattle as a point of comparison, the Baras in south-west Madagascar, or the *llanos* in the Orinoco in Venezuela, which yield four or five kilograms of live meat per hectare per year, then it is true that more can be gained from wild antelopes and hippopotami.

Hippopotamus meat is already appreciated in various areas. As soon as feed is produced, even in unfavourable areas, the quantity of meat will climb from 100 to 400 kilos per hectare. This just goes to show that the theory held by the 'friends of the animals' does not stand up.

The CINAM-SERESA report for the preparation of the Senegalese Plan shows an enormous difference in the relation of revenue to capital invested in 'small' versus 'large' livestock: it is six times higher for the small (goats and sheep) than for the large. The latter is ruinous as long as it is not modernized, yet it has occupied all the attention of the experts. One of the primary needs is to produce milk richer in protein than in fat. Goat's milk fulfils this condition,

---

[1] And they call the African herders' system 'sentimental'!

FALSE START IN AFRICA

and goats have the further advantage of being able to digest thick, cellulose feed more easily. In semi-arid zones, leaves of trees, shrubs and shrubby trees are sufficient nourishment if their protein content is high enough.

UNESCO accuses these accommodating goats of increasing erosion on the periphery of the Mediterranean, and of advancing the Sahara towards its northern and southern borders. Let us not deprecate this brave and hardy beast: the best breeds (Murcia, Malta or Alpine) are very productive, and the yields (when milked, which is rare in Africa) are as high as 800 to 1,500 litres, easily surpassing, despite their much smaller size, the African cows. If they are provided with a higher quality feed, they will require less in quantity per feed per unit of food they produce. The herder is responsible for this wastage; he wants to feed them without making any effort, without even seeking to organize the use of wild feed resources.[1]

The goat-farmer in the Sahelian zone, in the Senegal valley south of Lake Chad, breaks off branches of thorny acacias to feed his flock of small black goats. He stacks them into a pile of dry wood around the tree trunk, which, during the brush fires, destroys the still living tree. The foresters forbid him to use axes; he should be taught instead to carry the branches further from the trees, and above all not to cut too many. If he exploited this wealth intelligently, by replanting or simply protecting its growth, it would bear far more.

The forester of the Dauphin, under Louis XIV, had orders to break the right front leg of any goat found wandering in the royal forests. The unfortunate peasant could take his beast home with him, but from then on had to feed it in the stable, where doubtless it provided him with more milk. In Greece two categories of goat are distinguished, useful and destructive. Taxes were lifted on domesticated goats fed at home on feed crops and by-products, because they are much more productive than the nomadic goats, the only destructive ones.

In the Sahelian area 'feed forests' exploited in moderation can produce more food in the form of goat's milk than grasslands fed on

[1] These two reactions of UNESCO seem to come from the FAO, 'colonized' by the foresters, who have perfected a theory of conservation of soils and have not come up against any coherent programme of agrarian development to answer their arguments.

by meat cattle. It is the nomadic herder who is the enemy of the cultivator, whose fields he freely devastates. Controlling the animals by keeping them under obligatory watch in delimited sectors is the first step in the development of rural areas. If he has to fence in or guard his fields from wandering animals, the effort required of the cultivator is excessively increased, and he becomes discouraged. Modern livestock-raising, which demands feed crops, seems more suitable for the peasant used to hoeing, ploughing and weeding than to the 'wandering herder', who is scornful of these jobs. It is the rice cultivators from the high plateaux in Madagascar, and not the Bara herders, who are developing livestock farms, with good breeds, around the capital.[1]

8. PROTEINS – FERTILIZERS

1,300 tons of weight gain for cattle in Cuba, 63 tons of gain on barley in Puerto Rico, 14,000 litres of milk produced from cattle eating pure clover near Mexico, 2,000 litres even in the semi-arid savannah of the Alagoas, with Indian fig and cottonseed cakes – all these figures, reported per hectare annually, are a brilliant demonstration of the very high livestock-raising potential in tropical countries. However, tall grasses harden quickly in a hot climate to a state where they retain more cellulose than nitrogenous matter. The lack of cheap proteins is the most important stumbling-block to rapid expansion in this industry. It is already making an appearance on the ranches in the south-western United States, and there they can overcome it with massive doses of feed cakes.

When the crop is situated far from the coast and oil factories, tropical livestock-raisers have to find other solutions. Research on leguminous feed crops to find varieties richer in nitrogen must be vigorously pursued. The grasses themselves can furnish this element in abundance if grazed on while young by a regular rotation of pastureland, particularly if enough nitrogenous fertilizer is applied. But it must not be too expensive, in other words, not have to bear too excessive transport costs.

---

[1] Appendices V and VI will discuss certain possibilities for dealing with sheep, pigs and fowl.

Lack of nitrogen constitutes the principal factor limiting the development of tropical crops. The traditional necessity for a fallow period, during which time bushes and shrubs grew up, is the main cause of this deficiency. Nitrogenous fertilizer, by increasing vegetal development, increases harvests and also deposits of organic residues in the soil. Since it is more appetizing to the cattle, and therefore more completely grazed, grass in cultivated meadows which have received nitrogenous fertilizer is also preferable because not as much 'woody' waste is left, and this almost completely prevents the spread of bush fires.

Along with phosphates, found in abundance in north and west Africa, and Gabonese potassium, nitrogen is the essential lever of African progress in agriculture and livestock-raising. Through its use, the vicious circle of poor soils and under-production can be completely broken. (The use of dung as fertilizer is only a very first step to be taken in areas not yet able to afford nitrogenous fertilizers.) The manufacture of commercial fertilizers will have to be started soon and accelerated for they will soon be indispensable. Often several stages of development will have to be superimposed.

It has been suggested that Europe assume the cost of education and health in tropical Africa, its other expenses being all it can take on without a superhuman effort. If adopted, this proposition should be accompanied by the strictest possible economy in these essential areas. Since the need for schools is an obvious one, the Africans will pay for them. I fear that the relatively small amounts being invested by these countries cannot create satisfactory development. I would much prefer to see the investments in major projects increase still more, in order to harness rivers and dams more quickly and acquire the necessary energy to manufacture nitrogen, among other things. Nitrogen cannot be underestimated as a stimulus to progress, and is much more urgent than tractors, although it, too, will not obviate the need for great efforts. 'Give us enough fertilizers, we'll take care of the rest,' an Indian colleague told me in 1959. They took care of the rest so ineffectively that the fields, although better fertilized, were as poorly maintained as ever, and covered over with weeds. The hand plough must be perfected, and ploughs drawn by animals brought into general use before fertilizers are introduced. They became widespread in Europe only after centuries of good farming and decades of rapid agricultural progress. Nitrogen, however, remains essential for more rapid African agricultural development because it will facilitate the extremely difficult integration of agriculture and livestock-raising.

Between 1947 and 1961, France spent about 50,000 million old francs on the Sahelian area, in Mauritania, Senegal, Mali, Niger and Chad, to provide water wells and artificial or controlled natural ponds for cattle herds. Certainly the mortality rate of the animals was diminished as a result. But there is no point in keeping old cattle alive in the traditional 'sentimental' framework. The areas near the wells have been over-grazed and vegetation much reduced. The points of water supply were set up before a map of the pasturelands was drawn up, which would have established them on a more intelligent basis. The wells spread along the North Dahomey highway are not utilized; they should have been placed along the traditional animal routes, and not along the modern road.

The Sudan has developed ponds which do not require installation and pumping expenses. A policy in French Africa which provided the herders with good leadership and concentrated on the systematic development of feed resources would surely have produced much better results at less cost. Before I discuss ways to achieve the agricultural advances thus outlined, let us take a look at problems in the forest region.

CHAPTER THIRTEEN
Developing production in the forest region

1. PROTECTION OR PRODUCTION? FORESTERS ARE CONSERVATIVE

'Africa possesses 17 per cent of the world's forestland, but only 9 per cent of the exploited forests, 7 per cent of the lumber, and only 1·5 per cent of the world production of industrial wood,' the FAO inquiry on Africa points out. And yet this same study maintains the traditional, conservative distinction between protected forests, where 'exploitation of lumber should only be an accessory', and productive forests. The Ivory Coast is at present taking a million cubic metres of lumber from its four to five million hectares of primary forests and old secondary forests, by skimming off the cream and cutting down all the valuable species. This policy will come to a disastrous end well before the end of the century.

To ward off the disaster, the national forest service is seeking a lesser source of wealth, depending on natural forests to provide it. Young trees of value have to have a clearing, so that they will dominate the less valuable species. It is difficult work. Few good species are found and, since they are dispersed throughout the forest, an arduous search throughout the entire forest must be made at each clearing time. Estimates of timber production after sixty to seventy years vary only from 50 to 200 cubic metres per hectare. This comes to between one and three cubic metres per hectare annually, a very poor yield for the work involved.

French forestry came into being after the Renaissance, at a time when world population was small, genetics unknown, and agricultural techniques very primitive. It began as a battle to protect forests against peasant depredations, in order to obtain the 200-year-old oaks needed for the navy, the basis of power at the time. Thus forestry was mainly concerned with 'conservation'. It taught the peasants to respect nature, and not to direct it except very timidly. In tropical Africa, which is full of forests, the result of this policy is a net annual loss of thirty to forty millions of dollars in forest products. Although Africa exports a great deal of wood in a raw state, manufactured products of much higher per unit value are imported. The traditional fallow period of fifteen to twenty years in the forest zone has no purpose except to regenerate soils devoted to food crops. This is a complete absurdity when modern fertilizers are available. The fallow theory means that only 5 per cent to 7 per cent of forest zone lands can be cultivated at one time, and this is done at the price of enormous efforts to clear the land of the bushes and shrubs that have grown up during the fallow period. Often 150 days per hectare must be spent, to produce just one crop on the land – and this destroys all the timber produced in the interval.

2. A 'FOREST REVOLUTION' IN WET ZONES

Continuous cultivation is now possible, with a constant vegetal cover on the soil, ploughing in of organic matter, and fertilizers. Modern forestry is also moving towards the idea of planting forests, just as agronomists are replacing poor grazing lands by planting grass as another crop. Cultivation of trees is beginning in the dense forest regions, starting with the limba, okoume and niangon trees in Gabon, in the Congo at Mayumbe, and in the lower Ivory Coast. Production has reached ten to twelve cubic metres, at times even fifteen to twenty, per hectare annually. This is four to ten times more than in enriched forest areas, and twenty to fifty times more than in the unimproved natural forests.

The consequences of this 'forest revolution' are multiple and even cumulative, according to Gunnar Myrdal. A hundred thousand hectares of planted forest would produce as much as the four to five million hectares of 'wild' forest in the Ivory Coast. As these plantations would be localized along waterways, railroads and large highways, transportation costs would be far lower. Costs of cutting and exploiting would be lower as well, since each of the necessary access roads would handle much more lumber.

The costs of the initial 'blanket' felling necessary to plant the new forest can be borne by installing a provisional crop. In the Middle Congo a contract was signed with the banana planters under which they receive an indemnity if they allow foresters to plant limba or another species. In the Ivory Coast, the Cameroons, Ghana, and Nigeria enormous areas of old coffee plantations exist, too old to be productive, but where the natural 'forest' *milieu* would be conducive to new forests. In general, new plantations (cocoa, *Elaeis*) will do better on cleared forest land.

It is possible to have a rotation of long duration between different varieties of cultivated trees, some for their fruits or grains (cocoa, *Elaeis*, coconut, coffee), others for their sap (rubber) and others for their wood. In the middle of the niangons and the obeches, varieties which grow well in large masses, mahogany trees can be dispersed to advantage, as they are susceptible to parasites if planted too densely.

3. TEAK AND CASHEW IN DRIER SAVANNAH REGIONS

Since the samba tree can grow in deciduous forest zones where there is no rainy season, teak also seems to be indicated. From central Dahomey right up to the north of the oil-palm region, beyond Abomey, to the pre-forest zone savannah at Bouaké in the Ivory Coast, and over to Guinea and Casamance, this tree can produce twelve to fifteen cubic metres annually per hectare, in good soil. We are in the habit of keeping the best land for agriculture, leaving less fertile areas for the forests. Yet intensive agriculture is often better able to turn degraded soils which lack organic matter to good account if fertilizers are applied, while forest plantations can be more easily installed on old fallow lands in good condition.

President Apithy of Dahomey threw up his hands in horror when I indicated that teak plantations would reach full production in fifty or sixty years. The drive to enrich the national inheritance and take actions with such long-term results is not a natural one for such young countries. Nevertheless, twelve to fifteen cubic metres a hectare annually comes to around 75,000 CFA francs in annual receipts for standing timber, ten times the average income from a hectare of corn. Felled, sawn and transported to the pier its value would be tripled; but the income is deferred for a very long time. It can, however, be an important source of wealth for each of the villages in these regions. After as little as four years, on good soil, small poles can be cut for huts; after six years, larger poles; and the first lumber can be brought out in fifteen years when the forest is thinned. Each village in the semi-humid regions could thus, like those in the Vosges and the Jura areas in Europe, bring in enough income unaided to provide eventually for a good many improvements in infrastructure.

Further to the north, teak does not do well unless there is a phreatic surface one to three metres deep, and the earth must be good alluvial soil. But the cashew can grow further towards the north, up to where rainfall is down to 800 millimetres, and even lower in the favourable conditions defined above. Its great advantage is that it provides very productive work in the dry season; good edible fruit rich in vitamins; balsa wood used in aviation, and firewood at the time of its felling at twenty-five years; and, above all, cashew nuts, which are coming into demand more and more, and which start appearing after as little as three or four years. This African cashew is now being ground in India and sold in the United States. A few bags even reach Africa, for *chic* cocktail parties, not far from the producing trees, but at such a high price! A small processing plant could be established now to handle roughly a thousand tons of nuts. This would require at least a thousand hectares of trees, but would be a fountain of dollars. This is why I have pushed the idea, from Senegal to Dahomey. The nuts would tide the villages over the long-term wait for revenue from teak plantations.

Some people have recommended planting firewood, but the needs are for one cubic metre per capita annually. Land which has been fallow a fairly long time can produce six to eight cubic metres of firewood in bushes or shrubs per hectare per year. If forty to fifty hectares per village of 300 inhabitants are protected from fire, and are close enough to the village to cut down on transportation, their needs can be met more economically than by planting firewood.

Many other producing aspects of the forest can be envisioned. The feed potential of the thorny acacias in the Sahelian zone has been somewhat overestimated. Their leaves have little food value, nothing to compare with a plantation of cactus or a good carpet of grasses. The most useful role of the forest in the Sahel is to protect the soil from erosion. In wetter zones many slopes can be as well protected by graded grazing lands, properly exploited and thus highly productive, as by the natural, so-called protective, forest.

4. TROPICAL FORESTS WILL BE NEEDED TO SUPPLY PAPER

Until now paper pulp has come mostly from Scandinavian forests, which will not be able to meet the demand after 1970. During the decade following that the North American and Soviet reserves will be called in, but they are not endless. Although there is too much pulp now because there are too many factories, the upward curve of paper consumption, a characteristic of our civilization, means that demand will probably be far greater than supply in twenty years.

The Scandinavian forest often produces only two to three cubic metres a hectare annually. In the Vosges four to six are reached with Norway pines. Tropical Mexican pines, grown on the high Malagasy plateaux, yield fifteen to twenty cubic metres, seven times more than in northern Sweden. Near Fianarantsoa, a factory is to be installed which will be very profitable if it reaches a level of 60,000 tons a year of white sulfate pulp.[1] In Fouta Djalon, the Bamiléké Mountains, and the mountains in East Africa with a water supply, the potential for this pine is great. At Perinet, on the Tamatave–Tananarive railroad, the eucalyptus saligna holds close to the world record,[2] producing as it does fifty to sixty tons of dry matter per hectare annually. It can produce pulp paper very cheaply, of inferior quality. The Caribbean pines can produce better pulps and grow in certain slightly cool tropical flatlands. Bamboo, in the lower Ivory Coast, supplies thirty tons of green stalks, or six to seven tons of cellulose,

[1] Low cost electricity is needed for industry; household electricity should be made more expensive, as it is a consumer item. Foreign aid to lower the price of electricity would be very valuable as a stimulant to industry. The *conference*, a quasi-monopoly of shipowners serving Madagascar, asks 100 new francs per ton of pulp transported from Manakara to France, while a tramp ship will take it for 60 to 70 new francs, M. Bellouard tells me. It is curious that the Le Clère report defends the *conference*.
[2] Perhaps held by Hawaiian sugar canes, with their twenty-five tons of sugar, as much in by-products, and ten tons of dry leaves.

per hectare annually. Because of its long fibres, superior pulps can be obtained from it.

Given these statistics, the problem of the cotton crop is very much open to question; the eucalyptus can also be used for viscose pulp, the raw materials for artificial silk and rayon. Over-populated countries like China and India, which will be even more crowded in the coming century, will not be able to give cotton and other plants used for textiles the two dozen million hectares of good lands now considered essential. But they can clothe themselves from wood, using the eucalyptus, grown on the most depleted soils, which it thereby makes valuable.

Modern policy towards forest land is rapidly becoming intensive and productivist, instead of limiting itself to the sterile framework of protection and conservation. Actually, protection and production go hand in hand. Humanity may go over the twenty billion mark by the end of the twenty-first century, unless effective birth control measures are imposed. In that case it will obviously not be able to 'conserve' thirty-six million square kilometres of forests, as against only thirteen million of ploughed land. Like cultivated plants, the planted forests of tomorrow will benefit from the development of good species, fertilization, irrigation and plant health measures. The twenty-first century will thus see forestry schools closing down, because forest cultivation will be taught along with orchard cultivation, in agricultural institutes. I hope that Africa does not copy our current arbitrary division of disciplines, which are already out-dated without our realizing it.

Tropical Africa thus reveals great possibilities for development, although it will be difficult to get it started, as is the case throughout the world. Industry will play a fundamental role in the modernization of the economy, and its results will be more rapid and greater if it is established on rational bases and without dogmatism. It will have a limited role for a fairly long time, however, while agriculture can absorb almost all of the rural unemployment quickly and productively. We have seen that the traditions of land tenure and gerontocracy, moneylending and share-cropping are holding back development.

7

Once these traditions are overthrown, the agrarian potential will be immense in the dense forest zone, the area of the richest plantations, on condition that humus is applied, that protective measures are taken against erosion, and that a series of crop controls are adopted, the strictest being for oil palm and rubber.

In the savannah, the problems appear at first to be more difficult. However, modernization of cotton and peanut crops can mean immediate advances. The decisive progress will consist of replacing men and picks with donkeys and oxen, pulling harrows, ploughs and wagons. Intelligent livestock-raising will 'capitalize' on dung by putting it back in the soil; the more productive soil will then enable them to pay for chemical fertilizers, which should be manufactured locally as soon as possible.

African agriculture can then start using machines and, progressing gradually to the more complex models, will feed its livestock well and regularly, and graduate to the concept of capital exploitation – capital, let us not forget, derives from *caput*, head of an animal.

Many will wish to skip steps, and acquire the most up-to-date tools immediately, particularly tractors. A hundred billion CFA francs would be necessary to mechanize agriculture in a small country like Dahomey. The four-year plan calls for eight billion in agricultural investments in four years, however, and it is an unprecedented amount. Plantations of shrubs and forests and modern fisheries would be less ambitious but more effective.

It is relatively easy to draw up a basic outline for agrarian development in tropical Africa. The real difficulty is of course to put the plans into effect, in a framework I shall now discuss.

PART 3

In order to develop, Africa must reorganize the whole of its educational system . . . and set to work

_____

CHAPTER FOURTEEN
Education, Cadres, Activism among the Peasants

1. JOBLESS GRADUATES AND LEADERLESS PEASANTS

I have discussed in Chapter Seven: 1, the inadequacy of the present school system, entrenched in an unimaginative imitation of the European model. A heavy parochial heritage weighs on teaching traditions in Europe. The first purpose of education was to train priests, who need Latin, the language of Catholicism. Young francophone Africans therefore still devote more time to Latin than to English, Spanish, Russian or Chinese. Until 1924 the Oxford professor who lived in his College was not permitted to marry; and certain British Fellows still give tutorials to groups of two, much as the tutors of young noblemen do. In France the secondary schools created for the bourgeoisie were scornful – and still are – of primary schools for 'working-class people'.

As late as 1931 a law passed in Madagascar specified in particular that schools should train clerks and civil servants; not a word about peasants, workers, artisans or technicians. This type of abstract education, cut off from reality, costs far too much, for the buildings as well as the teachers. In addition to Upper Volta, already cited, the 11 per cent of the Mali children who are in school absorb 18 per cent of the national budget. The village teachers are apt to lord it over the rest of the villagers, and are contemptuous of the modern African worker. The schoolboy son of an agricultural worker is taught to have only one desire, to escape the land and his dependence on it. Opinion polls taken of Senegalese schoolchildren are very revealing: agriculture is the last of the professions they chose.

Economic progress requires an exodus from rural areas, at a

controlled rate, only in so far as a man can find productive work in urban areas. If he cannot, the result is a new unemployed and parasitic class living in the urban shanty-towns.[1]

Agricultural modernization requires peasant organizations to encourage and develop co-operatives and mutual benefit societies. When they fight for the necessary credits for rural development, peasant unions will come up against the *élite* class in public office, and bring out into the open the excess of the latter's share of the national wealth. This 'class war' of peasant-worker against bourgeois-civil servant may upset some orthodox Marxist ideas.

The co-operatives and mutual-aid societies are desperately lacking in competent, honest groups dedicated to the peasant cause. To be effective they must come out of the peasant *milieu* and also remain very much a part of it. School should not detach the young schoolboy from his original rural world but train him so that he is in a position to make it modernize. This will necessitate total revision of the basic concept of the system, which calls itself 'humanist' but which more than anything else increases the scorn for manual labour.

2. REVOLUTION IN RURAL EDUCATION

As soon as education is almost universal, rural schools should train agricultural workers above all, since practically all of the students will, or should, remain in agriculture. The teaching staff should be trained as much to be instructors of agriculture as to be traditional schoolteachers. Convincing African Ministers of Education, themselves taught in academic schools, of the importance of this will be difficult.

This revolution in education cannot be effected unless there is a vigorous peasant demand for it, coming from associations of rural youth, composed of those the schools had no room for.[2] Illiterate at twelve years old, even older sometimes, these young people can scarcely hope to enter even secondary school. They nevertheless

[1] In England enclosures were necessary to drive off the peasants. The attraction of the factory was modest, compared to the small farms with two cows and six hectares producing 1,200 kilos in Western Europe. Who would not be tempted to leave the land in Africa, faced with two hectares producing 500 kilos, often without cattle?

[2] Because of the lack of teachers in Chad, classes sometimes have more than three hundred pupils.

have the right, and it should be part of the various Constitutions, to minimum basic education and vocational training. (Cuba called 1961 'the year of education'). The new states should proclaim themselves 'educational' and not 'welfare' states, which India did prematurely as far back as 1947, in England's image. The comfort thus given to Indian villages by virtue of this principle was at the expense of development.

If organizations of young people in rural areas, arbitrarily turned away from the privileges of education, claim their 'minimum legal education', governments, in Mali and Chad particularly, can reply: 'We haven't the money to provide you with the traditional schooling, it is too expensive.' This self-awareness might help to eliminate the inexcusable expenses of this schooling.

Young people led by rural activists (whom I shall discuss later) can build an improvised school with the aid of the other villagers. In the beginning even the shade of a tree can do very well in the dry season, in the Sudano-Sahelian zone. It will be a matter of improving very basic education, preferably taught during this transitory phase in the vernacular, since it will not be a preparation for higher levels. Its prime interest at first will be to conquer illiteracy rapidly, and this can be accomplished by a volunteer from the village, given a modest salary by the village itself. As soon as possible it should press on, and add accelerated vocational training, an apprenticeship to the vocation of modern farmer.

3. REHABILITATE THE FARM-SCHOOL

The farm-school can satisfy the two requirements, basic education and vocational training. It should be small and modern, of a size adapted to available labour forces, built on land given it according to traditional custom, as I have tried to outline. A donkey pulling water from the well could water a large garden and orchard, which would supply the school canteen. Any excess can be sold through a co-operative, thereby teaching the students how to manage a small co-operative: excellent training in practical economics. The villagers will buy the vegetables and fruits if only to support their school. The irrigated areas would later grow feed, to supplement wild resources, and enable the school to feed a small amount of livestock the whole year, often dairy goats, attached to a stake or fed in a paddock.

Even before it supplies the canteen, the goats' milk would provide local milk for the *goutte de lait*[1] in the villages, which is urgently needed, and thereby eliminate imports of canned milk. Next will come, depending on local conditions, the herd of sheep, which should be large enough to pay for the cost of watching them, and will require the rapid training of a young competent shepherd. Pigs are also a possibility, if inexpensive feed is available. Fowl will require a nearby urban market in the beginning. These livestock will need grains, tubers, cultivated grazing meadows. The majority of the children's food should be produced by the school, with the exception of mineral salts, condiments and vitamins. Additional economical proteins can be furnished by peanut meal. Thus, through actual experience, an excellent education in nutrition can be given.

A number of present teachers would be incapable of running the school, a real agricultural enterprise, as they know nothing about agriculture. In a large town, one out of four schoolteachers should have been graduated from an agricultural school. Meanwhile, one can begin with young rural school graduates, preferably those who have not lived long in towns. An accelerated training course of six months at least, comprising an agricultural season, followed by an academic apprenticeship of the same length – two years would be better later on – would teach them basic methods of education as well as modern and economical agricultural techniques, those of the I R H O or of the C F D T. The use of donkeys with seeders and small ploughs, harnessing oxen to ploughs and wagons, simple cultivating techniques, installations for watering, preparation of manure and hay or silage, planting coconuts and coffee, with cover plants and secondary crops between the rows, in forest zones: all these would be the basic courses.

They would be taught in a deeper way what is now being taught to the 'organized' peasants, and would become the first rural school-

---

[1] The *goutte de lait*, literally drop of milk, provides milk to those who particularly need it, the pregnant women, nursing mothers and children. At Ambalavo, the *goutte de lait* is financed by 'voluntary' contributions from the whole area, particularly the villages, but only urban mothers can come and get the milk, because the cans are delivered in bulk. One more instance of anti-rural discrimination.

teachers, necessary to get the farm-schools going. As a next stage, more solid training would be offered in real rural 'graduate' schools. These could later be merged with the schools training agricultural teachers, with two different specializations: one giving practical courses to adults, the other providing basic education,[1] first of all for the very young, later for teaching the illiterate adults.[2]

In the first transition stage, farm-schools would recruit children from ten to thirteen years old, when they are able to work, and for three or four years try to get the largest number possible from children who have been unable to attend the regular schools. They would work four or five hours in the morning, from dawn on when weather is good, with the more productive modern techniques, including draught animals wherever possible. They will be able to devote the afternoon, when it is hotter, to basic education, oriented towards agricultural development. The school should seek as soon as possible to make ends meet, or almost: this presupposes good work from the students, careful management, and a low salary for the teacher.

4. REFORM OF GENERAL EDUCATION

If such a school were inserted into the present system, it would hold no interest at all, because students would have to work very hard, knowing that the other schools were continuing on their merry way, with no physical effort required, towards the *élite* jobs. Its success requires first of all a general reduction of salaries, private and in government, beginning at the top. Salaries should never, at the current level of economic development, be more than 50,000 CFA francs a month, and this for ministers and general directors only. This would simply bring them down to the level of Greek or Portuguese salaries.

Next, every school, whether primary, secondary or graduate, should introduce manual labour, to be considered as another form

[1] Other departments could train future members of agricultural co-operatives and mutual aid societies, later heads of rural activist centres, all in a spirit more agricultural than bureaucratic.
[2] It has been said that this is impossible, yet Cuba achieved it in one year (1961) by mobilizing young people from ten to eighteen years old. Africa has not as many educated young people, and, more important, is not activated by a revolutionary spirit.

of education, into its programme. There should be at least one hour
a day for smaller children, and two hours or more for children over
twelve. Teachers in rural schools, with their different training – it
must never be considered inferior – they should receive a salary at
least equal to that of their colleagues in the cities, plus a 'bush
bonus'. By paying more to urban teachers – Libreville salaries are
double those in the bush – the injustice of the town versus countryside conflict is aggravated.

In the same context, technical personnel should receive higher
salaries than administrative staff on an equal level: the agricultural
engineer more than the sub-prefect. Only then will technicians, the
irreplaceable element in development, be respected and their work
attract the best students.

This kind of rural staff will be difficult to recruit in the beginning
if it offers no prospect of a prestigious career, such as that of wearing,
one day (after a stage of accelerated training), the golden tricorn of
the sub-prefect. What better training for a future rural administrator
than that of a country teacher, who has lived a long time in a
village?[1] Why require, for this position, a jumble of French juridical
training, evolved to make the fortunes of lawyers and defend the
fortunes of landowners, which is often completely irrelevant in
Africa? The education given in schools of administration often
seems inapplicable, more often preoccupied with maintaining order,
a static formula, than with the dynamic problems of economic
development.

A school of trades would be better training for a sub-prefect, as
it would allow him to be a real 'works foreman'. The current agricultural schools have nothing of value to teach an administrator.
Starting in 1970 two-thirds of the sub-prefects' positions should be
reserved for the best educators, both in general and agricultural
schools, who have been able, while brilliantly performing their tasks,
also to complete their general education. The evils of bureaucracy
should be avoided like the plague by underdeveloped countries,
which must try to create an atmosphere of austerity in which those
who work hardest have the best opportunities for promotion. It will
be a pity if African governments copy French civil service ratings,

[1] The best prefect in Dahomey is a former works foreman of Congolese peasants.

and base salaries on diplomas (sometimes easily granted) and not on the quality of the work done.

Africa should simplify its legal system, because it cannot afford to maintain the parasitic group of notaries, lawyers and litigants who exploit the peasants in Europe. Certain minor delinquents would be sufficiently punished by a couple of humiliating slaps administered in public. Those who steal from the Public Treasury, on the other hand, deserve to be sentenced as murderers. The delay in development they cause results in the death of children, by prolonging malnutrition. Administrative simplification would avoid the accelerated expansion of 'Parkinson's Law', of which there is already damning evidence. For instance, buying a truck only after a contract is signed does not *per se* prevent misappropriation of funds: a specification can be included which is only found in one make. And because of the delays the truck is only bought after the agricultural season is over, or after the insect to be destroyed has done its damage (e.g., cocoa capsids in the northern Congo).

Although graduates of the transitional farm-school are primarily the modern peasants of the future, the best of them should be able, with accelerated courses, to attend the rural 'graduate' schools, where their practical knowledge will be appreciated by their classmates from regular schools. They may make more spelling mistakes, but they will be better at harnessing oxen. It will be important to make sure that this quality is as appreciated and respected as the other.

Eventually, economic resources will be increased, thanks to this utilitarian education. (Its utilitarian nature need in no way prevent it from offering as good a general education as other schools.) It will then be possible for all rural children to have a reorganized general education, which begins between the ages of five and seven. The farm-school, which is only a transitional stage, would then take students from ten to fourteen years old, after four (later six) years of primary school, and give them agricultural training in depth. They would be taught to lead a pair of oxen, make an irrigation ditch, plant a tree, raise an animal, and measure out the feed. But, for heaven's sake, they do not yet need the theory of photosynthesis! The primary school would have its own garden and

7*

orchard, with a donkey for watering and weeding, and a small quantity of livestock. All would be adapted to the abilities of the children, who would be aided on occasion by older students.

5. TRAIN EACH CHILD FOR A SPECIFIC PROFESSION

It is time to give every African child exactly the training he needs to perform a future vocation effectively. Europe tries to adorn its youth with a lot of knowledge, not much of which is useful in practice. Africa is too backward to indulge in this luxury yet. The sub-prefect in the bush has to know exactly how to make emergency repairs on a motor, and he won't learn this in two years at the Institute of Overseas Studies, but in two weeks of training in a local garage.[1]

Manual labour in urban primary schools will be directed towards training qualified workers and artisans, in metal and wood. Continued in the technical and secondary schools, these practical skills will result in useful objects, given to the students. They will start on construction and mechanics in some schools, weaving, basketry and pottery in others.[2] Each student, returning to his village or urban district, should be able to teach his fellow citizens to use their ten fingers better. In this way the scorn of manual work can be rooted out; right now it is an appalling obstacle to progress.

I must emphasize that it is not a question of lowering the standards of teaching, but of 'decolonizing' it, of diffusing it more rapidly, therefore at less expense, in the rural areas that have been neglected up until now. By making it more efficient and directly useful to economic development, it will procure the resources which can be devoted mostly to the education of the following generation.

6. ORGANIZATIONS AT THE GRASS ROOTS LEVEL

The need now is to take the African peasant in hand, with under-

[1] I am thinking of the sub-prefect of Gambona in the Congo with his two broken-down motors, the truck used to harvest palm oil and his husking machine. I saw him again later at the Institute of Advanced Overseas Studies.

[2] It is a great mistake to over-emphasize the last two trades or the tourist item industry (as in Senegal). They do not constitute the base of industrial development, like mechanics, and they decrease the size of the indispensable artisan class producing tools.

standing and skill, and show him the advantages and necessity of the modern techniques of cultivation and livestock management. Only individual action, on a direct man-to-man basis, will be effective in this area, by creating confidence and a personal relationship. This, of course, will require a great many leaders, perhaps one for each hundred peasant families, two for a large village of a thousand inhabitants.

Faith, dedication, and civic and moral qualities will count most, particularly in the beginning. They will be more important than a high degree of training, which is often now only found in men with a totally different background: the jacket, tie and car prevent such people from establishing contact with the peasants, and the very small number of them means that they pass through each area very rapidly. Moreover, the techniques I have discussed are simple to execute, as we have seen for peanuts and cotton. The same will be true, when they have received the attention they deserve, for the sorghums, millets and other food crops. On farms in the forest zone crop discipline has to be more meticulous, but it remains simple to learn. In the beginning, as for farm-school teachers, rural school graduates can be recruited from regions where they are numerous, near the coast.

As the leaders should work in the area they come from, even less education will suffice in areas where it is not yet widespread. Gagnoa, in the Ivory Coast, took those who failed the high school examinations, and turned out good qualified men in four months of training in an agricultural research station. They went to work without payment pruning on coffee plantations, without the owner even being always present during their work. Potential village leaders should never become unpaid workers furnished by the state to planters. They should not, however, be chary about lending a hand and picking up a shovel – like my guides from Katibougou, who accompanied me in Mali and never touched a shovel – because their role is to teach people how to do the job. But teaching is not the same as working. To train African peasant leaders, renewed European co-operation would enable things to go much more quickly.[1]

Although willing to help, the peasant leader should be greatly

[1] Chapter XIX, 1.

respected by the villagers, even the richest of them who never work with their hands. To achieve this, the first group of peasant leaders should be installed with great pomp and circumstance, equal to that given a President of the Supreme Court, on the village level, by the head of state himself. The latter would point out, with all desirable publicity, that the peasant leaders are in a way his personal representatives to the village, so that they can benefit from a reflection of his prestige. The sub-prefect should install the others, stressing the importance of their role for the future of the country. National deputies and party members can put all the weight of their authority behind work for rural activism. Alas, in October of 1961 the sub-prefect at Obala had not yet 'found the time' to visit a single one of the pilot cocoa plantations. Some of his staff still hardly conceal their contempt for technicians. They are the 'non-decolonized' ones, like their colleagues in India. I advise all Africans to go and see where the latter are leading their unhappy country, to judge for themselves whether they want to go the same way.

7. A UNIFIED DEPARTMENT OF RURAL DEVELOPMENT, WITH NO CIVIL SERVANTS

The peasant leaders will have to be many-faceted, because it is impossible to supply as many men on the grass roots level as there are technical departments. The departments themselves – Agriculture, Livestock, Forestry and Agricultural Engineering – will have to co-ordinate action on the local level, in order to stop pulling the peasant in too many directions. The most natural way to co-ordinate functions will be to fuse all these technical departments into one organization of rural development. Perhaps by so doing they will show that they are oriented towards a firm policy of agricultural expansion. In the Ivory Coast and the Cameroons, a good number of Livestock Department chiefs, separate from those in Agriculture, have inherited the prejudices and rivalries of the colonial era experts, at times carrying them to still greater extremes.

The unified Department would have at its disposal experts, veterinarians, foresters and agricultural engineers. The latter could be further specialized, some in irrigation projects, others in building or agricultural equipment. Under present conditions, there is no effective method of making a good number of the civil servants work well, or firing those who do not, and they contaminate the rest. The title of civil servant should only be given to representatives of 'law and order', as the English say, and of the Treasury. In the technical departments, this status can be limited to a very small body of advisers to the Ministers who ensure that programmes of development are drawn up, fitted into the Development Plan, and are then given the authority to oversee their implementation.

The other officials would be under contract, as it were, concentrated in development areas and fairly autonomous regional development societies. Their salaries can depend on their performances, and be increased more rapidly than those of civil servants, if a raise is justified; also, if the occasion arises, salaries can be lowered or cut off entirely. Under present conditions the danger is that the people recruited for these jobs will be the relatives, friends and tribal or political dependents of those in power, who will look on the jobs simply as a free living. To make room for them, others, however competent or well-trained, may be fired as necessary. I am thinking of members of the Department of Geology, or the representatives of the SEMA in the Cameroons, who were so quickly and unfairly replaced by 'friends' of those in power: 'tribalization and mediocrization'. A whole fabric of bad habits and the political atmosphere which encourages them must be destroyed. In these 'republics of friends', all hope of any kind of rapid development must vanish as long as clan and caste ties dominate national and patriotic ties. How can one escape this morass? By the intervention of new leaders from the peasant masses.

8. RURAL ACTIVISM

In this discouraging atmosphere, training rural activists, as the I R A M[1] has done, sounds a hopeful note for the future. Begun in Morocco,[2] the method has succeeded better in Senegal, where it

[1] *Institut de Recherches et d'Application des Méthodes du Développement*, 32 rue des Bourdonnais, Paris. G. Belloncle has made an interesting study of it in the *Archives Internationales de Sociologie de la Coopération*, 1961, 10.
[2] G. Belloncle has remarked on 'the absence (in Morocco) of a definite desire on the part of those in public power and in the technical departments to orient themselves firmly towards development.'

trained nationals to be more quickly capable of taking over as directors of activist centres from the Europeans who started them. Its objective is 'personal participation in development, not just awakening the populace, the second aspect only being a preparation for the first.'[1] Its method consists of seeking out dynamic activists among the peasant population. 'A peasant subjected to the exhausting problems of a backward economy and technique soon crosses a psychological barrier and becomes inaccessible to change. . . . It is also impossible, for sociological and technical reasons, to take men too young; the remaining margin is between thirty and forty years.' In three or four weeks the directors of activist centres, men 'full of respect and profound sympathy for the people they work with', teach them about their own new country, and the necessities of local development, by showing them that it is their business too, and that they can contribute a great deal. They have to be weaned away from the concept of the omnipotent state, in which individual contributions are meaningless.

After this training stage, which takes place in the off-season, the new activists, who have also made personal contact with technicians and authorities, return to their villages and duties, and their neighbours continue to regard them as 'one of us'. But they bring a revolutionary ferment and a new concept with them. They show that the village can make progress on its own, and create the conditions for its own economic expansion and development; that many of the complicated modern techniques are within the reach of the average peasant, particularly if the villagers band together to use the modern techniques economically; and that misery, sickness and ignorance are no longer inevitable, still less a religion.

I inspected a group of activists being trained in the Senegal valley and was pleasantly struck by the simplicity of their accommodations, which contrast with the luxury of the former French administrative offices, a tradition that the Senegalese are unfortunately carrying on. The Four-Year Plan for Eastern Senegal has provided ten million francs for the Regional Assembly's 'Palace' at Tambacounda. There are twenty members in the Assembly, who already have at their

<hr />

[1] Yves Goussault, *Tiers-Monde*, I, 1961.

disposal several spacious buildings in which to convene. Less than eight million francs are provided for production departments, as against 31·6 million for education, health, and water supply; more for luxury than for production and four times as much for 'welfare'. In contrast, the activists train their oxen as draught animals, and create small rice basins.

The activists have been most effective in Casamance. The story which struck me most was that of the villagers on the border of Portuguese Guinea, to whom the activist explained the great harm being done to the national economy by smuggling. The villages immediately mobilized to track down the smugglers. In other places, they make sure that unlicensed businessmen get their licences and pay the fee, or drag anyone who has cut down a classified tree to the Chief of Water Supply and Forests.

Their newly acquired knowledge is beginning to bear fruit in helping to spread modern agricultural methods. But the peasant leader, to whom the activists are in principle the auxiliaries as they gain for him the support and confidence of the population, is too often lacking, so that the activists cannot be of enough use. Their essential role is to persuade peasants to 'invest' their time in development projects. Thus, also in Casamance, in the Bignona area, a road thirty-five kilometres long was undertaken on their initiative; but the collaboration of the Department of Public Works seems to have been insufficient. And when they have been invited to construct first-aid stations, the villagers are evidently disappointed that, although they have been long finished and are falling into disrepair, no nurses or medicaments have yet been sent.

Activists are no more a magic formula than co-operatives. Results will depend on the dedication felt and communicated by the heads of the activist centres, and on the careful choice of activists, who have to make this faith their own. When they return to their village, many run the risk of sinking back into old habits and dormancy. Periodic refresher courses of two or three days on the problems of development and the best ways of attacking them will be indispensable. In the same way, training three or four activists from each large village will be a help, as they can lean on each other and work together. Activists are an essential link in agricultural improvements and rural development, although they cannot complete the task alone, and their role will soon be expanded.

Once the peasants' determination has been awakened, equipment should quickly be made available to profit from it. This involves a planned development of credit and co-operative groups. Activists will also have to expand their area of operations, because in order to obtain large credits from a very limited national budget they will have to compete with the time-servers in the privileged class. I have mentioned the possibility of conflicts between the worker-peasant and the exploiter-businessman-civil servant. Rural activists cannot be effective where Moslem *marabouts*, Nigerian emirs, or the all-powerful traditional district staff exist, as they leave no room for collective peasant initiative, but instead exploit the peasantry. The purpose of training activists is to organize the peasantry with men who have issued from it, and who remain devoted to its service. The two sides will soon be irreconcilable.

The recent revolutions in China, Cuba and Yugoslavia were essentially peasant revolutions, judging by the composition of their armies. They were not totally so by any means, but they do disprove the exclusive revolutionary role of the worker.[1] In Havana, the workers waited for the complete triumph of the rebels to join the movement, and the revolutionary fraction of the proletariat in China was wiped out in 1927. In any case, this working class is in the process of disappearing; soon only technicians will remain.[2]

If the activist movement is closely allied with the peasant leadership it cannot ignore the political situation: activism in Senegal has avoided cutting itself off from the party in power. If the latter really did its job, rural action in the villages would be twice as effective, and would be reinforced by political activism. But the militants in power in Africa have not understood, or do not want to understand, that their essential role should be one of civic education, to install enthusiasm for work and achieving the Plan. Idealists are needed

[1] 'Reality is always richer than theory; you have just proved it once again,' Mikoya said to Fidel Castro in January, 1960.
[2] In a dispersed subsistence economy, the African peasant will be difficult to mobilize for a revolution. But now he is being confronted with the problems of markets. Furthermore, tanks and planes prevent towns from rising against the military. Nothing remains but guerrilla warfare, as Castro demonstrated.

who are dedicated militants and not career-seekers preoccupied with landing a soft job in an election that caricatures democracy.

The absence of rural militants excludes in general the possibility of rural political activism in the Ivory Coast. Party representatives were paid to facilitate negotiations to create co-operatives, which meant large loans from the Treasury. The difficulties that were involved because of rural ignorance should incite the peasants to demand a school for rural children. If this were done, activism could more easily contribute to train leaders of economic organizations for the peasantry, defence associations, mutual credit societies, and, above all, co-operatives of various types.

In this last role, activism will come up against another adversary, vested economic interest; it will need the support of the state, notably through newly created trade bureaux. It is not possible to conduct an action in the economic sphere without political repercussions: so-called apoliticism is hypocrisy. No one, unless satisfied with a static preservation of society, can stand aloof. Development is dynamic and demands structural reforms, a break with tradition and the elimination of exploitation.

Basic education, in other words teaching adults to read and write, should only be undertaken after the children have been taught, as they will be productive a longer time; only a Cuba can undertake both at once. But when it can be done, it will enable the peasants to comprehend the situation better, to understand that development requires great efforts and austerity. But the peasant will also have the right to demand that these sacrifices be shared. Like the European proletarian in the nineteenth century, he will doubtless be led to revolt against bearing the brunt of the work alone.

'Unless the economy is seriously planned and controlled, peasant efforts become simply a number of local peasant initiatives without real economic effect. Furthermore, efforts made within an economic framework that lacks coherence or control or unanimity are rapidly suffocated, and tribal pressure soon paralyses progress,' according to the I R A M. And Yves Goussault emphasized that activism 'is not politically indifferent, but firmly socialist, because of its effect on systems and behaviour.'

Activism will thus lead the peasants to collaborate fully in the drawing up of a plan which is not simply technical. Although it is conceived by the group in the capital, it should be quickly decentralized and regionalized – Senegal and Dahomey have made an effort in this direction – and explained, so that the peasants can judge it and weigh its consequences. They will then be in a position to explain what part they can achieve, and what means of production will be necessary to fulfil the Plan. Thus will begin a constant dialogue between the base and the summit, so necessary to a planned democracy. Let us install first the solid bases of development, credit and co-operative societies, with trade bureaux at the top.

CHAPTER FIFTEEN
Credit, Co-operation and Trade Bureaux: God helps those who help themselves

I. UPS AND DOWNS OF AGRICULTURAL CREDIT

In this field the list of failures is long, particularly when compared to the successes. Coming only from public funds, credit has often been distributed at the same time as grants, sometimes to friends of those in power, who were very apt to think of it as a gift. Loans have not always been granted where there was a possibility of a profit being made. If a man mechanizes his farm prematurely, running it just as inefficiently as before, because no one has explained the new techniques to him or exercised any control over what he does, he is not going to be able to repay a loan.

If a peasant receives everything from the State, he risks nothing personally. Five head of cattle were given as a loan in Guinea to help disseminate livestock, at present too confined around Fouta-Djalon. But the beneficiary was practically invited to take care of them inadequately since he had had no trouble in acquiring them. We have seen how loans encourage idleness among forest zone planters in the southern Ivory Coast and the southern Cameroons. The loans enable them to hire many more unskilled labourers.

When preference was given loans for co-operatives, the reaction was instantaneous. Under the law, up to five (and sometimes ten) times the registered capital, as in Europe, could be lent. Consequently a group of village planters pooled their available capital and made up the required amount to 'form a co-operative'. The credit they thus obtained was not used collectively but divided up on a pro rata basis depending on the amount subscribed. Each man's assets were thus miraculously multiplied by five. When I asked the members the aims of the fictitious co-operative they had established, I found them quite open about it: 'Tell us what we should write down, and we will do it at once.' Provided they got the money, they would have written down anything the white man could dream up as a reason for the loan. In one of these co-operatives, near Dabou, 90 per cent of the credits granted were used either to pay unskilled labourers or simply for day-to-day purchases. Only a tenth of the money was used to purchase equipment and plant-health products, and could be considered as truly productive. I am not even counting the misappropriations ('If they hadn't put me in prison I would have paid them back.')

For a long time agricultural credit was the essential lever of European colonialism, as in North Africa, established to help favour expansion by European settlers. For this reason the colonialists were not always 'looking' for repayment. When policy changed and credit was granted also to native peasants, it was done in a framework of 'political gifts', which I have already called an attempt at corruption. It was thought that one could in this way avoid, or put far off into the future, demands for political evolution.

2. THE COST OF PIECEMEAL MUTUAL CREDIT

Non-payment of loans has practically become the rule – 66 per cent in the Congo – and the confusion between loan and grant is bringing on the ruin of the banks. In these conditions, credit can only be re-established on a healthy footing if groups of borrowers guarantee to repay the loans of each individual in the group. This was the basis of the success of the Raiffeisen banks in the nineteenth century; it allowed German planters to liberate themselves from the corrupt practices of moneylending tavern-keepers. Most African peasants accept the principle of this guarantee clause, but many of them are actively opposed to having it put into practice when a loan falls due. By making the group responsible for the individual, a majority of the members should be free to reject any proposed member who is unreliable, lazy or dishonest. This presupposes a small group of people who know each other well, but not so small that the failure of one will make it too difficult for the others. Fifteen to twenty is usually a good number. Family and clan ties favour a grouping for some reasons, but for others are an obstacle to the eventual application of sanctions.

A second condition of success is the effective use of the loans. Only harvests which can be increased make an investment worthwhile, for the nation as well as the cultivator, and therefore easy to repay. The purchase of a pair of oxen and the complete equipment for draught animal cultivation is a large one. The payments will therefore be large, and to be able to afford them the new owners must use the new source of production fully. This will often require the association of four or five producers, each provided with a donkey, to buy the heavy equipment. The process will not be without its difficulties, as a jointly owned animal is never treated as well.

Credit, in my opinion, should be subject to the decision of the peasant leader, who will have final say on whether or not it is granted. This will reinforce his authority in the village. If the credit were offered independently of technical advice, the peasant would quickly take the credit and forget about the advice. Credits should go only to those peasants who have already achieved a certain amount of progress and made some proof of their 'assets'. It should be tied to an agreement to follow the directives of the leadership, in other words, to employ all the crop disciplines necessary to success (early and dense sowing, in well-prepared soil, carefully cleared, *et al.*)

Penalties for failure to live up to the agreement should be rapid. Instead of the loan being granted in its entirety at the beginning of the season, it should often be given out in instalments so that it can be withheld from those who do not follow the prescriptions. This is most important for large, average-term credits, meant for land improvements. In this way diversion of funds can be checked as well as the quality of work being done.

Up until the present, public financing in Africa, generally deriving from the mother country, was responsible for almost all the development projects. To bring these latter closer to the volume desired, the people themselves have to shoulder a large part of the financing. Credit banks should therefore only finance a part, half at most, of the projected improvements. The peasant and his family should work themselves, or spend their savings, if they are 'large' planters, to furnish the rest.

Lastly, to avoid wastage of these rare funds, and direct them into areas of high productivity, interest on loans should be much higher than in developed countries, as was the rule everywhere before development. The current low rates, which are patterned after the European rates, have contributed to the deficit in the banks. Banks have been unable to pay the costs of administration, which are of necessity high because they are dealing with a large number of very small loans. Low rates have also encouraged borrowers to go into debt thoughtlessly, the more so because the hope that they will not have to repay persists.

The credit co-operative of a market garden suburb south of Peking made loans in the autumn of 1955 at rates varying from 13 per cent for agricultural credits to 16 per cent for consumer credits, which seems reasonable.[1] It attracted rural savings because deposits received 3 per cent interest if they remained in the bank for one to three months, and 8 per cent if they remained over a year. Total deposits were eight times the total amount of loans. The co-operative was more instrumental in channelling peasant savings towards industrialization than in modernizing agriculture with public credits.

This serves as a good lesson: in the beginning of development, it is scarcely possible to give it the necessary push without making rural savings play a part. As far back as the Renaissance, English landowners financed the agricultural revolution of the enclosures by charging very high rents to their farmers. Individual French thrift furnished capital not only to industry but also for foreign investments. If Africans do not have a natural tendency to save, fiscal means must be found to make them do so; unfortunately, demagogy enters this realm also.

Usury is a plague in underdeveloped countries. Although it is not as widespread in tropical Africa as it is in Asia, it still exists. Madagascar is 'Afro-Asian' from this point of view also. Struggling along with public credits alone is not and will never be enough. It has

[1] R. Dumont, *Révolution dans les Campagnes Chinoises*, p. 110. Éditions du Seuil, 1957. Out of print.

been calculated in India that they furnish 6 per cent of the money needs of the peasant. To end this plague, it is preferable to lend more money at a fairly high rate than to distribute a little at a very low rate. Loans at a 'reasonable' rate, like the Chinese loans mentioned above, enable one to offer 6 per cent interest for deposits left over three months, which is an attractive offer. The country would then finally realize, on public funds placed in rural areas, profits that it could reinvest – the key word in development. The over-abundant capital in Europe and North America could be placed there at normal interest rates: Western aid should not be limited to grants.

3. CO-OPERATIVES NOT A MAGIC FORMULA

The Danish co-operative movement developed roughly a century after compulsory primary education, and fifty years after the creation of graduate rural schools by the Lutheran bishop, Grundtrig. They trained real agricultural *élites*, as well as a good many of the co-operative members. Almost all of these leaders were honest, competent, dynamic and dedicated to their compatriots. Although ambition was often allied to these qualities, it was legitimate. On their side, the members were disciplined, and understood that they had to support their co-operative even when it was not to their immediate personal interest: if, for example, business interests sought to ruin it by dumping, they made provisional over-payments.

French agricultural co-operatives, on the other hand, were unable to make notable progress without the financial support of the state. The Danes still reject such support, jealous of their independence, and claim to be on a real competitive footing with business. However, the co-operative dairies at Charentes and Poitou have required, particularly in the beginning when they had much less aid, the dedication of all. One hears of the schoolteachers doing the accounts after school at night for the first co-operatives. It will be more difficult to find such volunteers in the African bush. Our teachers did not belong to the *élite* class, and were more willing to identify with the rural workers.

But the African peasant cannot wait fifty or a hundred years to free himself from the claws of business interests, particularly since the population explosion 'condemns' him to much more rapid development than ours. This justifies the intervention of state aid, at least in the beginning. As a general rule, the state will even become the initiator of the co-operative movement. This may be sheer heresy to the militants in the old European co-operatives, but it is indispensable to cut down on delays and spread out the movement. This is doubly so because the cultural and economic lag between the peasant and the businessman is much more pronounced than in Europe.

Impetus and aid from the top must not, however, dominate everything, and one must guard against the co-operatives becoming tools of the party and instruments of power. It is still a period of 'tutelage', which must prepare for its successor, and its own demise. The Agricultural Services, in some places the Missions, can establish the first groups to sell rice or coffee, 'pre-co-operative' associations. But very soon a good part of the managerial functions should be taken over by delegates from the farmers, who should be quickly trained for this job. The first stage should thus educate while it is actually functioning, teach people how to swim by throwing water on them.

If everything came from the top, like the national organizations in Madagascar or the Agricultural Provident Societies of Africa, it would be easy to predict catastrophes. When too closely supervised control ceases abruptly, without an intermediate stage, many co-operative members go to prison for lying, and their directors are hardly less guilty. One of President Tsiranana's advisers is unwisely mixing trade unionism with co-operatives, and thinks that spreading a lot of government money around is all he needs to do. Public funds are thus largely diverted from their purpose, and hastily chosen directors, often dishonest, are in any case never suited to fill business functions, which are always delicate. The Chinese, the Pakistanis and the large companies rub their hands with glee: competition from co-operatives is ridiculous.[1]

---

[1] The Tananarive Foreign Service defined a similar phrase in my report as in the 'style of the political agitator'. From the viewpoint of these solid bourgeois, who else would take the part of Malagasy peasants?

4. TRAIN CADRES AND ACCUMULATE CAPITAL

Near Obala, to the north of Yaoundé, a co-operative to sell coffee has just been formed: its presidency was given to a schoolteacher. It was an understandable choice, as his education fitted him for calculating prices, verifying the accounts, and for understanding and therefore explaining the laws. But he was totally ignorant of how the pre-co-operative association to which his own succeeded had sold coffee the preceding season, thus of what he could hope to make. He had not the least idea of what tonnage had to be sold in order to pay the expenses of the co-operative, transportation and the salaries of the accountant-secretary and the weigher.

The education of leaders and directors is thus the first step in forming co-operatives. Training centres are springing up in Paris and Africa. The trouble is that trainees from Paris often demand a job in the capital when they come back to Africa, and excessive benefits. It is better to train ordinary leaders locally. Familiarity with our civilization has already given rise to enough illusions and false ideas among the higher echelons.[1] Also, a minimum of the co-operative mentality must penetrate through to the students during these courses. Some of the questions asked at a co-operative training course in Tiebissou makes me doubt that this is occurring. Altruism, patriotism and dedication to the general interest as well as to the peasant community seem to me to be too rare.

This is a great obstacle to socialism, which makes great moral demands, on the minister as well as the lowest civil servant or accountant in the smallest co-operative. African development must be based on a 'simple and honest' morality: work and unselfishness. The social revolution is not in a position to take place, as a young revolutionary student suggested to me; it will require more dedication and sacrifice. If, by misfortune, it finds too little of these, it will be irresistibly drawn along the road to fascism or stalinism, or at least to police terrorism, which has already made an appearance here and there.

[1] Some of them talk of industrial decentralization, although at the beginning of development concentration is necessary. An excess of training periods deprives Africa of its good leaders, each of whom busily tries to wangle a further training-period. Training centres for African peasants in Brittany would be preferable, or apprenticeships with good French artisans.

The members of a co-operative must understand the necessity for very great efforts, if they want to construct their co-operative on a solid foundation. Some of them will simply consider that the money they turn over to a co-operative is a good investment, if it succeeds in obtaining large credits. The amount of this deposit, and it is reasonable to require it to be in cash, will generally be insufficient to cover the needs of modern equipment, except in certain areas of rich plantations, such as coffee, cocoa, bananas *et al.*

The co-operative, however, must be provided with the means of production, to facilitate repayment of loans needed to establish stores and purchase equipment. As for the loans to farmers, it would thus seem reasonable to reserve credits for those co-operatives which have already made a certain effort to procure regular revenues, ensured by the work of the members. (See Chapter Ten, 3.) A co-operative plantation, wherever possible, interests cultivators more than a collective field. If the latter is sown the last in the village, as is too often the case, it yields practically nothing, and it would be better not to have one.

5. DIFFERENT TYPES OF CO-OPERATIVES

What should one start with? Should credit, services, production, sales and purchase all be in common? It is difficult to establish an order of priorities for new co-operatives which is universally useful. The worst stumbling-blocks, and the most profitable and most easily accessible kinds of progress must be attacked first. If a parasite is seriously menacing an essential crop, and requires powerful means of fighting it, out of the reach of the individual peasant, an insect-control co-operative is the most urgent. Other organizations furnishing communal services will be necessary also, on condition that, even in the form of a co-operative, technically and economically premature mechanization is not attempted.

Organizations to loan equipment for animal traction should accompany the increased use of draught animals. It would be too expensive to endow each tiny farm with its complement of equipment. The Low Countries still have such organizations.[1] More

[1] A farm of two or three hectares, hoed by hand, could become seven or eight hectares if it was supplied with two donkeys. An association loaning harnesses and equipment would facilitate the transition.

widespread would be harvesting co-operatives, in some places own-ing mechanical reapers, in others a small mill grinding corn or millet, with a pair of oxen supplying the power.

The co-operative would sometimes, for example in dairy farming, go right up to the point of preparing the product; later it could become a sales co-operative. It will generally be necessary to have the co-operatives linked in some way to the credit associations. It seems at the least imprudent to pay out all the money for his harvest to an indebted peasant at one window, and then tell him to pay his debts some time later at another window. Under the best conditions, for the most honest peasant, this could be real torture, given the temptations the poor man will be subjected to in the interval, each time he passes a well-stocked store. The joint co-operative would hold back the amount of the loan from the price of the harvest, before handing over his net pay, irrevocably his, to the peasant.

In order to compete successfully with business, the co-operative will often have to compete on the former's own grounds, and go into retail sales. This becomes more complicated, because of the number of articles involved, and the difficulty in keeping track of them, because of the long inventories. It would be interesting to study in detail the failure in Guinea in this area, but it in any case advises caution. Those who enter upon it should limit themselves, as at Ambavalo, to the everyday consumer goods that are in great demand, such as petrol, lamps, soap, matches, oil, cotton goods, and everyday household and hardware items, and avoid perishable foodstuffs. Above all, the manager must be honest.

Moneylenders continue to hold the peasant in their grip because of his need of money before the harvest. Credit for consumer goods may be useful to replace usury, although economically it is extremely undesirable[1]; available capital should be reserved for production and investments. A whole new outlook is necessary, which can be instilled in stages. The habit of saving can be acquired young, at the farm-school, by managing the co-operative of cultivation, sales and supplies. Deposits should be substituted for loans as soon as possible, as in China. This will place new credits at the disposal of the

---

[1] Corn, bought for ten francs a kilo at harvest time in Porto Novo, is presently resold for thirty francs four or five months later, and is not preserved at all well.

government instead of demanding more from it. Thus at each harvest-time the peasant can save the amount, partly determined from above, that he will need to get him through the dead season, at which time he can draw out his 'forced' deposit.

Once again, it is far easier to propose this than to persuade a still very deprived peasant class of its virtues.[1] More work and more austerity should have been the chief promises of Independence. Many understood these promises, when they were made, as applying mostly to the other fellow. The peasants must have a formal assurance that they will definitely be paid: this implies a government guarantee, bringing with it control of the management. The last payment should be paid earlier to those who complete all the sowing for the new season on time, as a new form of bonus for early sowing.

6. PRODUCTION CO-OPERATIVES: CRASH PROGRAMMES IN DAHOMEY

Should we advise African leaders to set up production co-operatives like the Soviet *kolkhoz*, the Israeli *kibbutz*, the Chinese commune or the Cuban sugar cane co-operatives, or to create state farms with salaried employees, like the immense *Granjas del pueblo* of the incautious Fidel Castro, or the *sovkhozes*? No, for the choice between these or other structures is not only technical but political, and should depend largely on the will of the people involved, the rural Africans. By their attitude and their vote, they will act in favour of the type of co-operative they prefer, when they have understood the problems.

The cultivation disciplines that are most particularly necessary to the forest zone plantations require very skilful technical, organizational and economic management. I therefore suggested formulas of authoritarian co-operatives for Dahomey, at times similar to the state farm. The principal decisions, which must be made within a highly technical framework, remain in the hands of the technician-directors.

Thus, 130 'blocks of crash crops', varying from two to 300 hectares, to which food crops are added, are grown around exploitation

---

[1] 'All you have to do is this,' 'All you have to do is that', is what Parisians visiting the bush are apt to say.

projects of about 500 hectares, with about 1,000 or 1,500 inhabitants, of whom 200 to 400 are workers. They will be directed by three technical experts, under state management, and workers will receive a salary of 100 francs a day, to assure the fulfilment of the objectives essential to the Plan; there will be a massive concentration of trained leaders. These are potential co-operatives, and can be made so once they make a regular profit and modern techniques have been assimilated. It will take at least five years.[1]

A form of co-operative will also be necessary around irrigation networks to provide for proper maintenance of fields and distribution of water, also to make sure that all the cultivators employ the precise crop rotations and crop disciplines necessary in modern agronomy. It will also insure that the expensive installations work at full capacity. It can be patterned after the *moshav ovdim*, the Israeli village co-operative, and give the peasant autonomy in running his farm, while obliging him to adhere to the crop regulations and integrate with the various co-operatives that maintain the irrigation network, and provide for pest control, harvesting and sales.

The collective fields around each village anticipated in the Dahomey plan will be for the peasants themselves, under the leadership of elected officials, members of the party, and tribal chiefs. These people can seek out technical advice when needed from the few available experts. President Maga of Dahomey had the excellent idea of holding back an obligatory saving, 2,000 francs per worker, from the sales of these crops. If the savings of 500,000 agricultural workers are deposited into the development bank, they would endow it with a billion francs, permitting it to guarantee very high loans from international banks. The village would be allowed to withdraw these obligatory deposits, which belong to it, but only for directly productive investments, which will be the case for all loans granted by the bank.[2]

The entire organization would, of course, work closely with technical leaders as well as with rural activists. Some of the regulations of the technical leadership would have to be obligatory: do not

---

[1] The ownership of the soil remains in the hands of the peasants, and their 'investments', in the form of labour at a lower salary than is normal, will give them part ownership in the plantation.

[2] In principle, anyway. Let's be optimistic about it.

be horrified. This method has had good results in the Gezirah. All civilized societies involve a certain amount of obligation, of red and green lights, which are necessary to progress. We oblige our citizens to pay heavy taxes, our children to be at school, even if they do not want to. Later society imposes work, at least on those without an income or privileges who do not want to put themselves outside the law.

African development must seek short cuts, because a rate of speed comparable to that of the European Renaissance is too slow. Africa must reject the constraint of a liberal economy, which puts all the onus of development on the poor, and adapt other, more imaginative methods. Co-operatives can play a crucial role in agricultural development.[1] Let me repeat again the essential condition of their success: the dedication, honesty and competence of the activists and directors. Next, the discipline, dedication and very hard work of its members, who are building their new country, and also constructing the systems of modern agronomy. The edifice is still incomplete, however, without Trade Bureaux, which I shall discuss now.

7. TRADE BUREAUX OR MARKETING BOARDS?

Generally, a co-operative agrees from the beginning to distribute payment once the fiscal year is over, as in Europe. This is demagogy. In Africa the lack of investments constitutes the principal obstacle to development, and the sums thus saved should be reserved for co-operative equipment for a long time. The cruel variations in prices of raw materials is another factor. Former French Africa has established Stabilization Funds, but the accumulated reserves are useless, as they are blocked in France, and do not serve in the development of the new nations. But the Funds do not prevent the experts from making large profits, by giving them a certain amount of leeway to manœuvre, playing on the rise and fall of prices, at which they are more adept than the peasant.

[1] Some new and better solution, with new legal foundations, must replace both state-oriented collectivism and the European co-operative, too formalist and bound up in red tape. In two specific types of co-operatives, large irrigation networks and plantations of coffee and other bushes, there is room for a great deal of innovation, which is waiting for young, dynamic Africans to do it. (Cf. J. Guillard.)

To compound the problems, preferential prices were granted which still apply in the franc zone, and are generally higher than those of the world market. The French consumer pays about one new franc more for his kilo of coffee for this reason. In the summer of 1961 the peasant in Souanké received eighty-five CFA francs for a kilogram of cocoa, which came to 104 francs delivered to Pointe-Noire. The world price there would have been sixty-six francs. The Congolese budget paid the difference, but because of it had an increased deficit, was unable to make investments, and 'held out its hand' for foreign aid to balance the budget, instead of 'rolling up its sleeves'. A certain standardization of prices can be useful if it does not penalize the favourable zones and support marginal productions.

The Marketing Boards for cocoa in Ghana, oil palm in Nigeria and meat in Kenya go much further than our Stabilization Funds. The first and largest, that for cocoa in Ghana, resulted from the 1937 crisis. Following a serious fall in price, the traders established an agreement of non-competition. Against this monopoly, the producers successfully organized a double strike, both on delivery of coffee and on purchases of imported products. During the war, the British government controlled prices to fight inflation, through the intermediary of an official purchasing office. An autonomous office was formed in 1947, and given the very substantial money reserves of the official purchasing office, which it continued to augment. Each Bureau now has a monopoly on purchases and sales, and bureaux are only established for the principal export items. Each one sets prices, and controls the local industries which produce manufactured goods from the raw material.

It controls the product right up to the wholesale markets in Europe and the United States. In doing this, it takes over the normal function of import-export firms, thereby breaking one of the essential links in the chain of economic exploitation. In contrast, Georges Monnet insisted in 1960 that his CCCA (*Centres de Coordination des Coopératives Agricoles*) limit themselves to delivering standardized lots of coffee or cocoa to the wholesale trade, in regional centres. Thus the ungrateful task of collecting multiple small harvests from very numerous producers was left to the co-operatives, while the easy profit on wholesale tonnage was the 'private reserve' of the large trading firms.[1]

The Chinese shopkeeper on the eastern coast of Madagascar often lives modestly and his profits are usually reasonable, particularly if his measures and prices are carefully controlled, and he is forbidden to lend money. It would be much better to socialize wholesale trade first, as it is much easier to administer. The example of Cobafruit, the co-operative of banana planters in Abidjan, has shown that it is within the reach of organized peasants, particularly when a solid European core exists.

The British Marketing Boards operate in an economic framework that is less demagogic, and more austere than that in the franc zone. They are not afraid to pay less for a product than the world price in order to accumulate large money reserves. These are used first of all for crop research, then for peasant organization and training. In Ghana, the enormous resources thus set aside helped to spur general industrialization, facilitating the first steps of the independent nation. There has even been enough for loans to Guinea and Mali.

On the other side, the Senegalese Agricultural Trade Office (OCA) paid a higher, stabilized price for peanuts. This, together with construction costs, was the basic cause of the deficit during its first fiscal year. Starting with the second season, 1961–1962, it bought more than half of the commercial peanuts, eliminating the large firms and forcing them to convert to industrial activity, an excellent move. However, if the same price is paid for peanuts everywhere, the result is the support of production in areas ill-suited to it, and the maintenance of marginal operations too far from the coast. The primary aim should be to increase yields, particularly in the best-adapted zones, rather than to extend the area under cultivation.

The Marketing Board announces its prices, which remain stable for the entire season, a long time before it begins its purchases, and gives them the widest publicity. In this way the small shopkeeper can still participate in rounding up produce, but his margin of profit

[1] Only the *Union des Coopératives de Café Arabica*, in the Cameroons, takes its product right into Europe.

is defined and remains within reasonable limits. If a similar institution is formed in French-speaking Africa, prices will have to be lowered. However, this can be compensated for to some extent by reorganizing the distribution of products sold to the peasant. A number of items are sold in Souanké for three times the price they fetch in Lomié, 180 kilometres away, from whence they are carried on the backs of peddlers.

A good road will make all the difference: one that doesn't wreck the trucks in less than a year, or leave them out of commission for weeks in front of a washed-away bridge – as has happened on the Souanké–Ouesso road. If traffic were well distributed, the price of a kilometric ton, now from thirty-five to fifty CFA francs in the Congolese basin, could come down well below twenty francs. Pilot stores, analogous to the Cuban *tiendas del pueblo*, or those being set up by Edouard Leclerc in Gabon, can provide if necessary for controls on the more obvious abuses, if honest managers can be found. This is easier to do with a revolutionary army, as in Cuba, or with catechism students. In Guinea, there is a fixed price on all goods throughout the country, without taking transportation costs into account. Naturally, stores far off in the bush are empty, which could have been foreseen.

Corruption and incompetence obstruct the formation of the Boards, which are an essential element in the evolution towards socialism. Perhaps the failures of premature Africanization will encourage Africans to turn over the administration of these Bureaux, under an African president, to the best of the young European experts, chosen for competence and dedication to the African cause. They will quickly train their African assistants to replace them, as soon as it is possible without affecting the success of the organization.

These Bureaux should not be a direct offshoot of the Treasury, but must guard their autonomy even better than the English Marketing Boards have done. If the reserves of these purchasing Bureaux exceed the forecast amount needed to stabilize prices, they should not be swallowed up, like present export taxes, by the Budget, where they will fatten the salaries of the *élites*. They should be earmarked for a national development fund, and reserved entirely for investments.[1] Business and individual taxes should suffice for the budget – the latter tax has the big advantage of forcing the peasant to do at least a minimum of work – along with taxes for licensing, and progressive income taxes, which should be levied on much smaller incomes than in Europe.[2] The monies received by these Bureaux and all other Customs duties should be strictly set aside for the creation of new wealth.[3]

We must now look at ways to speed up still further this development of the African economy, by persuading the peasant to make a greater effort.

---

[1] For a long time the Marketing Boards invested almost all of their reserves on the London Stock Exchange, although they could have been so useful locally. They are now deposited in the central banks of the appropriate African countries.

[2] Otherwise the peasant would be furnishing, through the levies on agricultural products, an excessive share of the taxes, another instance of discrimination against rural areas.

[3] New, well-run cocoa plantations, or new *Elaeis* plantations are worth more than paying the costs of fighting capsids on the most mediocre cocoa plantations, a politically inspired measure (1·2 billion C F A francs in three years) in the Cameroons.

CHAPTER SIXTEEN
Full employment a priority

I. UNEMPLOYMENT IN FOREST REGIONS; SERVITUDE OF WOMEN

It is not that the peasantry as a whole is lazy. This is the erroneous colonialist thesis. There are variations, first of all depending on the region. By and large the farmer in the savannah gives more productive work, 100 to 150 days a year, in a more difficult *milieu*, and does so in order to survive, than the farmer in the forest region, who works sixty to eighty days a year. But his big effort is very seasonal, and is concentrated on the ploughing and sowing in the beginning of the rains, then the weeding and harvesting towards the beginning of the dry season. Unemployment is very pronounced during the dry season, even taking into account construction work and repair of houses. Only the rare irrigated zones provide sufficient work during this period.

'Agricultural' work is itself a misnomer in certain dense forest zones, where even small plantations are few and far between. The care of food crops is left to the women, and the man, who is essentially a hunter and fisherman, cannot even be called a peasant. I note below the total work done by twenty-one 'active' men in twelve days, two weeks without Sundays, in a village near Fort-Rousset in the northern Republic of the Congo (Brazzaville).[1]

[1]Dams for fishing	431 hours
Harvesting palm oil	193
Individual hunting, with a gun	115
Group hunting, with a net	66
Net fishing	47
Construction of houses	73
Gathering wood	16
Gathering palm nuts	5
Total	946 hours

These twenty-two and a half hours per man per week are devoted solely to fishing, hunting and gathering food, activities that greatly resemble our leisure activities.

Still in the Congolese basin, in a village of coffee and cocoa planters near Ewo, the adult man devotes on the average fourteen hours a week to his cash crop, plus one hour for food crops such as manioc and peanuts. Women spend twelve hours at each group of crops, or twenty-four hours of agricultural work a week as against fourteen for the men. However, her household jobs double the work for her; manioc takes a long time to prepare. In Dahomey women have evolved more, and detached themselves from agricultural work except for harvesting. Women's time there is devoted mainly to transporting goods, preparing cooked dishes for sale, and engaging in all kinds of trading activities. In the Bamiléké tribe in the Cameroons it is the men who engage in trade.

Most African peasant women are fully employed, and many are clearly overworked. The men, on the other hand, are usually unemployed, at least part of the year in the savannah and most of the time in the forest zone, except for immigrant salaried workers. Agricultural vocational training, which is non-existent or very inadequate, is given only to the men. It should also be oriented towards women, who accomplish the majority of the actual tasks. Their education will provoke the hostility of their husbands, who fear their emancipation. Some Senegalese women have had to give up their work in centres of feminist rural activism because of their husbands' objections. The latter call themselves évolués, but want to keep a monopoly on the salaries and privileges of this evolution for their own sex.

The African woman is under a triple bondage: her forced choice of a husband; her dowry and polygamy, which increase the leisure time of the men, as well as their prestige; and the very unequal division of labour.[1] An African peasant revolt could begin with the women. The Chinese peasant woman was often glad of the revolu-

---

[1] Sorghum mills operated with animal energy and manually operated 'flour' processors are used in Brazil's *Nordeste*. These would reduce the servitude of women, which is made still more difficult by their tradition of spoiling the children, who are veritable tyrants. (J. Guillard.)

tion, which was to her a liberator, until 1957–1958, the year of the 'great leap forward' and the communes. These last overturned all her traditions and demanded too much work of her.

When enough schoolgirls remain in the village, the emancipation of peasant women will be practically at hand. In 1961, in the north half of the Congo (Brazzaville), three out of four boys had received schooling, but only one out of four girls. A rapid increase in this proportion will further the feminine 'liberation'; perhaps girls returning from study in Europe will take it in hand. The Souanké Women's Association is already adopting a resolutely feminist attitude. It is saving up dues to buy a truck, with which to start a business, so that the women can free themselves economically.

2. POTENTIAL UNEMPLOYMENT IN THE SAVANNAH

Many other examples of African unemployment could be cited. In Madomale and Pouyamba, two villages in central Ubangi-Shari near Grimari, the proportion of work done by men is 67 and 72, respectively, as against 100 units done by women. At Pouyamba the time spent in agricultural work is about the same for the two sexes, but the men use machetes, while the women hoe, which is often harder. Further, the bulk of the non-agricultural work, here worse because of manioc preparation (steeping, drying, transporting), falls much more on the women. They are eternal drudges, starting well before dawn. No village in the savannah ever needs an alarm clock, because of them. In Madomale the men devote 11 per cent of their time to agricultural work. The women spend 17 per cent of their time in the fields, or one and a half times as much, not counting household work.

On the over-populated hills near Rubona, in Ruanda, where a certain amount of intensive cultivation is necessary, the Belgians estimate that average working time, on days when there is work to do, is four hours and twenty minutes. The peasants leave for the fields without eating, which seems an adequate explanation for their rapid fatigue. Modification of eating habits is often a preliminary to increased exertions. Peanut and fish meals, to begin with, and fruits rich in energy-producing Vitamin C, like guava, can provide a protein supplement that will be the most effective lever to increase labour productivity.

Lastly, rational organization of current work habits can rapidly augment the amount of time available. A plastic hose, or a tank placed on a wagon, either pulled by hand or harnessed to animals, can eliminate or cut down the time spent on carrying water. If there is a protected forest fallow area around each small village, and another wagon, time spent gathering wood would be reduced by three-fourths at least. Using a donkey for watering will diminish the time spent on gardening, as it will aid in the transportation of fruits, vegetables and other harvests.[1] This will benefit the women in particular, who have traditionally done all the carrying. Already corn mills have replaced pounding by hand in South Dahomey. Potential unemployment is therefore much higher than surveys have indicated. These very basic improvements will result in an even larger labour force being available for development projects, to accelerate still further the rate of production.

Western Europe was developed largely on the basis of a peasant class that often spent as much as 3,000 hours on agricultural work annually. Africa cannot really get its economy off the ground with a thousand agricultural hours a year per male. This may maintain current production levels, with highly deficient nutrition, particularly in zones of tubers and bananas; but it cannot provide the labour for any noticeable progress. Other sources of capital will always remain inadequate: foreign aid, in the current political context, too often has political strings attached. A large part of the various budgets are wasted, as the proportion allotted for productive branches is much less than that for Internal Affairs and the Army.[2] Fiscal efforts have been mediocre.

3. INDIVIDUAL 'LABOUR' INVESTMENTS: CLEARING, PLANTING, MORE
   CULTIVATION

When a crop brings a good profit without involving too much work –

[1] Reduction or elimination of fallow periods is exhausting the vitamin content in fruits and vegetables and makes garden-orchards even more urgent in over-populated areas.
[2] The figure of 1·2 billion has been mentioned for the Congolese army, which could one day intervene in the other, ex-Belgian, Congo.

this is the case with well-established cocoa plantations in the Ivory Coast and the Cameroons – peasants are quick to plant it. I have just seen this happen again in Souanké, where production was increased a hundredfold in the space of eight years: from seven to 700 tons between 1952 and 1960. But care of the plants is completely inadequate, and the harvests show it. Hard work on new plantations should be encouraged by credits, when the crop is suitable to the terrain, is well maintained, and is 'desirable' from the point of view of the Plan. This applies to the oil palm and coconut palm, in the Ivory Coast and the Congo (Brazzaville) but not to coffee.

The labour 'investment' made by the peasant will be valuable only if credit does not cover all the labour costs, as in the Ivory Coast. In the case of planting, an incontestable creation of wealth, rates of interest, which are in general high, should be lowered (never below 6 per cent) for those that follow all the technical prescriptions and maintain their fields well. This will penalize the others, whose interest rate would remain at 12 per cent. Profits made by these planters would still be satisfactory, provided smaller oil palm processing plants were established, handling 200 tons of oil a year. By reducing the average distance from the plantations to the factory, the cost of transport, which is the largest expense, would be significantly curtailed.

It is necessary to clear and remove tree stumps if one plans to utilize oxen, wagons and ox-drawn ploughs. This takes several hundred days of work per hectare in the cotton zone in south Chad. It should be encouraged, always provided that disciplines are respected and effective measures to prevent erosion are taken. Granting of credits, representing at most a quarter of the expenses, should be dependent on the construction of combination stable-manure sheds, and building up reserves of feed for the animals. The Chinese agrarian civilization, much superior to the Indian, has used organic fertilizer, which is the principal basis of intensification there, and brings economical mechanization closer.

From the Congo basin to south Dahomey, a number of investigators have come to the conclusion that salaries are the surest way to make African peasants work regularly, particularly the men. The potential interest of the 'crash cultivation programmes' in Dahomey appears therefore to be very high. The 'fishermen-hunters' of the north Congo despise agricultural work, particularly as they consider it essentially a woman's job, unworthy of truly virile men. They must be given the lure of an immediate salary, preferable in their view to payments on a future crop harvest. Foremen on land improvement projects can also seek to re-establish an equal division of labour between the sexes.

4. COLLECTIVE LABOUR INVESTMENTS – WITH DRAUGHT ANIMALS

Any agricultural system being modernized can provide enough useful projects to attain full rural employment immediately. One cannot avoid the structural reforms necessary for development, however, by sheltering behind an archaic artisanry like the Indian *Khadi*, weaving by hand and spinning. Work of moderate productivity is worth more than disguised unemployment, non-work, or the contemplative attitude. In any case, there is so much that needs doing that a provisional order of priorities should be rapidly established, and modified as needed, for the different types of small agricultural zones, and then applied to each village by the available local technicians.

Peasant enthusiasm for labour investments has been very restrained in Africa. It would be far easier to instil if the labour gave immediate results, and if peasant productivity rose through the use of the most modern available techniques.[1]

Clearing the land of stones, cited in G. Ardant's *Le Monde en Friche*, should have come before the small irrigation projects in southern Morocco. It would also have been more intelligent to put the stones along contour lines, instead of in piles. Lastly, each larger

---

[1] A small irrigation project can be educational; if local political leaders have participated in the manual labour, if only for half a day, their little speech on civics the same evening will be better received. King Sihanouk, now President of the Council, is perfectly willing to drag civil servants and workers from the towns of Cambodia out to the fields and show them how. 5,000 hectares of rice fields have been developed in this way. Works foremen need no longer fear they will 'waste time' explaining how to set up small dams, ditches, drains, contour lines, embankments and so on. The peasants they are teaching, in this accelerated 'practical course', can undertake smaller, similar projects when they return home.

project in the savannah zone should have a training centre for oxen and donkeys. Each peasant who owns animals will arrive with his oxen or donkeys, which are half savage, and learn how to harness and lead them when he returns to his fields. He will thus own a pair of well-trained and extremely useful animals. The idea of human labour as an investment thus ceases to be reminiscent of the forced labour during the colonial era. Here it is allied with draught animals and rendered physically less onerous. Any appeal to 'construct the country' will be better understood if everyone participates in a democratic atmosphere, including the urban rich and the political leaders.

The success of these projects will, of course, depend on the leaders who organize them: political militants and real rural activists are needed to whip up enthusiasm for the work. Experts would be responsible for the economical and correct utilization of the projects. The current dearth of such experts justifies the European Community's attitude: it stipulates that the projects it subsidizes be fulfilled by business enterprises. But this means that the companies, which are European, make a huge profit. The Community recently ruled against state-run projects, which could accomplish much more, more cheaply, with part of the work unpaid or almost free (food is provided). A last bastion of liberal capitalism, the Community rejected with horror any trace of socialism. Unfortunately, it is too often correct when it maintains that current administrations are not in a position to undertake projects efficiently.

The technical services will have to come up with some new ideas in order to utilize this new source of manpower as effectively as possible. It is more difficult to manage than salaried workers. It is essential if the rate of reforestation in Madagascar and tropical Africa is to surpass that allowed by skimpy budgetary resources. President Tsiranana was right to include retimbering projects in his 'grand programme of small projects'. The foresters, responsible for these works, will have to organize their unpaid teams of workers to get good and efficient results from them. 'Human investments' will require spending money on organization, but they can be well worth it.

These projects will be well received if delegates from the peasants
8*

participate in planning them and understand the need for them.[1] It will also help if everyone profits from the projects, and they do not simply swell the purses of a few, whether tribal chiefs and elders, political leaders or new leaders of the party. When land is developed and improved on an individual basis, the participants should have the guaranteed right to use a part of the worked land afterwards, proportionate to the amount of labour they donated.

5. FIFTY DAYS OF LABOUR INVESTMENTS ANNUALLY CAN DO THE TRICK

The European peasants themselves maintained the communal paths leading to their fields, bringing the necessary stones and sand, and using their own horses and carts.[2] Replacement of this 'fatigue' with local taxes has only recently come about in the West. It occurred at a stage of development far more advanced than that of Africa, which has at times monetarized these taxes prematurely. Money is not yet readily available in poor zones. Annual per capita income in the Congo basin was estimated at 700 CFA francs in 1961, 400 francs at Abala.

Available 'unused' labour is very plentiful there; men do not work more than fifteen to twenty-two hours a week, very little of which is spent on agriculture. Roads are very badly maintained by labourers paid by the day, who do not accomplish much. These road-menders might be paid per job, applying the socialist maxim: 'to each according to his work', whereby no one receives any income without working for it – no matter how highly placed he may be. I would prefer to see budgetary resources reserved for the industrial development of the country, and have these works done as a communal task.

Where enough money is available, as in the southern Ivory Coast and the southern Cameroons, a local tax would make large investments possible. The old area tax, spent locally on projects visible to

---

[1] In the Moroccan Rif, summer of 1960, the peasants made anti-erosion ditches on their plots of land, planting vines and fruit trees there for their own use. However, the yield was deplorable because they wanted to receive the pitiful subsidy allotted them for a longer time. Furthermore, planting was very badly done as nothing was explained to them.

[2] I have done it myself in the Ardennes.

all, was not unpopular. The repeal of the poll tax and the area tax on New Year's day of 1960 seems a purely demagogic measure. The extension of the measure in 1961 to the Republic of the Congo (Brazzaville), which exports virtually nothing and has very few resources apart from foreign aid and local French expenditures, is all the less justifiable in that it encourages people to cut down on agricultural efforts.

China demands superhuman efforts of its peasants, India only a land tax, often too low. A reasonable solution somewhere between these two extremes can be found. The real take-off of African agrarian economy requires fifty to sixty days of unpaid labour investments per adult per year, above and beyond the time spent on current agricultural production. No nation has even approached these figures. Guinea is far behind its Plan for seven days a year per adult, and perhaps half of what was done was devoted to clearing and maintenance and not to new projects.

In the Inca Empire, during the last pre-Columbian phase of Peru, 'the statute labour system held such an important place in economic life that even at the height of the Empire, "the tributes", in other words, the taxes, were all human, so that no Indian was forced to dip into his possessions. The idea of providing free labour was so deeply rooted in the Indian mentality that the Spaniards remarked with surprise that the natives, during the colonial period, still preferred to submit to forced labour, even for fifteen days, than to hand over a bushel of potatoes to the authorities.'[1]

6. A RURAL CIVILIAN SERVICE WOULD BE TOO EXPENSIVE

Faced with the lack of labour, the new governments are thinking of 'mobilizing' their youth into a civilian service, somewhat patterned after French military service. It would combine patriotic training with the achievement of public works. If it is fashioned in the likeness of the French military apparatus, the most wasteful in the world, far too much money will be spent. A young 'soldier', fed, lodged and clothed by the commissariat always furnishes, in the form of labour,

[1] Alfred Métraux, *The Incas*. Studio Vista, London, 1965.

less than the cost of his maintenance.[1] Such a civilian service would over-burden budgets, cut down the possibilities of investments even more, and lead to militarization and politicization of the service.

A voluntary work camp was set up for high school and college students in the south of India when I was there in January 1959. Their maintenance cost three rupees a day, three times the salary of agricultural workers. This is reasonable considering their background and standard of living. But because of their lack of experience, they only achieved half as much as these same manual labourers in terracing the land. The cubic metre thus cost six times as much as it did when terraced by local salaried labour. Furthermore, this very expensive 'free' labour increased local unemployment and brought on a revolt of the rural workers, deprived still further of work.

An African civil service, in the current framework of administrative chaos, would be even more expensive. On the other hand, cheap labour is available in the village framework, where costs of clothing, lodging and transportation can be eliminated. All the peasants, including the eventually 'mobilized' ones, are available at the important times, for sowing, weeding and harvesting. The rural activists can constitute the majority of the leaders, which means that much less in salaries for 'junior officers'. If the volunteers supply their own food, it would be helpful if a protein complement were added to it, consisting of peanut meal, vitamins and mineral salts.

Let us not deceive ourselves. Guinea and Mali, who had put great hopes in labour investments, no longer feel they can obtain results comparable to China's. Their recent rapprochement with France results in part from the fact that foreign aid given by France and the European Fund does not demand as much from African governments as do the Eastern countries, which furnish mostly equipment

[1] The army itself, nowadays totally inefficient, not adapted to the modern world, constitutes from the very fact of its inadaptability, a grave menace to African development, because of the fascist spirit that is coming to animate it more and more; this is yet another of the legacies of colonialism. There is a good possibility that it will soon be at the exclusive service of the ruling classes, into which its high salaries put it, and of the directors, who often seek to keep power for themselves without worrying too much about development, universal peasant education, raising standards of living. As the Malagasy Parliament had not voted the necessary sums for the Army and Foreign Service, a national subscription was opened to cover their expenses (for one year). Many peasants were 'voluntary' subscribers, although the local administrations officially collected.

on credit. The fifty to sixty days of necessary supplementary labour can only be obtained quickly if a certain amount of statute labour is instituted. We have seen the successes with reduced salaries in the crash cultivation programmes in Dahomey. The general lowering of pay made it possible to distribute a greater number of paid work-days. International aid is also orienting itself towards distributing agricultural surpluses of the rich countries. This means that they can allocate food, not for purposes of pure charity, but as a means of putting more people to work, and thereby speeding up development.[1]

Through the rural school and the peasant cadre, sustained by an effective activist movement, Africa is seeking to build a new men-tality, which will enable it to speed up the task of carrying out cultivation disciplines. The subsequent increase in production this will produce would only profit business interests – and quickly discourage the peasant – if a network of co-operative-regulatory agencies does not quickly crack down on abuses. This will have to wait until efficient Bureaux and Marketing Boards encourage the spread of such agencies.

A better controlled credit system should have as its first objective full rural employment and the creation of new wealth. 'Labour investments' can achieve this full employment quickly, if the prob-lems are fully understood. High efficiency, along with less arduous working conditions made possible with draught animals, will en-courage the African peasant. Unfortunately, one cannot build great hopes on labour investments at present, as long as the current political atmosphere remains. In too many cases it is oriented towards economic stagnation. The magnificent dream of African socialism may quickly evaporate unless the young people throw off the colonial ways leading them to 'South-Americanization'.

[1] Read 'Alimentary produce in the service of development, a system of utilizing surpluses.' F A O 1961.

PART 4
Africa as client of Europe – or developed for itself?

CHAPTER SEVENTEEN
Two pitfalls: South-Americanization and a rash type of Socialism

1. CARICATURES OF DEMOCRACY

The FAO study of tropical Africa mentioned above emphasizes the gravity of the situation, which 'presents to an extreme degree all the characteristics of underdevelopment. The handicap to be surmounted is so enormous, in every area, in relation to other under-developed regions, that its nature even becomes different. . . . The rigidity of social organization and the strength of traditions present an obstacle . . . misery tends to be self-perpetuating.' It is no longer the moment to persevere in mistakes, in the name of whatever dogmatism. The time has come to look facts and men in the face, to see what can be done with them.

The Brazilian President Kubitschek started the palaces of Brasilia fifteen or twenty years too soon. It was much more pressing to develop and intensify agriculture in regions already provided with roads and railroads, and to provide the *caboclos* with tools. Even in the areas bordering the Rio–Sao Paulo highway they still work with the African hoe, the *enxada*. He should also have worried more about feeding the starving people in the arid *sertão* better, and built more factories, from Rio to Recife and throughout the *Nordeste*. The wealthy in Brazil act much like white colonials, spending their holidays in Europe. Africa is also endangered by this type of neo-colonial vassalization.

President Houphouet-Boigny dresses the ushers – I almost said valets – of his air-conditioned palace in the 'French' style, turning his back resolutely on African civilization. Even in climate and dress he prefers to emulate Europe. Breweries and coco-cola or private car factories are springing up in Abidjan, while the Senoufo people around Korhogo cannot get enough to eat from the exhausted land, despite a great deal of hard work. The planter from the rich south, after working his Mossi labourers, drives up to have a spree in the capital. Its shanty-towns, from Treichville to the Plateau, are already similar to the Rio slums. Certainly, dynasties of great landowners do not exist yet, and any revolt would not be 'peons against haciendas' because fortunes are more of a commercial origin, and thus often from foreign sources. Already speculation on land, as in the suburbs of São Paulo, procure enormous incomes without work. The fortunes derived from politics are native, and also more recent.

The role of Parliamentary deputies throughout young Africa seems to be very often derisory, and often nefarious. What use are election campaigns, generally accompanied with demagogic promises, if there is only one candidate, or only one who has any chance in a one-party régime?[1] Why pay such high salaries for men who will approve in an hour the budget for the year? When the deputies modified the Senegal Plan in a demagogic direction, the government simply did not print it. It continues to apply the original, and better, text.

Parliamentary democracy does not really function in a reasonably satisfactory fashion, except in Nordic and Protestant countries, or very small countries where the possibility of direct participation of all the citizens exists. Elsewhere a presidential régime seems more indicated: Brazil at present, lost since the departure of Janio Quadros, confirms it. 'European' democracy should not be envisaged until years after universal elementary education is in force, and a minimum of economic development achieved. When for all practical purposes there is only one Party, could one not think up better methods of designating representatives of a region than certain Congolese libations of red wine? One would avoid the losses of time and money for election campaigns, which caricature democracy.[2]

[1] A deputy in Northern Cameroon attempted to force, by persuasion and penalties, his constituents to clothe themselves; he has a textile business.

[2] In a Bamiléké section of the Cameroons, where terrorism made an election impossible, the government candidate miraculously received 90,000 votes. In a corner of North Cameroons, where 500 Moslem Fulanis exploit 120,000 Kirdish peons – some of them are taken to Mecca as slaves – the three deputies are Moslem, as well as the fifty deputies of North Cameroons: The chief or *lamido*, it is true, does the voting for everyone. (Letter from a missionary.)

The delegates could be chosen for each session, two or three months of the year, and only receive their (small) salary during that period. If the position carried less privileges, and did not free the holder from productive work, it would be less sought after by status seekers. The lack of imagination of European advisers has led new States to copy the French Constitution, truly a poisoned gift. No economic representation is provided for the peasants, although this would have facilitated the drawing up, as well as the carrying out, of the plans, and introduced democracy and political apprenticeship in the villages.

If salaries of civil servants were dissociated from those of members of parliaments, they could more easily be brought down to reasonable levels, comparable to those in Brazil, Greece, Syria or the Soviet Union, where the living standards are much higher.

The one-party system helps avoid the spectacle of parties out-doing each other with extravagant campaign promises; but this can occur anyway. And the system tends towards the abuse of power by the ruling group, if there is no minimum opposition to make its protests heard. To be truly acceptable and effective, the party must have a real popular base, organize the peasants, and help them to stand up for themselves; their complaints must be heard by the government. The system should facilitate the 'dialogue' between the base and the summit, in both directions: first, to transmit to the peasants the provisions of the plan and necessary crop and economic disciplines; and also to find out what the peasants think of it, what they need to carry it out, and what organizations are best able to put all of them to work.

Evolution along South American lines is already dividing, much too clearly, the rich towns from the poor countrysides. Luxury goods, cars and Ministers' villas are purchased before basic equipment; a privileged class is being created which thinks first of profiting from its power. The situation varies from country to country, of course.

The atmosphere in Dakar, and even more in Bamako, can already be distinguished from that in Tananarive, Yaoundé and particularly in Brazzaville. But if this continues, Africa may find itself in an even more difficult situation than South America, because the population explosion is already at work, and the level of economic development is much lower.

Although the political situation reminds one at times of Renaissance Europe, the aspirations are definitely of the twentieth century. Only rapid development can fulfil them, particularly if the already flagrant social injustices are not to be aggravated still further. The greatest obstacle to progress remains the lack of elementary morality – work, honesty, and dedication to the country – of a good percentage of political leaders, even more than the lack of revolutionary drive. A camp closer to socialism exists in Ghana, Mali and Guinea. Let us look at the first results of it.

2. MALI'S PROBLEMS

Development in Mali has been undertaken with a certain prudence, without the passionate impulsiveness characteristic of decisions in Guinea. Nevertheless, it is drawing up a Plan which, given the anticipated rate of growth, is too ambitious, and cannot possibly be fulfilled. There can be no doubt that it is a political document, a declaration of intentions, because the government has neither the finances, the equipment, the organization, nor the personnel to carry it out. They have allotted a budget for equipment more or less equal to that for administration, which other countries in Africa are not doing, but the percentage for administrative 'equipment' is much too high. The part to be played by labour investments and stronger fiscal laws as envisaged in the plan is great, but nothing as of May 1962 leads me to think that they will come near to achieving it. The incidents at Bandiagara in March of 1961 indicate that the population is at times unwilling to make a great effort, when it does not understand the purpose.

When political leaders, and particularly civil servants, address the Mali peasants, they give them orders, in much the same way as the colonial administrators used to. They do not understand rural problems and therefore cannot help the peasants effectively. Also, there has been no fundamental change in the peasants' attitude. Their interest in innovations and technical improvements has not been sufficiently stimulated. Several manure-sheds have been established, but only some of them are being used. Credits to purchase equipment for farming with draught animals are seldom utilized.

However spectacular they may seem, the results of the CFDT in cotton (see Appendix III) have cost too much. This is to be expected at first, but rural and political activism must quickly disseminate the results throughout the country and make agricultural popularization efficient and economic at last. One must seek also to bring the administration closer to the producers: the bureaucracy in Bamako is too removed from reality, from daily life in the bush. Decentralization in this sense can mean the crystallization of traditional positions, but it is still necessary because credits granted on the national level are too often whittled down at different administrative levels along the way.

The battle between partisans of Franco-European aid and of Eastern aid sometimes leads each side to conduct a kind of scare policy. The former seek to show that one cannot get by without Western aid, and the path they favour is certainly, at the present time, the easier to follow.[1] The latter seek to increase the exchange deficit, and bring on a crisis with the franc zone. The two sides join in refusing to utilize the Dakar-Niger, out of a self-destructive sense of pride. The loss to their country is close to the total amount of investments.

It is true that government ministers in Mali have worked a little with their hands, but this is very rare now. Some of them require Frenchmen, their friends from the time of the anti-colonialist fight – when they called each other by the familiar *tu* – to address them as 'Your Excellency' now. This kind of thing is a great pity, particularly since the Mali peasants, perhaps the best in West Africa along with some Ghanians and the Bamilékés in the Cameroons, seem to lend themselves better than most to a massive agricultural modernization programme. The French technicians are leaving the country at an accelerated pace, especially from the Niger Office, and they will doubtless be replaced by Eastern bloc experts. In geological research or industry the substitution offers scarcely no difficulties except linguistic ones. But in agriculture the knowledge acquired

[1] France was asked for credits to build factories to house equipment supplied by the Eastern bloc: she refused.

over the years by French agronomists represents a fund of acquired experience which is irreplaceable for the time being.

Obviously, Chinese experts will arrive also, but after how long, at the price of what errors and how much deceleration in development? It would be too bad to see a truly neutralist country like Mali, with its undeniable good qualities of hard work and organization,[1] spoil its chances of getting off the ground rapidly, and of demonstrating the possibilities of socialism in Africa. This is especially true because its leaders have a good grasp of the economic problems, and the somewhat totalitarian atmosphere of Guinea does not exist here. The future is more hopeful because the peasants are 'responding' in certain areas of development; in one year they built one hundred and fifty schools although this does not always lead to agricultural development.

3. THE GUINEAN VENTURE

I have described elsewhere[2] the atmosphere of euphoria – completely unjustified by the facts – that prevailed in Guinea in the summer of 1959. Not long after, early in 1961, Jacques Charrière, in the conclusions of a study that appeared in the *Cahiers Internationaux*,[3] sounded the alarm.

He pointed out a basic lack of balance in six fundamental areas. First, the gulf between foreign aid and national capital resources: the latter were to supply only eight billion C F A francs out of total anticipated expenditures of fifty billion for the three-year plan. This 18 per cent he compared to the 88 per cent and 96 per cent respectively represented by national capital resources in the first Indian and Chinese plans. Investments (accumulation, in Marxist terms), were to supply only 4 per cent of national revenue, against 8 per cent in India and 22 per cent in China at the beginning of the Plans. The

---

[1] André Blanchet writes in *Le Monde*, January 13th, 1962, that 'The Malian organization, which, greatly impressed M. Houphouet-Boigny and his Ivory Coast companions during their recent visit, is in any case irreconcilable with the Senegalese vagaries, which it professed for a while to control under the aegis of a joint federation, and also with the pragmatism of the forest peoples, in the Ivory Coast, Nigeria and Gabon, for whom food, clothing and shelter from the weather come first.'

[2] *Lands Alive*, Chapter XII.

[3] No. 118, February, 1961. See also the article by Charles Bettelheim in the preceding issue.

three billion in labour investments in three years would only have represented, if it had been achieved, seven days per adult per year, as against more than sixty in China.[1]

Investments capable of increasing exports are very inadequate, given the deficit in the trade balance, a legacy of colonialism, and the 2·5 to 2·7 billion per year of payments on foreign loans. 'The total national accumulation of capital in 1963 will scarcely reach this level, which signifies both the impossibility of honouring foreign commitments and the obligation, starting in 1963, to cut down the rate of new investments.'

The more serious imbalances, as I see it, are in the last two areas (I summarize): 'The disparity between the vastness of anticipated efforts, creations of enterprises, co-operatives and services, and the actual lack of technical and political training of personnel . . . Between the extreme national tension that the vast three-year plan presupposes, and the delays in initiating the fight against illiteracy and mobilizing the masses for the plan . . . These disparities all stem from an underestimation of the real amplitude of the efforts required to achieve such an ambitious plan . . . Definite delays have occurred in decisive areas: co-operatives, a coherent system of price and salary stabilization, industries . . . The disparity between the institutional superstructure and the degree of political morality will swallow up all the others.'

Guineans could say these warnings came too late, because just before the publication of the above article the Guinean agency for Internal Trade had to be dissolved 'as a result of the imperfect workings of the organization'. I can personally testify that previous warnings, oral and written if not published, were not lacking. However, its various European advisers pushed Guinea too far in the direction of nationalization of foreign and wholesale trade, and of creating a national currency independent of the franc.[2] They would have been wiser to overestimate rather than underestimate all the problems they would encounter in applying these measures, and adapt them to actual possibilities rather than set them in a theoretical framework.

[1] In 1958 and 1959 the figure was close to 100.
[2] The measures are described in detail in the above cited article in *Cahiers Internationaux*.

Since then, most of the national Guinean companies have failed, and the country has also admitted its political failure in another way, by pursuing Marxist intellectuals and students, even by seeking a rapprochement with France. The decision to summarily remove all the French technicians and administrators in October, 1958, certainly did not help the 'experiment in socialism'. However, Guineans have not been willing to bend themselves to the efforts and disciplines necessary to carry out the measures they adopted, even when they were advised by Communist countries, some of whose nationals have left Guinea quite discouraged.

The failure of socialism in Guinea could be fruitful for Africa if serious and profound analyses of its many causes were undertaken now. Precious lessons for the future of socialism in Africa could be learned, by outlining the pitfalls to avoid, and pointing out the most important conditions for success. In the absence of such studies,[1] let us try to lay down several general principles.

4. SOCIALISM AND DEMOCRACY MORE EXACTING THAN FASCISM AND CAPITALISM

It was mainly the lack of morality that caused the failure of the two attempts at socialism in Mexico, in 1919–1921 at the end of the civil war, then from 1935–1940 under Lazaro Cardenas. By nationalizing the petroleum industry and then placing it in the hands of an administration as corrupt as Pemex, they were only able to maintain previous production levels, while neighbouring countries raised theirs more and more quickly.

The problems of Guinea have resulted from a dearth of competent and honest local leaders. To some extent, a lack of knowledge can be compensated for by complete honesty, and vice versa: but a

---

[1] The reporting of P. Decraene in *Le Monde*, December 28th and ff., gives interesting aspects of this economy 'adrift', but could not yet analyse all the causes. Let me extract this passage: 'The proof is in any case made that the different State Companies charged with importing foreign products have failed one after the other: Alimag, which specialized in general foods; Libraport, in books and paper; Ematec, in technical equipment; Pharmaguinée, in pharmaceutical products, and all the "sister" companies have had or are having scandals, frequently denounced by Monsieur Sékou Touré himself. Corruption and intrigue make a good working pair in these companies. This no doubt explains why rice – a basic food for the native population – has been lacking for six weeks.'

country cannot do without both. When the whole financial power of a country backs a nationalized enterprise (e.g., CGOT in Casamance, Chapter Four, 1), management errors can lead to enormous losses. In spite of all its faults, capitalism does penalize failure. No doubt, pure profit seeking does not rate investments according to social and national utility, and does not accord priority to the most urgent needs of all the people; it can nevertheless stop errors of orientation in time. The worker on a capitalist plantation who does not perform is fired, while the lazy civil servant is retained (in Africa, not in China).

Gunnar Myrdal reminded the Indian Parliament in 1958 that Europe evolved its diverse forms of democracy only after it had achieved a high degree of economic development. He felt that India's attempt to install an analogous type of democracy before some economic headway had been made was extremely hazardous. In my opinion, India has established only a very poor caricature of democracy. The African continent runs the risk of doing the same.

Many Africans revel in the sound of these two words, socialism and democracy, which seem to denote a high level of development in the economic and political domain. A government will profess itself democratic even when no freedom of expression whatever is allowed to the smallest opposition, even if it is constructive. Another government calls itself socialist while protecting the interests of private business.

Africa would have a far greater chance of developing if it were able to assess more accurately its present stage of evolution, and choose the political and economic institutions most suitable to it. It will make a grave error if it copies present-day Europe, in just the areas where it is rarely exemplary and is in fact re-examining its premises carefully. Western socialism is regressing, from the English Labour Party to the German Social-Democrats,[1] because it is firmly woven into the constricting framework of the semi-privileged nations, and does not think on an international scale. It cannot renew its dynamism and unleash the enthusiasm of the young unless it seeks international social justice more forcefully and sincerely.

[1] Without even mentioning the 'betrayed socialism' of Guy Mollet, as André Philip called it. The influence of the SFIO does not seem beneficial in Madagascar; in Senegal, it is fortunately tempered by the PSU elements.

The true proletarian of today is the tropical peasant, and the child in an underdeveloped country. Why should these be the last to continue to suffer intolerable injustices, as if they had to carry the weight of original sin? Europe discovered Christ, but Asia carries the cross, as a Chinese Catholic pointed out.

The Soviet Union and China were further developed in some areas when they became socialist than Africa is today. Russia had a certain amount of industry already, and the Chinese peasant had reached a level of technical knowledge and agrarian civilization in 1949 very superior to that of the herder in the Sahel or the Bantu cultivator in 1962. The most essential difference, however, is in the way independence was acquired. Colonial Africa became independent often without other fighting than that carried on by Algerian *fellaghas*. Among other reasons, the French army could not have simultaneously carried on other wars in the tropics.

The Chinese Red Army fought during more than twenty-one years, almost a generation, under the most arduous conditions. Its political organization, its administration, and even a good number of its technicians were forged during the struggle. The weak and faint-hearted were quickly eliminated, leaving only a hard core at the head of the country, which was courageous, honest and austere, having withstood the incredible hardships of the Long March.

Supposing that African communists come into power with the support of a large part of the population, in Mali or in Stanleyville. They probably could not attain a rate of development comparable to China's. Certain Guineans who were graduated from our higher educational institutions thought it was possible, with the help of modern equipment, to surpass the Chinese rate of growth, with less work: a dangerous naiveté! This would require tight controls at least equal to those of the depth of the Stalinist era or the 'great leap forward'. Already extremely questionable for China, the latter does not seem advisable for Africa, where the human problems are much more difficult than the natural conditions and resources. Recriminations and regrets are superfluous: it is with men, with all their qualities and failings, that the New Africa must be built.

From now on it belongs to the Africans, for which we must all rejoice: may they watch out for the dangers of political paternalism!

Yet young Africans ask my advice, and sometimes reproach me for purely technical answers, in which I leave the political decisions in their hands. Others remind me that it is their business. I cannot satisfy everyone. An objective that can be realized within the framework of the various political structures would consist in putting the peasants in their rightful place, in repairing the enormous injustices that have been done them by refusing them all education and vocational training and sparingly measuring out for them local leadership and credits. Strong pressure will have to be exerted on the government by an organized peasantry to arrive at the 'night of August 4th' of the new *élite* classes. But the peasants are not organized yet, and recently governments have seemed to keep from the countryside students returning from France, fearing that some of them will organize and lead the more discontented rural elements.

The only recent revolutionary union, in Cuba, was first of all the work of a small band of students. Disembarked eighty strong from the boat *Granma*, they numbered only thirteen after the first battles, but they triumphed because of the help of the poor peasants in the Sierra Maestra, and later that of workers from the large estates. Although large estates scarcely exist in Africa, discontented peasants are already beginning to grumble and to refuse to pay their taxes, a first step in revolt. Sometimes their sons enter school, but the privileged class has just closed the doors of access to itself, and the peasant cannot become a clerk. He wanders in the cities and towns and starts to dream in the shanty-towns lining the capitals, throughout Africa.

5. DO REVOLUTIONARY AFRICAN STUDENTS EXIST?

Revolutionary students are the ones who would provide a large proportion of the organizers in an eventual peasant revolt, and prevent it from simply being an anarchic peasant uprising, or turning into a disastrous Congolization. A great number of those who study in French universities are members of the *Fédération des Étudiants d'Afrique Noire en France*, the F E A N F. It calls itself revolutionary, and places itself firmly in the anti-imperialist and socialist camp. On the basis of this very clear stand on foreign policy, the Federation, at its fourteenth Congress in December, 1961, 'reaffirms that the unity of Africa will come through total and unconditional independence . . . the rupture of all the institutional and organic links with the former colonial powers and the imperialist powers; the denunciation of the so-called agreements of "co-operation", which maintain ties of the colonial type between the states of the Brazzaville group and France . . .'

Guinea, in the first three years of its independence, took a position quite close to the one above. It would be interesting if the F E A N F seriously studied concrete ways to translate this policy into reality, and did some research on why Guinea has been incapable, despite sincere efforts, of eliminating corruption, which seems to me to be the most important step to take before introducing socialism. Ghana is already taking steps in this direction, but not Nigeria.

If the F E A N F really does want to prepare the way for socialism, it should make realistic analyses of the African situation. Only in this way will the students be in a position to play a decisive role soon. Since 1960 their Algerian and Moroccan counterparts have placed primary emphasis on agrarian reform. They have discussed it a great deal, from prisons to union and student associations – I participated in the discussions several times.

At Easter, 1962, the Dahomey Student Association, a member of the F E A N F, asked me to discuss the Plan drawn up for their country. Marcel Mazoyer, a young agronomist back from Cotonou, and I each gave a talk and then answered the various questions asked as best we could. During my lecture, M. Dieng, president of the F E A N F, interrupted to make a long speech, at the end of which he declared, among other things, that 'talking of all this planning is like building castles in the air, it does no good and cannot succeed. it is worthless . . .' I won't dwell on the lack of 'form' involved in requesting a lecture, in the full knowledge of my political orientation, simply to affirm afterwards that it was useless.[1] The really serious aspect of their attitude is the refusal to attack economic problems that are real, concrete and immediate for Africa.

If M. Dieng, whom I liked in spite of his attitude, had shown how

[1] I had come into Paris especially from the country, interrupting work on this book to do so.

the form of government he envisaged would draw up the Plan differently, I would have been extremely interested. Studies on planning are being undertaken now in Africa, and can only be done in the concrete terms of existing socio-political conditions. Research on the changes necessary to adapt them to socialism would be difficult but very useful also, provided always that the necessary preparations for the success of socialism are made. Since the failures so far have been caused mainly by a lack of competence and honesty, this area should be attacked first of all.

Furthermore, we are no longer in mid-nineteenth-century Europe, but in Africa near the end of the twentieth century. A good many of the tenets of socialism are outdated. To 'get along' with the masses, particularly the peasant masses, I advise African students to reread Frantz Fanon,[1] then *Clefs Pour La Chine* by Claude Roy. The latter describes how a young Chinaman, a doctor of law in Paris, was sent by the Party to direct the agrarian reform in a lost corner of central China. He began by living for two months with the poorest peasant in the village, working as the peasant did and eating at his table, sleeping in his one room, beside the refuse pail. . . . If the African students really wanted to prepare for their role as socialist leaders, they would benefit from working for a summer on a French farm, in a German factory, a Cuban *granja*, an Israeli *kibbutz*, a Soviet *kolkhoz*, or better, a Chinese commune. On their return to Africa, they would bring back simple tools to the peasants who remained at home, tools capable of raising productivity and living standards quickly.

Marcel Mazoyer, the son of peasants and artisans and accustomed to manual labour, gave the students an extremely important but little-known idea in his 'useless' lecture. The *coupe-coupe*, or machete, practically the only tool used in the South American and African countrysides for clearing, cutting and sawing trees, has a yield one-fourth less than that of the combination axe-hatchet-saw and billhook. If the African students were really anxious to improve the lot of their peasant countrymen, and if they worked with their hands, they could have made such observations long ago, and proposed a number of similar improvements. Hand-ploughs, harrows,

[1] The F E A N F encourages this also, but it is not evident from the discussions.

hoes, rakes, spades, or, even better, Wolf tools, all have a yield at least one-third greater than the African *daba*.

The students must stop scorning[1] manual labour, and protesting strongly when we propose introducing work into education, as has been done in the Soviet Union. 'Manual labour is nothing but demagogy': let Dieng try to explain that in China. They are already of the privileged class, by virtue of the standard of living which enabled them to receive 'middle-class culture', and they are protecting their privileges. I seek in vain in the resolutions passed by this student congress for a proposal for massive reduction of salaries of high officials, to bring them more into line with those in socialist countries. Since some of them will soon be occupying these high posts, they carefully refrain from such proposals. Yet if I talk to them of officials who exploit the peasants, they accuse me of divisive tactics.

When I chided President Dieng for his 'revolutionary' speechifying, he replied, with justification, that his French education was responsible. But is he making a real effort to rid himself of it? This book was carefully rewritten as a result of many discussions, often vehement, that I had during the academic year of 1961–1962 with African students. Dieng's position during all that time did not budge an inch.

I understood why a little better after rereading a letter from geography students, who were communists, inviting me to speak to them on Cuba in May, 1962. 'As Marxist geographers, we think that the ideas that you express and the solutions you suggest, while they are always interesting and permeated with the greatest honesty, are not always completely correct.'

The difference between us is irreducible, because, as I said before, scientific exactitude and doubt will always prevent me from considering my proposals absolutely 'correct', no matter how much observation, thought and study has gone into their formation. If I arrive at honesty and objectivity, which is very difficult, I am pleased. Even the concept of 'correct positions', in political and economic

[1] The only ones invited to Israel, with all expenses paid for two months, who refused to work for a week in a *kibbutz* were the young Africans. The school at Katibougou founded a production co-operative cultivated by and for the profit of the students, they hired salaried workers to do the labour for them. There are many similar examples.

matters, seems to me a scientific absurdity in the absolute sense. If a student speaks of this concept, it is because his education has not really 'got through' to him. It is also a very dangerous concept, because it justifies the evils and cruelties of Stalinism, evils which held back the establishment of communism and are still doing so through the people who are not completely destalinized (we have them in France).

This concept, along with the socialist betrayals, has constituted the main obstacle to a regrouping of the Left in France, and has also favoured personal power.

I nevertheless share the attitude of the F E A N F when it defends Patrice Lumumba, the African martyr; or students in prison; and when it fights for the re-establishment of freedoms. Their elders used to speak this way, but today, instead of teaching the alphabet to peasant children as in Cuba, they are comfortably installed in the privileged class. It would be greatly to their benefit to reread the recent declarations in China, which has been forced to adopt more modest goals because of economic difficulties. The Chinese are now saying that 'revolutionary zeal does not replace technical ability'. For a very long time they had been proclaiming that one has to be 'both red and expert', as much a good communist as a competent specialist. Lately, however, technical knowledge has been put in first place. One cannot trust European revolutionary jargon, which fared very poorly regarding the Algerian war.[1]

In this fourteenth F E A N F Congress, I also seek in vain a resolution on the problems of underdevelopment, or on the need to study the best methods of conquering it in a socialist framework. I do not find any allusion to the almost superhuman efforts which will be demanded of young African *élites* if they want to 'catch up' economically without support from the 'former colonial power and imperialist powers'. I understand their position very well, but I would hesitate to share it, for one reason. I realize, perhaps better than a number of young African friends, the awesome amount of

[1] In his interesting *Révolution Algérienne* (Feltrinelli, 1962), Fr. Jeanson states on page 130 that the revolution is 'profoundly hostile to all anti-communism . . . and yet does not accept the attitude of French communists towards the Algerian revolutionaries, which betrays their conviction that they can only advance in the direction of socialism if they do not accept the diagrams which the dogmatism of the French Communist Party has made "colonial-socialist" use of . . .'

work and austerity this policy would mean for Africa, given the limited aid available at present from the socialist camp. Since I have an indecently high standard of living, I do not feel qualified to invite others to make such sacrifices. My African students certainly have the right to ask it, on one condition, that they themselves set the example, by working very hard and depriving themselves of luxuries. Their sincerity will be more freely recognized if they accept this preliminary, massive reduction of average and high salaries.

The Algerian students have put all the scholarships they received from different sources, in differing amounts, into a pool, and redistributed them evenly. The F E A N F protests against the cancellation of the grants to some of its leaders. I agree with them, just as I demanded the liberation of Assane Seck. However, they could react more effectively by banding together to support their deprived colleagues. This could easily be done, since a number of their scholarships are higher than those given to Europeans. Furthermore, many of their elders, like Jules Razfinbahiny, earned a living while studying, as is still done a great deal in the United States. There is nothing degrading about it. The officer of the Algerian Liberation Army receives twenty-five francs a month, the same wage as a common soldier. This is the kind of thing that creates an authentic revolutionary atmosphere.[1]

A Dahomeyan, a cousin of the Director of Agriculture, received a scholarship for many years to study the manufacture of Louis XV shoes in France.[2] A country with a really revolutionary spirit cannot prosper with such disastrous misuse of funds. There must be more patriotism, and students must set the example for it in their daily life. In an underdeveloped country, the opposition should be constructive – which does not prevent it from fighting for its principles. But for a number of young Africans opposition seems to be an alibi, a refusal to take on responsibilities, and an excuse to adopt a policy of 'waiting', and meanwhile making demands, J. Baboulène told me.

On the other hand, the F E A N F is right to denounce 'African'

[1] However, absolute egalitarianism, as preached by certain elements of this army in May, 1962, would take away incentive to work, hope of promotion, and discourage future technicians from attaining the necessary training.

[2] Failure in final examinations means an extra year of scholarship is necessary, equal to 'the price of a primary school', a Dahomey student said to me. He at least has understood his responsibilities.

socialism. Too often it is just a cover for neo-colonialism, or else a not always honest attempt to reconcile the communal ideal with African tradition. The latter cannot be reconciled with progress, which requires discipline and control, and rejects family parasites. However, it is not enough either simply to proclaim oneself a revolutionary, ideals have to be lived as well.

The chances of quick and successful revolutionary action are not great, but this fact in no way justifies resigning oneself to the present situation. Ways must be found to speed things up, to lay the groundwork for socialism and make its eventual realization smoother, and the transition less difficult for the African peasant, worker and student.

6. SWEDEN, ISRAEL, YUGOSLAVIA, POLAND, CUBA, SOVIET UNION, CHINA

In the course of study I am proposing to young Africans to help rid them of 'speechifying', I have purposely eliminated the 'lessons of the Western imperialist camp', from the 'American way of life' to the Fourth French Plan. The methods by which the latter were drawn up are extremely interesting, nonetheless, although not sufficiently democratic. Economic developments in Germany and Italy are hardly useful to Africa at her present stage. The Japanese example, with all the ingenuity it required, would be closer. In Scandinavia, the solid co-operative organization demonstrates how peasant and consumer initiative can hold its own against the most powerful monopolies. I have already discussed how the economic and cultural level in Africa would slow up the realization of such a movement, if it was not initiated by the government.

Israel offers the most complete range of agrarian economic structures, from citrus plantations run by a corporation to the *kibbutz*, where not only production but also consumption is collectivized, even more than in the Chinese commune. The organizations most directly applicable to Africa are not these communities, however, as they are brimming with idealism, but the administrative farms, which to some extent inspired the 'crash' cultivation programmes in Dahomey. The *Moshav ovdim*, or village co-operative, could somewhat guide the evolution of the tenant farmers at the Niger Office, perhaps in competition with the state-owned and collective farm of the *Moshav shitufi* type.[1]

In Yugoslavia, only a small family plot limited to ten hectares is privately owned, and as in the *Moshav ovdim*, all commercial and industrial activity in the village is co-operative. It tends to put the factory in the hands of the workers, through the intermediary of the producers' council, and gives the latter a share of political power.

Since the October uprisings in 1956, Poland has sought to achieve socialism 'without totalitarianism or dogmatism', Czeslaw Bobrowsky tells us. 'The new forms of economic life are an attempt to avoid the errors of a blind faith in the perfect automatic working of the market[2] and the errors of a blind faith in the infallibility of planners.' Family plots still exist here, and less than 1 per cent of the land in Poland is accounted for by the *kolkhozes*. But 'agricultural associations' are seeking to promote technical improvements within the framework of a flexible co-operative group, which on occasion is similar to the French co-operatives that share agricultural machines. Saving is mandatory, as in Dahomey. However, here again, mechanization has, it seems to me, been accorded excessive priority, and it may prove to have been very costly.

Cuba demonstrates the immense possibilities of a revolution in full swing as regards education: it has broken the world record for conquering illiteracy. But its economic difficulties invite more prudence: too many beautiful houses, too many tractors at the beginning, and State farms that are much too large. I advised more efforts to spread technical improvements, brochures to spread knowledge of them, and all the forms of agrarian intensification. A paid vacation of one month per year is also a world record, this time questionable, particularly as massive slaughtering of livestock results from salaries climbing faster than production rates. The absence of harvest norms, in the *granjas* as well as the co-operatives, seems to have reduced the work effort. The sugar harvest in 1962 was not especially brilliant, being a 27 per cent cutback, and it was terminated too late. But the revolutionary potential will make good yields easier to

---

[1] *Lands Alive*, Chapters XIII, XV and VII.
[2] Gunnar Myrdal also denounces this theory.

obtain, particularly if the communists stop their discouraging dogmatism.[1]

Except between 1954 and 1960, when agricultural production increased at a rate of 6 to 7 per cent a year, the Soviet Union has had nothing but difficulties with agriculture. A primary cause was the lowness of prices paid for *kolkhoz* products, and another was the obligatory deliveries of goods.[2] In his excellent book, *Les Paysans Soviétiques*, C. de Lauwe has put the lack of technical personnel in its proper perspective, as well as the heavy burden of the bureaucracy. But these faults have been recognized now and will therefore be easier to deal with. Although plans for milk and meat production in 1962 still seem extravagant, it seems probable that they will be cut down to more modest levels.

The Chinese model seems much more valuable for the African economy, because levels of production were lower there, and the structure was semi-colonial. The period from 1952–1957, during which the Han peasants were mobilized for a 'reasonable' level of achievement, is full of lessons for Africa. Certain modifications will be necessary to avoid the excesses of the subsequent 'great leap forward' and the communes. The lesson of manual labour for organizers and leaders (which Dieng calls the romantic conception of revolution) seems to be particularly relevant for Africa right now.

---

[1] In *Le Monde*, May 16th 1962, page 8, J. Julien reports a speech of Fidel Castro given on March 23rd 1962.
[2] Prices paid for potatoes do not always even pay transportation costs to the places where they are stored.

9

CHAPTER EIGHTEEN
Africa would be more efficient if unified

1. CUT SALARIES DRASTICALLY

There is no magical solution, including socialism, that will relieve Africa of the hard work necessary to pull herself out of under-development. The work will be practically unbearable if she refuses to accept all foreign aid or too narrowly limits its source. A revolution would have the advantage of forcing Africans to see problems as they are, and preventing them from avoiding these problems. But the cost in the short run would be higher. Meanwhile, a number of measures are possible, and some are absolutely necessary, to speed up development. The Soviet and Chinese methods are consistent with speed, at the price of a generation. But their views on priorities for investments are not the best possible ones, and they have a great deal to learn in this area. Furthermore, it is extremely doubtful that an effort comparable to China's can be dragged out of the African peasant.

Above all, let us not speak of socialism as long as a Minister or Member of Parliament, in a month or two of 'work' in his air-conditioned office, can earn as much as a peasant during a lifetime of arduous toil under a scorching sun. The Congolese unions which (like the parties) are run from the top, support the highest salaries, and therefore support the *élite* class, but not the peasant-workers.[1] The worker at Pointe-Noire, with a salary of 3,000 CFA francs a month, and the peasant in the Congo basin with 700 francs of money income a year, cannot be expected to feel much solidarity with a Deputy receiving 165,000 francs. In the USSR the range of salaries, far too wide in Stalin's time – which had its privileged, and tremb-

[1] Unable to lower the salaries of political leaders in the Congo, trade union leaders in Leopoldville seek to reduce them by provoking inflation (May, 1962).

ling, class – has been reduced, and now goes on a scale from one to twenty. The misuse of cars, which were put at the disposal of the whole family of each Director, was abruptly stopped in the beginning of 1959.

In China the range of salaries goes only from one to six, from one to four in the communes. The multiple services and facilities given certain leaders make the differences greater, but the ministers do not sport European suits and ties as symbols of their status. They have preferred to wear the dress of the worker. The fact that independence was acquired without serious fighting in Africa has prevented it from eliminating all the 'collaborators' and corrupt officials. Perhaps certain results could be obtained if the Chiefs of State declared war on underdevelopment, economic backwardness, misery, ignorance and sickness. In this way sacrifices, reduced salaries and work would be justified . . . in an atmosphere of general mobilization.

It is unforgivable that a professor, on becoming a Cabinet member, should receive two or three times more for his new position, which he should have assumed out of dedication to his country. In May, 1961, the majority of the officials in Brazzaville found that appearing for three or four hours – I have not said working – was sufficient. In principle their working day ran from six-thirty a.m. to one p.m. Some of them still spend more time in night clubs than in their offices. They will be able to buy still another wife. If this means that the impoverished peasant cannot have one it does not seem to bother them for the moment. In the long run, polygamy, the most deeply resented form of social injustice, will increase the number of revolutionaries in both sexes.

2. A FEW PROGRESSIVE MEASURES

A fiscal system that does not discourage initiative, in other words, native capitalists, but which especially encourages investments made in the framework of the Plan, would constitute a first step. Next, the tradition of parasitic relatives must be stamped out, as it stifles both motivation to work for personal and family success, and the idea of saving.

Wherever anticipated initiative does not materialize, State capitalism should develop, in so far as honest and competent managers are available. In the beginning, if necessary, this can be done with the help of European organizers. At the same time the co-operative movement can be supported under the conditions I have discussed. It will be preferable to have the State and co-operative sectors roughly equal to the capitalist sector at the beginning, and then surpass it.

The business sector should be the most severely controlled, for at least two reasons. It must quickly stop holding back the development of industries. The creation of shops at moderate prices and reduced distribution costs will encourage the peasant to increase his efforts. The goods that he wants will thus be put within his reach; at present he does not feel that he can ever obtain them. It has to be accepted now, as an unavoidable fact, that the African refuses to accept the bleak, harassing and anonymous effort involved in 'labour investments' of the Chinese type. Therefore, the peasant must be made conscious of the problems of development, by playing both on his patriotism – the role of activism – and on his self-interest. Ways must be found to facilitate his passage into a trading economy, which will help break the mental structures found in a self-sufficient subsistence economy, permeated with resignation and stagnation.

The high cost of a modern trading economy cannot be borne unless peasant productivity increases quickly enough to pay for it amply without lowering standards of living, especially as regards nutrition. This occurred in Senegal with the development of the peanut crop and its corollary, the replacement of home-grown millet by purchases of rice. Draught animals and fertilizers, which alone could have doubled the harvests, were not used.

Such a framework would provide the largely parasitic white-collar bourgeoisie of today with the incentive to become enterprising and useful to his country. Economic development would therefore take place at first within the framework of a plan protecting the general interest and guiding a certain amount of private initiative. A government operating in this direction would be effective if it was careful to place the general development of the nation first.

Regarding foreign capital, the countries in the Brazzaville group have adopted investment laws that seem more favourable to the capitalists than to the new states, from the point of view of tax immunity and repatriation of profits. And yet capitalist groups are not pressing forward to invest, as the units are often too small to interest them. To encourage foreign investment, France was thinking in terms of certain guarantees, which I shall discuss a little further on.

It was proposed in Dahomey that an investing group be able to repatriate all the capital invested gradually, in the form of profits, plus a 'normal' interest, between 8 per cent and 10 per cent. In France, 'normal' interest was in the neighbourhood of 7 per cent in 1962. Once the capital and interest is completely reimbursed, the installations would become the property of the State, whose share in the profit would increase regularly. At the end of this phase, the contract would provide that all African experts and technicians necessary to run the factory would be trained. In this way, young African engineers would have a job market. To further attract investors, since the profits are on the whole fairly small, I suggest that the contracts between the African governments and the foreign investors be countersigned by the trade unions, which would give the investors a certain socio-political security.

Governments must also act to prevent a capitalist evolution similar to Japan's, where a small *élite* has become very rich and the backward peasant mass is supporting the entire weight of development. The dangers of this are already very apparent in the Ivory Coast. This tendency will be even more disastrous if imports of luxury goods continue. On this point, popular uprisings against Packards, Cadillacs and Mercedes would be very helpful, as they would force governments to put excessive Customs duties on these imports, or even better, prohibit them entirely.

3. AID WITH NO STRINGS ATTACHED

Can a government accept foreign aid from France, England and Europe without sacrificing its independence, and ability to develop autonomously? The actual facts are more complex than the Marxist views on neo-colonialism suggest. It is possible to accept aid and reject political dependence if one knows how to guard against the potential dangers. Mali is resolutely neutralist and continues to receive aid from France, which proves the point. For this to happen, the Guinean revolt against France was certainly necessary. In order to establish this position on firm ground, the Plan should be drawn up by men anxious to increase to the maximum the wealth of their countries. Thus, foreign aid would be directed only towards productive investments: long-range investments for social services, education, and professional and vocational training, both universal and accelerated; intermediate-term investments for industry; and, above all, short-term investments for agricultural modernization.

A richer country can protect itself better. France, after receiving aid through the Marshall Plan, has rejected American leadership. The state of her economy allows her to do without aid completely now, as she has attained economic independence. The path that leads Africa to that stage is longer, but not inaccessible. A country resolutely battling for its revolution is in a better position to accept large amounts of foreign aid without fearing the political noose: thus the Algerian F L N signed the Evian agreements. In saying this I may be called a neo-colonialist. The Algerian signatories to these agreements were exposed to the same charge by Ben Bella.

In its relations with the Common Market, or France, or all other governments or groups, Africa must first of all assure herself of markets. It cannot break all its ties with the West without first being sure of markets for its products in the East, or it will create serious economic disturbances. Guinea has shown that it can be dangerous to make the break prematurely. The Polish leaders have complained bitterly that they are forced to buy more Guinean bananas and Cuban sugar than their plans had foreseen.

Next, the new African states should firmly safeguard their right to protect their new industries, above all by Customs duties, even if these are directed against those providing aid and buying their products.

Such a policy will be easier to uphold if a group of nations are involved, who confront the rich nations with an African bloc. It will be stronger if it includes all of Western and Central Africa, without stopping at former colonial or linguistic frontiers. If it is conceived as a federation of States relinquishing all sovereignty to a supra-national organization, the bloc will be a very long time indeed in forming, particularly as at least two different political concepts are involved. The Casablanca group, comprising Ghana, Guinea, Mali, with Egypt and the Maghreb, is on one side, and the twelve so-called Brazzaville states on the other. The latter are allied to the Republic of the Congo (Leopoldville), which will be an important power once it straightens out its internal affairs, and to Nigeria, which has considerable weight all by itself.

A confederation of states which are completely autonomous in domestic policy, with a more or less liberal or socialist policy, would have even a better chance of success. Agreement on basic issues, particularly foreign policy, would be necessary. President Sylvanus Olympio's recent proposal for a purely economic union seems more realistic. It would first of all abolish the endless Customs frontiers, impossible to guard adequately (particularly with present unreliable agents), and move them back to the frontiers of the bloc. Lastly, the most important advantage is that it would permit the nations to compare economic plans, and make them complementary, thereby avoiding duplication and marginal enterprises. This enlarging of markets would facilitate industrialization: a 'war of factories' would be fatal to young, developing economies.

To an economically unified West and Equatorial Africa, an *entente* with North Africa, the Maghreb, could be of very great value. It is true that the 'moral fibre' of the Tunisians and Moroccans may not be very strong: too many privileges remain, and agrarian reform has been very slow.[1] In the Algerian students, who call each other 'brother', one can recognize exceptional moral values, formed in battle; contact with them can be a great stimulus to youth groups from tropical Africa. Two 'common markets', the Maghreb and

---

[1] Seven years after independence, Moroccan agricultural production can be considered stagnant, in general atmosphere. Uneasy about the future, the *colons* are no longer investing, are even cutting down on current expenses. The efforts of the Moroccan *fellahs*, often blocked by feudal and trade structures, share-cropping and money-lending, have not picked up where the colonialists left off. If it is true that roughly the same amount of food is available for a population that has grown 18 per cent in seven years, the proportion for each inhabitant is that much less. If the curve is prolonged much further, economic problems will lead to a very disturbing political and social situation. A foreign policy that veers to the left as an alibi cannot replace necessary internal reforms.

western Africa, could meet on an equal basis with the European Common Market, if the two African ones join forces first.

Whatever form it takes, a West African Union should first of all unify all road and rail networks, and establish the necessary transverse roads. Why connect Chad with Bangui in such a bloc, if a railroad via Douala or Nigeria is more economic? To telephone from Porto Novo in Dahomey to Lagos in Nigeria, you still have to go through London and Paris. A convertible monetary system will be easier to establish if England joins the Common Market. The monetary problem is extremely complex, as ties will be necessary with the pound sterling and the franc: the problems Guinea has faced in this area, as in others, will be instructive. An African banking system would facilitate an autonomous development, no longer conceived as an appendage of Europe. All these problems deserve much more detailed and complete treatment, but I am not sufficiently conversant with them to press further. The question of bilingualism remains, as all African *élites* will soon need both French and English. Both are already spoken in some places, such as Douala.

The development of large regional complexes depending on the same river basin – Senegal, Congo, Niger, and the Voltas – will furnish concrete bases for the economic development of a unified Africa.

The question now is whether this African bloc, after achieving the first stages of development, somewhat along the lines I have been discussing, can achieve a certain synthesis of Eastern and Western methods of development in building socialism. One of the problems is the international atmosphere: will it be sufficiently relaxed to give Africa a free hand in this attempt? This search for ways and means is not limited to Africa, but is the essential problem now confronting all of the Third World.

4. A COMMON FRONT FOR BACKWARD COUNTRIES

An African common front, even if limited to economic affairs, would enable Africa to safeguard more efficiently against political strings being attached to foreign aid, particularly French, English or European. Later, it would be to its advantage to join with organizations of economic defence formed by other underdeveloped areas. These latter should safeguard the buying power, particularly for machinery and manufactured products, of their raw materials, agricultural or mineral. In short, they should seek parity, somewhat similar to that obtained for a long time by American farmers, and demanded by French peasants. It would now be extended to a world-wide scale. In the framework of the liberal economy, it will be very difficult, as the problem is not a simple one.

Organizations set up to protect products, like the one recently formed for coffee, seek only to avoid a fall in prices. This policy, if applied to many products, runs the risk of leading to quota systems or even of cutting down on production to maintain the value of the product. If it goes too far, it leads to Malthusianism, and thereby to scarcity. If each organization cuts down on production, whether it be sugar, cotton, coffee, milk, or cocoa, the poor, the very ones who are doing the producing, will no longer even be able to clothe themselves cheaply. Where will new groups of consumers come from? This is what the primary objective should be, increasing markets.

In relation to cereal crops, typically 'colonial' products are relatively overestimated. The coffee grower and the metallurgical worker exploit the rice grower. Flexible methods of defence must be drawn up, and intelligent ones, that can rapidly adapt to changes in the situation; in a word, methods that are not dogmatic.

Nothing in all this should justify the massive and universal fall in the buying power of tropical products. For more than a century, England, and more recently Germany, has been fed very cheaply, at abnormally low so-called 'world' prices, as a result of dumping of agricultural surpluses. Thus the rich force the poor to feed them on very advantageous terms . . . for the lucky. If the emerging nations form a common economic front, they would be able to reduce and then eliminate these flagrant abuses, until such time as a world-wide agricultural plan is drawn up.

The best general orientation would thus be an intelligent defence of relative prices, and of the buying power of basic products, meanwhile tending progressively towards a world plan of constant expansion of all useful products. National Bureaux would federate into African, later World, Bureaux; only the latter would be able to

9 *

prevent speculation. One cannot count on large trading firms to support such projects. As late as 1946 they torpedoed, at the First Congress of the FAO in Copenhagen, the much more modest proposals concerning anti-speculative stocks drawn up by Sir John Boyd Orr and Tanguy-Prigent.

Africa will be in a better position to protect itself if, while diversifying its agriculture, following the outline I have made here or another (reducing imports, improving nutrition, planting industrial crops, then feed crops and livestock), it seeks at the same time to increase its markets. Instead of orienting itself only to the rich Atlantic area, which will make it too dependent on the West, Africa should turn also to long-term markets with the Eastern bloc, which is willing to guarantee maintenance of African buying power. In the framework of a kind of economic neutralism, exchanges inside the African bloc should be developed first, then in all of the emerging nations, which could grant each other a mutual preference. Close and exclusive attachment to the European bloc is, of course, unacceptable, no matter how much aid is promised, if it slows down industrialization and general development. This would be satellization, and one could then legitimately call it neo-colonialism.

After solving internal ethnic problems[1]– which some of the recent political quarrels have revived – the idea of nationalism should quickly be transcended. Perhaps the concept of African unity will give the peasants a deeper motivation and reinforce propaganda for economic plans and progress.

The Africans, peasants and rulers, officials and students, are being asked to furnish absolutely exceptional efforts and sacrifices for their development: in short, to be heroes and saints. What right have we, who have such an easy life, to ask this, a life made easy because of the work done by our ancestors, and our workers and peasants? And what have we done up until now to give Africans more effective help, what real 'sacrifice' can we put in the scales? It is high time that we offer Africa truly 'disinterested' aid, concerned above all with Africa's development, and not with prolonging abuses and privileges.

---

[1] A European bishop dies, and the local deputy asks a Legate passing through to give him an African successor. Since the priests of the deputy's ethnic group are very young, the Legate proposes a bishop from a neighbouring tribe: 'Then I prefer a European,' the deputy quickly replies.

CHAPTER NINETEEN
Underdevelopment can be conquered in twenty years

1. A 'CIVILIAN' MILITARY SERVICE

Although the word 'co-operation' is replacing 'aid' and 'assistance', which imply charity and the generosity of the rich to the poor, there is nevertheless a certain amount of hypocrisy involved. However, at least affairs have progressed so that 'vice renders homage to virtue'.

France finally regained its 'honour' by ending the degrading colonial wars in Indo-China and Algeria. The forces thus liberated, in terms of both men and money, should be used in a more effective way than to create the paltry and ridiculous *force de frappe*, France's nuclear striking force. War is no longer a viable concept, only world suicide is within our reach, and no one is reaching for it at the moment. Too many in the French army were dishonoured under the banner of 'Honour and Country', because of the tortures, murder and destruction of which they were guilty. To some extent the army is out of step with the modern world. The 'traditional values' no longer mean very much. From now on the only honourable battle is against hunger and misery, ignorance and sickness, and for the dignity of all men, liberated from their diverse forms of servitude.

The young must be helped in this search for a new ideal if they are to be kept from fascism. The pioneer spirit, and the idea of sacrifice and dedication are inseparable from this difficult task. Instead of learning how to kill, one should learn how to help and understand. Military service could be replaced in Belgium now, for its doctors and engineers, by a 'civilian' service performed in emerging nations. France could have been the first to make this fine gesture, had it known how to use the dedication of its conscientious objectors, instead of putting them in prison.

Now that the colonial wars are over, a 'civilian service' could be extended to include all volunteers: young audiences at my lectures are numerous in calling for such a solution. The agreement of the African states, of course, is a prerequisite. Some of the African students reject this kind of aid *a priori*; perhaps they see in it a kind of competition. They take on a heavy responsibility for their attitude, as it slows down their countries' development and increases peasant misery, since not enough trained Africans are available. Look at the consequences in China of the departure of the Soviet experts. If you call that neo-colonialism, then try your own hand at it, but with more ardour, and don't hesitate to roll up your sleeves instead of holding out your hand. Such a 'service' would have no connection, overseas, with the army: it must be totally civilian. These young people, who would remain on our payroll during the legal duration of service, would cost less than experts, who are sometimes overpaid in relation to the value of their work,[1] and are too old to get around much in the bush. The agricultural war will not be played out in the capital.[2] The young people can perform very useful functions, complementing what is already being done, not replacing it.

If they are able to make themselves accepted, and respect the Africans, both men and women, and African ways of thinking and living, these young Europeans can accomplish a great deal, each in his own speciality, by helping to avoid the pitfalls of premature Africanization. Young peasants would be the most useful, particularly those from poor regions who can still yoke and ring oxen, and hold and repair ploughs. Skilled labourers would also be welcome: the blacksmith could beat out and strengthen the ploughshares, and repair harnesses and farm equipment, while the cartwright could teach his trade. They would show the Africans how to make and repair the simple tools of farming and woodcutting so necessary at this stage. The peasant's sons from Auvergne and Brittany have invaluable qualifications for backward countries: and we make chain

[1] The 'Rotival Plan' for Madagascar is a scandal pure and simple, as R. Gendarme has shown.

[2] 'Like a cloud of grasshoppers, experts, often quite mediocre and of slight moral and human value, swarm over our country.' *Al Istiqlal*, Mabat, March 12th 1960.

gang workers of them, or even, the worst possible waste, policemen (M. Mazoyer).[1]

Workers would come with their boxes of tools, and teach the Africans how to use them. Working in conjunction with the foreman, they would be particularly useful on all the labour investment projects. The many technical short cuts known in Europe, which engineers are not always aware of, would quickly raise current production in Africa. Mechanics would repair trucks and other motors owned by the co-operatives. Economic mechanization would thus be brought nearer to realization.

Medical students and young doctors would be the most appreciated, for obvious reasons. High school graduates would become schoolteachers, aided by agronomists if they are in farm-schools. A fruitful collaboration would thus take place in the training of peasant organizations of all kinds, teachers, heads of co-operatives and self-help organizations. Naturally organizations would have to be set up to receive and utilize these young people, whose role would be above all accelerated vocational and practical education, and the training of leadership.

Training African teachers on all levels to conceive of education first of all as a lever for economic development – which in no way excludes general culture – would be another and extremely important step towards the new education. Along with the sections for academic and agricultural teachers, sections for heads of activist centres, co-operatives and self-help associations can be added more quickly, thanks to the 'civilian service'.

The young students would participate in the research necessary to draw up the Plans, more and more of which is needed. Each would work with an African destined to replace him. Needless to say, young people dedicated to the new African states, liberals in the largest sense of the word, will be more effective. Others would probably not volunteer, and would be more at home in garrisons in Germany. There should be no trace of anti-communist propaganda in this work, as compared to the United States Peace Corps, nor for that matter any kind of propaganda.

[1] The French agronomists were mostly of middle-class origin, which reduced their practical value. They have not improved the basic tools. Sending African peasants and apprentices to Europe would be a useful complement to the 'civilian' service.

The aid that I propose would rapidly improve the human resources of Africa, essential to development and even more important than capital investments. The lack of organized initiative is the primary stranglehold on progress, as A. Sauvy has shown so well in his books.

2. FRENCH CO-OPERATION

The French have felt that industrial investments should be in the hands of private companies. An influx of private capital would, of course, be extremely valuable, if it met the needs of the country, and fitted the purposes of the Plan. The Plans no longer – at least in principle – put primary emphasis on profits, and the private investor is consequently losing interest. He is greatly concerned about the political future of the new African countries, fearing that his installations or investments will be nationalized. Lastly, the policy of making French or European taxpayers provide the money for the non-income-producing investments, and inviting private investors to furnish the rest, seems questionable.

As I have repeatedly said, the industrialization of Africa will be far too slow unless it obtains a massive amount of capital from African, English, French, European, American and Soviet sources. I am not speaking simply of grants, which occupy too prominent a place in Western aid programmes, but essentially of loans. They should be long term, with low interest rates, payable in local currency or products, like those made by the USSR. In this way more money would be forthcoming, but the borrowers would be forced to use it profitably and efficiently. They have been spoiled by 'political gifts'.

As in the Alliance for Progress (already compromised) for South America, I would prefer to see the capital partly supplied by the recipient country, even if the proportion set by the Americans, which is half and half, cannot be attained everywhere in Africa. In agricultural projects the share of the beneficiary can consist of labour, following a formula similar to that of FERDES, but effectively applied this time. New plantations, reforestation, erosion prevention and especially irrigation projects should no longer be planned without a minimum of semi-unpaid participation on the part of the country. This is necessary not only for the sake of speeding up development, but also for the self-respect of the Africans. Without work on their part, one cannot speak of co-operation, but only of assistance: it again becomes charity, dangerously close to dependence.

New sources of funds for this renewed co-operation will be easy to find even before general disarmament, the best source of money, is achieved. The abolition in a year or two of grants to balance budgets, which are simply hand-outs unworthy of both parties, would be a first step. They compromise the real independence of African governments and allow the *élite* class to regale itself at the cost of discouraging workers and holding up development. From the donors' point of view, the idea is to seek a 'dependent' client, who 'votes right' at the UN, whose economy remains dominated and who is a source of big profits for business interests, which carry great weight with the leaders of France.

If large sums are granted to new agricultural credit associations – which would guarantee repayment – agricultural modernization, if provided with activists and cadres, can be speeded up. Everywhere priority should be given to directly productive investments. At the same time, aid would be in a lump sum, so that each country would be able to count on receiving *x* number of millions, but only to achieve its plan, for which it would become truly responsible. In the beginning wastage might increase: but present aid, given in bits and drabs, contributes to the irresponsibility of the African governments.

I do not, of course, eliminate investments in the basic services which help speed up modernization, such as transportation and communication, nor in the 'social' services, because education, like health, is an essential element in development. This should be only on the condition, however, that education 'decolonizes' itself, and becomes practical. A healthy balance must be observed between 'social' expenses and economic investments, particularly as regards the amount of labour involved. Thus, increases in yields on cleared and improved fields, the added tons of cotton and peanuts, coffee and cocoa, palm oil and rubber, will supply the funds needed to run the schools and clinics.

3. INCREASED AID FROM THE EUROPEAN ECONOMIC COMMUNITY

The Community has just provided Chad, greatly in need of increasing production, with 11·8 million dollars. Yet 5·7 million are for medical equipment, 1·5 for schools, 1 for sanitation improvements in the capital and less than 3 million for water supply and irrigation projects in the countryside and villages. Nothing for industry, nothing for crop cultivation.[1] What will the country use to maintain its new school and hospitals? The text of the agreement associating these 'territories' with the Community anticipated only outright grants of funds, which limits the possibilities of co-operation and at the same time gives Africans the disagreeable impression of charity.

The new association being worked out could diversify methods of supplying aid. The proportion of outright grants already anticipated, however, seems still excessive. Credits of any kind are preferable, and they can take the form of international guarantees of loans or of reductions of interest rates. If the Germans or the Swiss lend money at 6 per cent, the Community could take over at least half of the interest, and bring the rate down to about 2·5 per cent, the Soviet norm. By financing national development banks, the Community would aid 'large-scale programmes of small projects' and provide the necessary resources for the labour investment projects, following schemes similar to those of FERDES.

To facilitate preparation and achievement of these plans, more sustained technical assistance is necessary. It would be even more useful if it supplied the experts needed to carry out government-sponsored projects, which would include a large part of the semi-unpaid projects. Completion of the Central African Republic's programme of rural water supply has been held up for lack of an engineer.

The creation of a European Development Institute is a good beginning, provided it associates operational and concrete research with training African technical and economic experts, and uses to the utmost the best available European technicians and economists. Too many of the existing 'study associations' or 'institutes' have no

[1] Not counting the government 'palace', Fort Lamy has consumed more than a third of Chad's foreign aid. Cement prices are sky high, but when J. Guillard proposed school-shelters with walls of woven straw, he met with a barrage of protests.

value whatsoever. The idea of working out a common philosophy of aid and development disturbs me, as it is too apt to be done in a vague liberal framework, and remain too theoretical. This will prevent it from trying to find the concrete solution to each specific problem, the solution that most favours development.

In the economic sphere, association with the Community will open up new markets to tropical Africa in an atmosphere entirely different from that of the protection – at times excessive – granted in the franc zone until now. There will be no more strict quota systems, but the right to impose low Customs duties, which will not turn away other suppliers, notably from Latin America. The Low Countries and Germany would therefore be unable to obtain monopolies on supplies to Africa.[1] Africa itself might be able to equip itself more cheaply that way, but it would be the loser, without any doubt.

The countries most opposed to granting excessive privileges to former French Africa are the African states in the Commonwealth. The negotiations for British entry into the Common Market, if successful, will enlarge the economic framework of the Common Market and prevent it from discriminating against former English colonies. Economic structures like the Marketing Boards, of which we have already discussed the great possibilities, will become even more attractive. Tropical Africa should unite quickly the better to resist the ascendancy of this powerful European economic bloc.

Self-protective measures should go beyond price defences, and include industrial development. If necessary, industries can be sheltered behind Customs duties, as in the nineteenth-century United States. This does not exclude any kind of trade or supply of raw materials, or economic co-operation fruitful to both sides. But such co-operation should always favour the underdeveloped nation.

If Europe decides to maintain a form of economic domination as outdated and unacceptable as colonialism, it may find itself some day cut off from Africa, as well as from all other underdeveloped areas. It would thereby lose its principal sources of raw materials, and a large percentage of its markets. The West has a clear interest in

[1] Cf. the author's article in *Le Monde Diplomatique*, November, 1961, page 8.

developing Africa, to transform it into a valuable economic partner. In 1946 the United States sold more to Sweden than to China; England sold more to Germany in 1961 than to India.

Aid remains completely insufficient, if it is true that the amount of official 'Western' aid to tropical Africa represented a little more than 300 million dollars in 1961, of which 200 were supplied by France. The Soviet Union lent 35 million dollars to Guinea[1] and China gave 25 million dollars and 10,000 tons of rice. 'This aid represents less than 2 per cent of the gross national expenditures of the countries . . . and makes only a relatively small contribution to development. . . . Through lack of co-ordination with development programmes, utilization of domestic or foreign resources has not always been the best possible. . . . Aid has at least prevented transfers abroad made by Europeans on salary and lenders of European currencies from reducing economic activity and investments.'[2]

4. AMERICAN AND SOVIET AID

United States 'aid', the greatest in terms of volume,[3] has for a long time had a military emphasis in its grants. Priority has been given to Korea, Formosa, Laos and South Vietnam. A good part of the rest was directed to Europe through the Marshall Plan, where many private investments are concentrated. Three-quarters of American aid to underdeveloped countries in recent years has been to Latin America and European 'dependents'. It has mostly consisted in outright grants, a form of generosity all the less appreciated in that it was at times ostentatious. A great part of it was in agricultural surpluses, and other goods 'in kind'.

In Vietnam the massive arrival of certain industrial products strongly impeded creation of new industries, and even caused difficulties for some existing ones, such as textiles and sugar. In India, the seventeen million tons of cereals which are to be turned over in a four-year period, March 1960 to March 1964, will give the Indian government a useful respite, and prevent inflation by maintaining

---

[1] And 40 million to Ghana.
[2] F A O Africa.
[3] If the rate of growth of the American economy remains half that of the Soviet Union, this aid superiority will soon be lost.

stable prices, even with insufficient harvests. They will also allow the government to plan the fundamental modifications of structure needed to modernize agriculture rapidly, like the abolition of share-cropping and moneylending and radical agrarian reform. When this 'help' ends, however, the lack of food in India threatens to assume even greater proportions. It is reminiscent of French grants to prop up budgets, more harmful than useful, for which France has justly been criticized.

Soviet aid started much later and is still more limited. It is more concentrated geographically: India, Afghanistan, Egypt, Yugoslavia, Ceylon, Cambodia, Burma, Ghana, Guinea, Mali, the Sudan, Cuba and Argentina absorb most of it. In the last few years it has grown rapidly, so that in a few countries it already largely counterbalances American aid. It consists mainly of loans, and the USSR takes great care to make clear that its few 'political' gifts are given as a friend – the gesture of an equal to an equal – and not out of the generosity of the rich towards the poor. Lastly, Soviet aid provides above all for large industrial complexes, like dams and electrical installations, which are basic levers of development.

In Cambodia, the bags of American sugar and flour are forgotten as soon as they are consumed, while the four Chinese factories remain. These modern monuments make unbeatable propaganda, and bear witness to the intelligence of their great neighbour.

I am certainly not going to advise the new African governments to prefer this or that aid, or become involved in political value judg-ments. A unified and neutralist Africa can more easily defend its economic and political autonomy, and at the same time profit greatly from the collaboration of the two great blocs. The essential is that this aid allows it to modernize agriculture and industries rapidly without forfeiting its independence. One can trust the better judgment of many African leaders, but unfortunately others seem susceptible to arguments of hard cash, like Katanga bullion. In 1961, in the middle of all the turbulence in the Congo, *Union Minière* still announced profits of fifteen billion old francs, as against twenty-three in 1960.

5. THE AFRICAN METALLURGICAL INDUSTRY

Here is an interesting bit of information: a deposit of more than a billion tons – one of the three largest in the world – of 63 per cent iron ore was discovered in Mokambo, Gabon, by an American company. Since it is situated 700 kilometres from the Coast, in the middle of dense forest, its exploitation is not a priority. Those in Mauritania and Liberia are in better locations. But in order not to let its permit lapse, Bethlehem Steel nevertheless seeks to persuade Gabon that the railway necessary to bring out the ore represents the future of the country. The 150 billion old francs that it would cost could be better invested in exploitation of the forests.

By keeping control of the best metal deposits, capitalists are entering a new form of exploitation. The profits, as in the oil business, are made in the refining process, and not in extraction. The present context of bilateral relations between Africa and France-Europe is to prevent the emergence of real poles of development which can animate the entire economy of the African continent. Nevertheless, the future must be controlled, first of all by establishing a rational calendar, on an 'atlantic' then a world scale, to use these African mineral resources. The regulations drawn up would respect the collective interests of Africa: in exchange for exploitation permits, the companies would agree, wherever possible – which is more frequent than they claim – to establish metallurgical factories right in Africa. Nigerian coal and Gabonese and Liberian minerals would mean three series of blast furnaces that can be built, and Mauritania can follow, with its anticipated natural gas.

In discussions with large Western companies, small nations do not carry much weight. Even Guinea is hesitant when dealing with representatives of F R I A. On the other hand, a large economic unit would be in a good position to defend West African interests and project a realistic future by planning large economic complexes to assure the real development of the continent. Despite the pressing need for unity, many obstacles stand in its way, and it will be more feasible to limit it at first to the economic domain.

6. WORLD SOLIDARITY: MASSIVE TRANSFER OF INCOMES

The national income tax was vehemently attacked in the beginning of this century, and its detractors insisted that it would ruin all businesses. Yet the different kinds of social security, and the increase in the buying power of the masses which resulted from it have been essential factors in the rapid economic development of our time. Without it we would have had difficulty in competing with Communist countries. Massive aid to underdeveloped countries can have the same effect on world economic expansion. It should be financed by a national income tax of comparable importance, or it will remain appallingly insufficient, as it is now. We have seen its modest effectiveness in the case of France, and yet we devote from 1·4 per cent to 1·7 per cent of our national income to foreign aid, according to the estimates, which would be the highest proportion in the world.

In South America the gulf between rich and poor widens each year, between the golden swimming pool of the Archbishop of Rio and the *favellas*, the shanty-towns on the hills overlooking the city; between the agricultural workers of Alagoas,[1] the Recife prostitutes and the Matarazzo in São Paulo. A similar gulf in income is widening every day on a world scale, separating the developing states in Asia, Latin America and Africa from the rich nations. The distortion is increasingly rapidly because the difference in ability to invest is even greater than that in incomes. One can save a high proportion of a high revenue without any sacrifice.

Two separate worlds are forming; soon they will have nothing in common, and they may one day confront one another even more tragically than East and West. The idea that an American businessman's son and the son of a Congolese or Indian peasant have an 'equal opportunity' at birth cannot be seriously entertained. The rich world calls itself the free world, and thereby thinks that its conscience is clear; but a 'defence' of liberty which is allied with defence of privileged status is fairly suspect. The situation is too unbalanced, and foreign aid, if it continues to grow as slowly as it

[1] The torture and massacre of these workers by private police and even official policemen reported by the peasant associations of Francisco Julião show, alas, that I was not well enough informed in *Lands Alive*.

has these last years cannot correct it. As the French peasants have demanded, the West has to start thinking in terms of massive transfers of funds to the 'disinherited' social groups, like the developing nations.

Should this concept materialize, it could one day lead to an apolitical aid, as it gradually becomes world-wide. I recently[1] outlined an idea for an East-West accord which would be easier to achieve than most because it would not abolish all competition, but would place it in a more 'sporting' framework. If former French Africa is associated with the Common Market, a large percentage of the rich world would be aiding a much smaller percentage of the 'deprived' nations, and in this union could be considered more advantageous at the moment than a totally international solidarity. The admission of England to the Common Market, if it brings in the former British colonies, would reduce this temporary advantage.

In any case, a great increase in world aid, in effect a large-scale transfer of incomes, would free tropical Africa from the dangers of neo-colonialism and dominance by the West, without its losing anything in terms of amount or effectiveness of aid. There are a number of prerequisites, however. Disarmament is necessary to raise the contributions of the rich to a decent level. It would not even lower their standard of living; on the contrary. The need to 'up the ante' of the rich nations through disarmament is as great as the need to reduce the dangers of an East-West confrontation. Disarmament should not be considered an essential preliminary, however, as this would justify a delay until disarmament is achieved, which may be a very long time indeed.

Total volume of international aid at present is estimated at about six billion dollars. Several authors have estimated that from thirty to forty-five billion dollars a year would be needed to raise by 2 per cent a year the standard of living of the Third World. In contrast, the United Nations has estimated that 120 billion dollars a year are spent on armaments.[2] By adding the amounts devoted to space

---

[1] *Lands Alive*, Conclusion.

[2] The estimate seems small. W. W. Rostow estimates them at 10 per cent of the gross national product in the United States, 20 per cent in the Soviet Union, amounts similar in absolute value. W. W. Rostow, *The Process of Economic Growth*. New York: W. W. Norton & Co. 1952.

exploration and the indirect expenses of national defence, one could probably double that amount.

The contributions of the rich nations should increase gradually as structures to receive aid in Africa and the Third World permit them to use larger amounts of money more effectively. This could occur rapidly if more efforts were made to train local organizers. As early as 1965 France and Western Europe could turn over 2 per cent of their national income, and the United States 4 per cent.[1] In 1975, the proportions could be raised respectively to 5 per cent for Western Europe, 10 per cent for the United States, 7 per cent for Australia. This would cost a great deal less than continuing armament expenses, following a geometric progression, and far less than a world war, which will be more difficult to avoid without this aid.

Such measures will ensure that a world economic organization can be built on solid foundations. In progressive stages it can draw up a world economic plan, a logical path towards world federal government.[2] A Utopia, certainly, but it is Utopias, or visions of a better world, that have furthered progress, in Greek and Renaissance times as well as our own. Utopia could be defined nowadays as 'long-term forecast'. At least, as long as raw material prices are not stabilized, and the buying power of emerging nations not protected, the liberal slogan of 'Trade not Aid' is pure hypocrisy.

Such an organization would be responsible for humanity, which will be gravely menaced by famine around the year 2000 – a modern version of the suffering in the year 1000 – if we follow our present erroneous ways and do nothing to improve on them. It would co-ordinate economies, establish the amount of contributions, and study their optimal utilization. They would go first to the poorest, for desperate needs. The great majority would be directed to points of maximum effectiveness and high potential, and towards 'bottlenecks' that affect the world economy. Lastly, it would give special advantages – God helps those who help themselves – to those that

[1] At the March Preparatory Conference of the Vienna Conference, organized in July 1962 by the Korner Foundation, the American Peace Corps delegate proposed 1 per cent of the national income of the United States. They have not yet understood the scope of the problem.
[2] It could be a renovated UN, but with supranational economic and political powers: above all, not a 'UN of nations'. The fact that its present Secretary-General is a representative of the Third World is a big step forward.

themselves furnished the most serious and applied efforts, in production as well as education and intelligent organization of the
economy. On this hypothesis China would receive the largest
proportion.

'The East,' replied one of my students, 'will never consent to help
a capitalist nation.' Nevertheless, Nepal, Argentina, Afghanistan
and even India, all of which receive Soviet aid, are far from achieving
socialism. 'The West will never be willing to aid a country oriented
towards communism.' And yet the United States has already given
very large credits to Yugoslavia and Poland.

A better division of wealth would eliminate the fantastic wastage
of money by land-owning potentates in poor countries, Nizams and
Arabian sultans, and above all, by nations which have more than
enough. Stalinism was a monstrous deviation from communism,
but this scandal, in retrospect, should not blind us to others. More
than a third of some raw materials – more than half the coffee – is
consumed by the 185 million inhabitants of the United States, out
of the more than three billion people in the world: an eloquent
testimonial of the aberration of our civilization. It cannot be
defended as long as it countenances such abuses of its power. The
failure of the landing in Cuba in April, 1961, is a good demonstration
of this.

Before giving lessons in socialism to Africa, let us set our own
houses in order. Such a world development would be easier to
achieve if the idea of socialism, raised to the level of real international
solidarity, was progressing in Europe; and if communism became
more liberal on the political level. By lessening the gap between the
Russian and Western standards of living, the Soviet Union is now
able to take steps in this direction, which at the present time China
cannot do.

7. UNDERDEVELOPMENT CAN BE CONQUERED IN TWENTY YEARS

W. W. Rostow estimated at sixty years the interval which up until
now has separated economic 'take-off', when investments total more
than 10 per cent of the gross national product, from economic
maturity, when the economy effectively applies the full range of

modern techniques to all of its resources.[1] But he tends to make a universal law, valuable for the future, of this time-span. It would perhaps be true if backward countries were left to their own devices, and the take-off itself may be delayed for a long time by the political situation. But on the hypothesis of constantly increasing world co-operation, which seems a probability, and taking into account constant technical advances, Rostow's view seems very pessimistic.

Gunnar Myrdal is more carefully optimistic.[2] He points out first that people in underdeveloped areas tend to blame the world economic system for maintaining them in misery, and that development, reaching only ports and towns, leaves the rural areas in stagnation and misery.

He refutes the thesis of the spontaneous and automatic stabilization of the social system, stating that a change does not attract a compensating change, but additional changes which carry the system further along in the same direction. Thus development, if well directed by a Plan detached from the forces of the market, which tend to increase inequality between nations, can create a spiral of economic expansion which increases more and more rapidly.

In sum, if people all over the world who are disturbed by present policies can make themselves heard by their leaders, and impose wisdom on them, in other words disarmament and brotherly aid, Myrdal's intelligent optimism can cease to be a Utopia and become a concrete hope. It would then be necessary to find effective ways to use the enormous production potential made available by the abandonment of rockets and thermonuclear bombs. This would bring us closer to a world production plan, or, let us say, a plan to accelerate constantly expansion of production, moving towards increased co-operation.

A flexible method of approaching the Myrdal Plan comes out of a recent study by G. Ardant.[3] It aims at stabilizing the market in raw materials, in order to protect the buying power of backward countries. The author emphasized two problems: price-fixing,

---

[1] *The Process of Economic Growth.*

[2] *Economic Theory and Underdeveloped Regions*, London, Duckworth, 1957. This book should be on the bedside table of all political leaders, as well as economists, in emerging nations.

[3] *Le Monde Diplomatique.* May, 1962; *Tiers Monde*, 1962. 'La Réforme des Échanges Internationaux par la Création d'un Fonds de Stabilization des Matières Premières.'

which, if it puts prices too high, will lead to over-production and quota systems, or Malthusianism; and financing, which would be facilitated at first by the fact that contributing countries would profit from reorganization of the world market, in itself an essential factor for expansion. An original proposal by Ardant is 'the issuing of money by the stabilization fund as a guarantee against its purchases, international money which is guaranteed by an ensemble of necessary commodities, and not by one alone.'

In this framework, completed by an international tax which will answer all the real needs of the world, even the hypothesis of an economic crisis like the one from 1929–1939 is absurd. Constantly accelerating expansion will no longer be the exclusive province of the Communist bloc, Western Europe and Japan. The problem of markets, a primary obstacle to development, being thus resolved, American steel mills could at last function at maximum capacity; and automated shops could turn the steel into machine tools. In some cases international aid would start by feeding workers on the labour investment projects, if necessary (the FAO plan). But it would become much more effective by supplying the majority of the equipment to harness African rivers and equip their farms and factories – until such time as Africa is made capable of producing this equipment itself.

Before we get carried away, still more is needed. The job of training qualified workers, modern craftsmen and peasants as well as technical experts on all levels, must take first place. Until now, everywhere, emphasis has been placed on high school and college students, despite the fact that in Europe such students were effective in great numbers only after workers and peasants had made great technical advances. Africa, at our suggestion, has put the cart before the horse.

Political leaders who have the full confidence of their people will also be needed to make this international aid effective; aid which, if the West is willing, can rapidly become massive. The development of the Third World is inconceivable without active participation on its part, the kind of participation which will enable it to achieve full independence. Even if it were materially possible – and this seems doubtful, even on a very small scale – it would be morally and therefore eventually politically inadmissible to develop the Third World without sincere efforts on its own part. We do not want to open up the perspective of charitable assistance, which would ultimately end in an impasse, but rather that of effective co-operation.

'The capitalist trusts would oppose these measures with all their forces.' No doubt, but the problem is to see whether President Johnson and his successors will be able to resist them: Kennedy after all managed to prevent a rise in steel prices. Furthermore, public opinion counts in Communist countries more than is generally thought in the West. The essential basis of my optimism is my belief in man, because in the final analysis everything will depend on him. The Soviet Union has shown that, after a certain extension of education, Stalinism itself cannot last. China will also come to this.

The future of the world is in our hands, if we make up our minds to grasp it firmly. For the first time, I have hopes of seeing great progress made in the war against hunger, sickness and ignorance.

In all this, what will Africa become? Its fate in the future is also in the hands of the Africans themselves; but it is often now in those of leaders set up by the West, which exercises control. Yet its peasants, students and workers will also play an essential role in its future. Let us hope that they do not falter in the huge efforts needed to bring on the great destiny surely promised to Africa.[1]

This book is only an outline,[2] and a very partial one, by an author unqualified to go into all the aspects, particularly the sociological and political ones, of such a vast and difficult problem. I was criticized, especially by *France Observateur* and *Démocratie Nouvelle*, for not taking a clear political stand. This was deliberate, in order to avoid political paternalism: I am not, after all, an African citizen. But when one proposes to reject all at once the salary reductions needed to increase investments, and also all European aid (F E A N F Policy, Chapter Seventeen, 5), then I must point out that this is an untenable position, as I said at the time to M. Dieng publicly. It can only increase peasant misery still further.

---

[1] I have just read an account of the tortures inflicted on slaves in British Guiana in the eighteenth century. Leaders of rebellions were roasted over slow fires, and 300 guilders paid for the right hand of a fugitive. How quickly we have forgotten all this!
[2] This paragraph and the following were added to the fourth edition.

'If we had several Cubas to support, the burden on our economy would be too great,' a Soviet economist told me in Moscow. But Cuba has less than seven million inhabitants, and there are two billion people in underdeveloped countries. We have got to face facts. I have sent up a trial balloon; it is up to the Africans to answer me, and above all to criticize me. If any reader finds that my book is banned, openly or indirectly, I would appreciate his notifying me.

'Africa has not got off to a false start, it has not started at all,' I hear on one side. Another tells me that 'It was left in a bad way.' Yes.

CHAPTER TWENTY
A note on English-speaking Africa
JOHN HATCH

Since 1966 radical innovations have been made in African economic policy. They were spearheaded by Tanzania's Arusha Declaration of early 1967 and President Kaunda's Mulungushi speech in April 1968. Both these statements and the attitudes which they embody have been influenced more by René Dumont than by any other individual. For this assertion I have personal testimony. Late in 1966 I was visiting Dar es Salaam. My ministerial friends there jokingly grumbled to me that they had been set homework by the President. I discovered that this book had become required reading for every Tanzanian minister and high public servant. A few weeks later I found a similar situation in Lusaka. When discussing Dumont's ideas with President Nyerere and President Kaunda I suggested that it was not sufficient to read his book; he should be invited to visit both their countries in order to report personally on economic planning and development. Since then René Dumont has visited both countries and the influence of his investigations is clearly reflected in subsequent national policies. This is not to suggest that Tanzanian or Zambian leaders accept all he says or writes, a situation which Dumont himself would be the last to welcome. But it is undoubtedly true that his book has already had a profound effect on these two trend-setting English-speaking African states and that these same states are now engaged in trying to put into practice policies based broadly on his ideas. Unfortunately they are so far the exception. Indeed, in the few years which have elapsed since this book was first published the warnings sounded in it have been amply justified by a series of coups arising at least in part from the malpractices portrayed by Dumont. Unless these are eradicated in the near future still more régimes can expect to be overthrown. Despite the encouraging examples set by Tanzania and Zambia, Dumont's constructive criticisms are as valid now as when they were first made.

As Professor Dumont has done, I shall quote African criticism as substance for my own. For Africans, entering the international jungle for the first time, cajoled, bullied, ingratiated, condemned from all sides, are inevitably sensitive to criticism. Nevertheless, like others who have participated in African campaigns against colonialism and feel involved in African affairs after independence, I cannot shed my urge to offer constructive criticism where I believe the cause of a just African society is at stake. Sycophancy is false friendship. And those who fought colonialism did so not only because they preferred to see black rather than white faces behind ministerial desks. We all fought because we hated the indignities and inequalities of colonial rule; because colonialism, like capitalism, assigns power arbitrarily; because it combines wealth and non-representative government as unbridled authorities; because it stems from the principle of innate inequality between human beings. But the fight was concerned with African *people*, not simply with constitutional changes nor with the replacement of arbitrary colonial administrations by equally arbitrary African oligarchies. The aim has always been to help to create healthy, just, democratic societies. And the most profound evidence that Africa has indeed made a 'false start' is that in virtually every African state the socio-economic gulf between the peasant masses and the urban *élites* is even greater than the gap between those *élites* and the European and North American norm.

Again, with Professor Dumont, the main burden of my criticism is laid at the door of the colonial legacy, while I entirely agree that some African rethinking, together with international co-operation, can still transform African society within a generation. It is in order to raise some intellectual challenges to those responsible for African development that I offer this small addition to Professor Dumont's sympathetic, profound critique of African trends.

Much of the criticism he directs to former French Africa applies equally to the ex-British territories. Yet there are certain significant differences. There are probably more exceptions in English-speaking Africa from the general trend towards imitating Europe. The Gezira scheme in the Sudan proved that agricultural co-operation can be successful in Africa given intelligent, devoted leadership. It has been followed by the significant example of co-operative self-help amongst the coffee-growing Chagga on the slopes of Kilimanjaro. Cotton ginneries in Uganda have reinforced the same lesson. I remember visiting Machakos in Kenya at the height of the Mau Mau war and being amazed at the transformation effected since my previous visit four years earlier. Under the persuasive leadership of the local District Commissioner and his tiny group of experts, what had been stark red beacons of eroded hills were now transformed into wooded, terraced slopes, dotted with trim, white-washed homes. By convincing the local Kamba leadership first, the administration had been able to show the tribe how to help itself by combining agricultural reform, community development and rural education. One of the finest and simplest films ever made in Africa was the Crown Film Unit's 'Daybreak in Udi', depicting the true story of a Nigerian village building its own maternity home.

The tragedy is that most of these instances have to be quoted from colonial times. In the first ten years after the second war a community spirit of self-help seemed to be engendered, only to be frequently lost just before and after independence.

The general experience of British Africans has been the same as their French cousins. Slavery disrupted the indigenous development of African society. Colonialism brought the economic and social life of Africans under the control of European governments and companies. Economic exploitation distorted African development to serve the needs of the metropolitan peoples. Even in the post-war period of aid and investment the pattern has remained unbroken. Capital has been mainly attracted to mining—to South Africa, the Rhodesias and the Congo—while much of the expanded infrastructure has been designed to facilitate trade to Britain. Even when large-scale development was attempted in the Tanganyikan groundnuts scheme, the major motive was to supply British oil needs and lack of intelligent planning resulted in a fiasco.

Meanwhile, Britain has been priding herself on her generosity in providing Colonial Development and Welfare Funds, as the French have in supplying F I D E S. Yet the same mistakes have been made in London as in Paris. Too often the funds were subconsciously regarded as conscience-money, with scant thought for the manner or consequences of their use. They were allocated by the Colonial Office to separate colonial governments, thus being confined to the strait-jackets of unviable political units which inhibited coherent planning. They were controlled by the Treasury, which automatically pared down estimates and thus often distorted plans. Above all, they were administered in the paternalistic spirit of British aristocratic tradition which assumed that African society should accept British values. Thus C D & W took its place in a colonial administration which was setting African sights on the British standards of a national establishment, an intellectual *élite*, white-collared superiority over manual labour, and social security. As one of Africa's most intelligent young men, the late Dunduzu Chisiza, once put it, 'Social security in an underdeveloped economy is something very close to a luxury. Scarcely any of the advanced countries ever provided it in the early stages of development. None could have afforded it without arresting capital formation. The same would seem to go for present-day underdeveloped countries.' (*Africa – What Lies Ahead*, D. K. Chisiza, New York, 1962.)

The consequence was that Africans at the time of independence were bequeathed a vicious circle. The more developed sector of their economic life was mainly geared to export crops whose production was not related to the nutritional needs of the rural masses. Research programmes were largely devoted to the same objective. The luxury demands of their *élites*, who imitated the social habits of expatriates, absorbed most of their foreign exchange earnings and endangered the reserves inherited from colonial rule. Meanwhile, as a result of population increases and decreasing primary product prices on the world market, many rural populations were actually becoming poorer with declining nutritional standards. And this cycle obstructed both the agrarian and the industrial revolutions essential to any satisfaction of 'rising expectations'. Without healthy rural markets viable industries were not possible.

It may be said – and many Africans do say it – that this disastrous economic situation must be laid entirely at the door of British colonialism. But this is to insult African leaders by treating them as purely passive operators – helpless victims of a predetermined situation. In fact, Nkrumah had shown an example of the potential power of African leadership long before independence when his government persuaded the cocoa farmers to eradicate swollen shoot disease after a complete failure on the part of the colonial government. However spurious the legacy bequeathed by the colonialists, African leaders cannot be absolved from the responsibility of meeting the challenges of those societies they have undertaken to govern. And when thousands of pounds are squandered on lavish weddings it is not only the British contributors to War on Want who are disillusioned but African dedication which is undermined. When, out of the Nigerian Federal Government's total annual expenditure of some £86 million, the eighty members of the government cost nearly £1 million, not to mention the expense of 160 members of Regional Governments – no one should have been surprised at the discontent which was expressed in military coups, nor in the failure of civilian government. Nor should anyone be surprised if the presently unorganized peasants eventually revolt against such 'colonialism of class'.

Once it became known in Africa that many public men were salting away private fortunes in Swiss banks, that dishonesty in public life was rife, retribution quickly followed. Despite Nkrumah's many exhortations the ostentation of public life in Ghana, the hoarding of scarce consumer goods by public officials, wives and relations, and massive corruption played a crucial role in the collapse of his régime. As the masses in other countries realize that public men are stealing their wealth similar repercussions can be expected.

Meanwhile, the use of import capital for luxury consumer goods, or even for non-nutritive foods like flour and sugar, and profiteering in administration, is obstructing the import of machines and essential raw materials. Even more important, it is corrupting the spirit of the community, destroying the effects of any appeal to the hard work and sacrifice which alone can overcome the obstacles to Africa's economic 'take-off'.

There is another facet of this imitation British upper-middle-

10

class life, this assumption of the comforts of an affluent society in the midst of their own people's poverty. Much of the public money is spent on urban prestige projects whilst the rural areas are neglected and forgotten. To quote Chisiza again, 'Neglect of rural areas stems mainly from the fact that modern African political leaders are creatures of the towns. Most of them grow up, live and die in urban centres – even if they may be born in rural areas. They tend, there-fore, to be more attached to urban areas than to rural areas. This tendency is reflected in development activities. Driven by their desire to have within easy reach a few "show pieces" to point to when distinguished foreign guests visit their countries, and made complacent by their rather superficial knowledge of conditions in rural areas, African leaders – and others in similar situations – devote most of their development resources to towns.' So the stream to the towns where modern amenities are available – even for the thousands of unemployed – which is denuding the countryside of many of its intelligent sons is accentuated. And meanwhile, scores of stadiums, monuments, conference halls, luxury hotels, palaces, motorways are built, expensive jet aeroplanes purchased, steel mills planned, television services opened – while the peasant finds his ration of rice or maize becoming ever smaller.

These circumstances are the products of policies controlled by men – African men – not by such abstractions as 'neo-colonialism'. And they can be changed by men. Of course, colonial rule left a bad heritage. Little had been done to increase the domestic markets and there was virtually no inter-African trade. Though primary exports were sometimes marketed through public boards, their prices were left to the mercy of the world market; and European social values had been fostered which led directly away from the measures needed for economic development. But this is no excuse for African leaders to pursue the same policies after independence.

It is true that some attempts have been made to break the mould of colonial socio-economic policies. President Nyerere of Tanzania has been moving in this direction since independence. The Arusha Declaration, with its emphasis on self-reliance, rural community development allied to small industries, and strict austerity in public life, marks the highest point of economic independence yet reached in the continent. President Kaunda of Zambia is following Nyerere's example, though with variations inevitable in his vastly different environment. Zambia's copper wealth provides resources unknown to Tanzania. It supplies the foundation for a vast national revolution in living standards, yet, at the same time, it imposes the dangerous problem of a large, privileged urban community, living on standards out of sight for the vast majority of Zambians. Nevertheless, and despite all the pressures arising from the rebellion across his borders in Rhodesia and the distortion of Zambia's economy which has resulted, Kaunda has kept steadily to his determination that social justice shall be established in his country. This has led him directly to try and concentrate on rural renaissance to raise the living standards of the mass of his people. The fact that in 1968 Zambia became self-sufficient in protein-giving eggs is one small, but significant evidence of success in this endeavour.

The case of Ghana is one of the most pertinent, though still ambiguous illustrations of this argument. In the early Ghanaian development plans the strongest emphasis was laid on rapid industrialization and the provision of widespread social services. Only about 10 per cent of development capital was allocated to productive investment. Inevitably this led to administrative indigestion and a constant drain on reserves. The nation's economic activities were simply not capable of providing the resources which were being used. Food production, badly neglected, could not keep pace with the growth of urban population. So imports rose rapidly to provide the food, raw materials and machinery needed within the new economic structure. Capital had to be sought abroad, whilst the overseas balances had to bridge the gap between export earnings and external expenditure. Always, of course, revenue fluctuated wildly as the price of cocoa, which provided three-quarters of export income, rose or fell unpredictably. In 1954 it was £562 10s. a ton, in 1965 £100.

By 1964 it seemed that the lesson had been learnt. The new Seven Year Plan allocated over 37 per cent to productive sectors, planned to rise to over 48 per cent by its last year. Production of food and raw materials was to be stimulated by loans to farmers and fishermen, farms were to be modernized, forests tended, agricultural research and education encouraged. The Minister of Agriculture was heard to declare, 'Instead of the farmers and fishermen producing enough to meet the bare needs of their families, they are now producing a little more to meet the needs of a few more. The target for the moment, however, is to get them each to produce as much as can feed themselves and their families and ten more people.'

It was too late. The wasteful spending of the past had exhausted reserves. Ostentatious luxury alongside poverty had sapped the trust of the masses. The public administrative machine had been rusted by corruption and was no longer capable of putting the new policies into practice. The full story of the coup which overthrew Nkrumah and his régime in 1966 is still to be told, but it is significant that no popular rising in his defence accompanied it.

So since 1966 the mantle of socio-economic leadership has been assumed by Tanzania and Zambia. Yet in each of them there remain large obstacles to the realistic policies which alone can produce essential socio-economic revolutions. In Tanzania the lack of trained administrators, misuse of local powers, shortage of materials, absence of co-ordination between local and central planning, often reduces excellent paper plans to chaos in practice. There also seems to be some danger that too many resources are being allocated to unproductive building in Dar es Salaam, where large hotels are now proliferating. The failure to secure an East African Federation and the difficulties of associating in a Common Market with Kenya and Uganda, whose policies are very different, raise considerable obstacles to planned development.

Zambia is also short of trained manpower, a shortage of which will be aggravated as ex-patriates and their wives (who provide most of the efficient secretarial services) return home. In 1965, Zambia had about 100 university graduates, about 1,500 people with full secondary education, and about 6,000 with two years at secondary school. But the toughest obstacle faced by the modernizers of Zambia arises from the multi-racial character of her population. This is a problem generally more severely suffered in British than in French Africa – except perhaps in the Ivory Coast. It is vividly described by Dudley Seers in his Report to the Government of Zambia on the Economic Development of Zambia. 'In every town there are Europeans enjoying in plain view vastly superior standards of living, housing, education and medical care. This very small minority have the best-paid jobs in the mines and the railways, work the most prosperous farms and own nearly all the financial wealth. They also hold almost every senior position in the civil service.

'But the Government is no longer in European hands. . . . Economic and social power has been abruptly divorced from political power. Since the great majority of the population are impatient for economic and social change, this dichotomy could prove dangerous.' (Chapter 1, page 1.)

This contrast between European and African living standards menaces both civil peace and economic development throughout British central and eastern Africa. It provides each government with the dilemma of needing to attract European-trained personnel, who at the same time will promote jealousy, friction, and destructive social examples. I recently stayed at an hotel on the Copperbelt where the menu included the item: 'Caviar, specially flown from Iran, 32/6.' What a use of foreign exchange!

Meanwhile, both Tanzania and Zambia are beset by the universal African dangers arising from unemployment. Accurate statistics do not exist, but the 1963 Zambian census showed 57,000 urban unemployed, over 40,000 rural males 'seeking paid work', and another half a million other males over the age of sixteen divided between 'self-employed' and 'not employed'. In fact, only about 250,000 Africans – one in fourteen – were in paid employment. In Dar es Salaam, despite Government coercion to return vagrants to their villages, the number of unemployed residents continues to grow. Because of the large number of children under the age of fifteen in both countries, these figures of unemployment must be expected to increase over the next few years.

It is in Ghana that the dichotomy between progressive economic development and destructive misuse of resources can be seen most vividly. We have already noted some of the most hopeful trends in the new Seven Year Development Plan. When the great Volta River scheme is added, together with massive educational advances and the constant exhortations to dedicated austerity, the broad lines of a progressive policy can be perceived. Yet we have also seen how the demand for luxury imports has diminished Ghana's ability to secure resources essential to her economic growth. President Nkrumah's frequent pleas for frugality did not lead to the disappearance of corruption or ostentation. The government itself, by spending scarce resources on expensive embassies, allowing regular supplementary allocations to government departments, purchasing the latest aircraft, tolerating inefficient state corporations, building unproductive palaces and prestige conference edifices, often belied its own principles. Moreover, its premature concentration on social services, industrialization and public building directed resources and attention away from the agricultural rejuvenation essential to underpin other forms of development. Thus food imports doubled between 1952 and 1962, becoming almost five times those of the West African regional average. And it is significant that only 4·5 per cent of these imports consisted of low income foods. The consequence of allowing these contradictory features to undermine her main policy is that favourable trade balances were transformed into unfavourable balances of payments, with the inevitable shortage of foreign exchange. Even more serious, Ghana now had to move into reverse, leaving many of her industrial and social projects uncompleted, whilst she tried to turn back her urban class from their expectations of comparative luxury and repair the neglect of her agriculture. Ghana's economic future, including the success of the vast Volta River Dam and its industrial complex, now depended on whether she could pare down unnecessary business and prestige expenditure, exorcize corruption, force her privileged urban class to accept heavy taxation (which led them to incite the working class to dangerous strikes in 1961) and radically increase her agricultural production before her constructive plans collapse into bankruptcy. She failed.

If Tanzania and Zambia are the most hopeful countries in British Africa, the story of much of the rest is similar to that told of French Africa by Professor Dumont. Promising agricultural development schemes in Kenya are menaced by tribal jealousies and the impending withdrawal of expatriate officers. Uganda is still rent by the struggle between the modernizers and the traditionalists, whilst luxury spending is by no means unknown in Kampala. Malawi, with her scarce resources, has to waste her slight wealth on fratricidal conflict, despite Dr Banda's calls for dedication to national development. Rhodesia remains a white man's country economically, its caste system perpetuating poverty for the masses beside luxury amongst the few Europeans. In Sierra Leone the heavy hand of traditionalism is reinforced by a slavish aping of British manners among the more sophisticated Creoles. Under such social conditions the economy inevitably continues to stagnate. In Nigeria a combination of tribal, political and social conflicts allowed a financial-commercial oligarchy to live in luxury. The conditions which precipitated the coups of 1966, and which have certainly not been entirely removed by the army, were described by a Nigerian:

'. . . a small privileged group lives in comfort and even luxury. They enjoy the fruits of office and make fortunes through their association with foreign business and other interests. Investments continue to yield even fatter profits which are not put into further economic development which is urgently desired but go to sustain a life of luxury for financiers and to cushion the "high standards of living" of people thousands of miles away from Nigeria. This small group of privileged men employ every method – from imprisonment through blackmail to bribery – in defence of the present system because their wealth and fortunes are tied up with the status quo. And whenever this small group of privileged men hint at the need for change, what they really mean are adjustments (especially in our constitution) which will strengthen their position in and their control over the Nigerian society.' (S. G. Ikoku, *Nigeria for Nigerians*).

There is widespread talk of iron and steel mills whilst rice is imported into rice-growing countries. (I once stopped to buy some nuts in a Sierra Leone village store. The village was surrounded by nut trees, but the only nuts sold were in tins imported from England. The storekeeper told me that this was because of 'imperialism'.) Ministers and public servants are driving Humbers, Mercedes and Cadillacs while the majority of the population are hungry; VC10s are flying to the international airports, but village roads are impassable; air-conditioning is found in new palaces and offices, whilst mosquitoes return to the neglected slums. Even agrarian development itself often favours the rich. In Nigeria, for example, a farm settlement scheme cost £3,000 per farm unit to raise output to £500 per annum. Yet the national average is under £50 per farming unit whilst the national average per capita income is only £30.

Professor Dumont has offered simple, inexpensive, grass-root remedies which depend more on a spirit of service than on new resources. I entirely endorse his suggestions and will not repeat them. But in one respect, I believe British Africa has got off to an even worse start than the French territories. This is in education. It is typified by the fact that although Fourah Bay College in Sierra Leone was founded in 1827 it is estimated that it will take until 1990 before universal primary education can be achieved in the same country.

One of the worst contributions made by Britain to Africa in the post-war period has been the universities. Short-sighted colonial educationalists have scattered around British Africa a series of 'Oxbridges' which are not only irrelevant to African needs but positive barriers to development. In their imitation caps and gowns African undergraduates recite Latin graces, retire to luxurious hostel rooms, are waited on by 'native' servants, study European history and learn to become 'gentlemen', contemptuous of those who dirty their hands. Voluminous academic gowns are hardly the most appropriate form of dress in tropical humidity, and even the common European accoutrements of jacket and tie are all too often used to indicate 'class'.

The consequences of this imitation British aristocratic educational system have been that the very type of work most needed in Africa – agricultural work – is now despised by the educated; unemployment among the educated classes is growing; and the gulf between the *élites* and the peasants – manual workers – party activists is rapidly widening. Yet the social values of the Europeans have been so deeply absorbed that few African leaders have had the courage to make a fresh start. The practical education of village schools closely associated with the agricultural skills needed for a rural renascence has yet to be conceived. Meanwhile UNESCO has entered the scene, only to increase the follies. Its 1961 Addis Ababa conference declared that the cost of formal education in the continent should rise from the $550 million spent in 1960 to $1,150 million in 1965 and $2,600 million by 1980. This would need $1,000 million a year in foreign aid to sustain it, about double the total foreign aid now provided for Africa. And the plan presupposes a continuation of student and teacher facilities based on European standards – i.e. £3,500 for a secondary school teacher's house, in countries where the average annual income is £20–£30!

If African leaders are genuinely concerned to use educational facilities and budgets for the welfare of their whole societies, they will close their luxury universities to their own undergraduates and offer them as pleasant (and expensive) resorts for visiting American scholars to conduct seminars on foundation resources! The money saved would be more than sufficient to finance the agricultural, technical colleges at which crash programmes can train young Africans to go back to their villages and revolutionize agricultural production or to supply the increasing number of technicians which will be needed in factories and workshops. The Latin and Greek can safely be reserved for the leisured classes of two generations hence after the fruits of the economic revolution have been gathered – though by then they will probably have found more interesting and realistic subjects for study.

Most African leaders talk of their policies as based on 'African Socialism'. Whatever adjective is used to qualify the term, the concept of 'Socialism' must always be directly related to the welfare of the mass of the people and to social equality. Yet it seems obvious from present trends that many African countries are running the risk of becoming Latin American racketeering oligarchies – or Arabian oil plutocracies. The masses – who are still the peasants – are being not merely neglected but exploited by the new politico-commercial régimes. This is not inevitable; it is the product of men's policies. Many of Africa's leaders will still see some of the peasant's soil adhering to their boots – if they are not too proud to look. The extensive family links have not yet been entirely broken, the opportunity for African leaders to remember the villagers from whom they sprang is still there and can provide opportunities for societies to be built on social justice. But, as Dumont says, 'Socialism and Democracy are more demanding than Fascism and Capitalism.'

This book is not only addressed to Africans; Europe and North
10*

America are also involved. It is a great tragedy that just at the historical moment when socialist ideals are most relevant to the Two Worlds, rich and poor, of the twentieth century, European social democratic parties seem to be losing the last vestiges of their internationalist spirit. They concern themselves with balances of payments, common markets, containing communism, blind to the fact that the social justice which is their justification for existence is now an international issue between the developed and the underdeveloped. Numerous excuses can be offered for Britain contributing just over 1 per cent of her national income to the underdeveloped countries – they always have – but they can only be offered in a *national* context. And to concentrate on *national* issues is to accept a world in which the gap between the poor two-thirds and the rich third steadily widens – with inevitable catastrophe for all national interests.

For it is time that a number of stark realities on the international stage were recognized. Despite widespread belief that the underdeveloped peoples have been supplied with massive economic aid by the richer countries since the war, the fact is that the worsening terms of trade due to low primary produce prices have more than wiped out the value of all public aid. At the same time, increases in population are drastically reducing the effects of development. In Africa the annual rate of population increase amounts to about 2·4 per cent – perhaps more, no one knows – compared with 0·9 in Europe, 1·6 in North America and 1·7 in the USSR. This population explosion and the lack of interest in agriculture has resulted in a failure of food to keep pace with people. Food production in Africa rose by no more than 13 per cent from the mid-fifties to the mid-sixties compared with an average of 21 per cent over the world as a whole. Production of food per head in Africa was actually 1 per cent lower than before the war.

It is thus clear to those who will see, that the gap between rich and poor in the world is steadily widening. The remedy for this dangerous international threat is greatly increased aid from rich countries to poor. It was estimated by the UN that if the rich states were to allocate 1 per cent of their gross national products to economic aid, the developing countries could reach half-way to the objective of the Development Decade – a growth in their national incomes of 5 per cent per annum by 1970 – and so keep pace with the rich. Even that would not actually decrease inequality, but at least this modest aim would allow poor countries to do no more than double their standards of living in twenty to thirty years. We are far from achieving it. The standard of living in Tanzania is still only what you can get for £20 a year.

Harold Wilson wrote a book, *War on World Poverty*, some time ago (Gollancz, 1953). In it he proposed that a World Development Authority should be created to make a concerted international attack on poverty. And he posed the question of what Britain should do if America refused to co-operate. His answer was unequivocal: '. . . she must be ready, in the American phrase, to "go it alone", or at any rate to go it with as much support as she can secure from Commonwealth, Scandinavian and other countries. She should propose the establishment of a World Development Authority, even without American support, and to show her good faith, pledge her contribution – the £350–£400 millions necessarily in sterling – to its work.'

Yet under a Labour Government with Harold Wilson as Prime Minister, Britain's contribution to international aid reached a total of only 0·6 per cent of gross national product – around £200 million annually. Moreover, part of this was allocated to loans to the ex-British colonies so that they might pay compensation and pensions to British ex-colonial civil servants! Making the newly independent states pay for the costs of their past colonial administration hardly comes under the category of 'aid'. Further, another section in this aid budget consisted of loans at commercial rates of interest. Again, this practice, necessitating the payment of high interest rates in addition to repayment, can only be classified as 'aid' by unjustifiably stretching the definition. It is to the credit of the Labour Government, and particularly of Barbara Castle, then Minister of Overseas Development, that interest-free loans were introduced in mid-1965.

Yet the burden of the charge remains. Britain is simply not facing up to the realities of mid-twentieth-century international life. It is not enough to plead balance of payments difficulties. This problem basically concerns only the rich nations of the world and their relations with each other. The least that can be done is to guarantee that when immediate difficulties have been surmounted, increased aid to the poor countries will become a first priority. In the meantime, surely tied loans and grants, even based on the 'in kind' principle, can be multiplied without seriously worsening balance of payment deficits. It has now become evident, and admitted by the government, that such economic aid is of great value to the expansion of British trade. A more virile, adventurous aid policy, reinforced by the kind of measures proposed by UNCTAD to allow the exports of developing countries to expand, could well pay surprising dividends for a trading country such as Britain.

Today there are many young people in Britain seeking a national lead to practise their humanitarian concern on an international stage – those who work for causes like War on Want, Oxfam, Freedom from Hunger, Christian Action. But charitable organizations, however laudable, can never meet the massive challenge of twentieth-century poverty; 'amateur' contributions are no substitute for the trained 'professionals' who are so desperately lacking.

Today, when a great part of the socialist battle has been won within the European states, its original international character is more significant than ever. For the domestic class conflict has been transformed into a struggle between the rich and the poor, privileged and deprived, master and slave, amongst nations. The significance of socialism today is its involvement in this international class war being waged between the rich and the poor segments of the world. The British Labour Party is uniquely placed to lead the fight. But this will only become possible when the British Labour Party is courageous enough to give a lead to the British people themselves; when its leaders are prepared to appeal to the same humanitarian sentiments, the same sense of justice as the slave emancipators and early socialists of last century. Nothing less than a deliberate call for the British people to forego a part of their rising living standards, consume less of their own production and allocate the surplus to the world's deprived can create the moral spirit needed for the relevant socialistic policies of today. If British Labour is not prepared to combine this spirit of international social justice with its exhortations to greater production it will find itself leading the nation towards the sterile values of the American consumer-gorged society – and faced by the rising wrath of the world's proletarian nations. Of course there is a new world of material opportunities to be gained from the potential expansion of markets from today's handicapped consumers. But it is only from conviction in social justice that the call to dedicated effort can be revived, its objectives given a moral purpose and the spirit of international socialism reborn. British Labour will have to choose between remaining a member of the exclusive rich nations' club or participating in the Third World struggle for international social justice.

Yet increased economic aid alone is not enough. A great deal of aid over the past ten years has been wasted or has actually impeded progress. Economic assistance used to bolster corrupt reactionary régimes is both futile and regressive. If the object of aid is to provide self-fuelling economies one of the objectives will be to stimulate social revolution. Whether the African peasants' revolts come through violence or peaceful transformation depends on the intelligence of African leaders. But until they appear, neither agricultural renascence nor industrial growth are possible. Paul Hoffman estimated that to raise income per capita in all the underdeveloped areas of the world by no more than £10 during the 1960s from its current £30 demanded an increase of development capital by £1,000 million a year. So long as the bribery and counter-bribery of the Cold War continues even this colossal increase could be well wasted. If America and Russia are genuinely concerned with removing the menace to world peace of international poverty they will have to forge the means of co-operating in economic assistance.

Even with existing aid programmes, greatly increased dividends could accrue from new policies. There has rightly been a great outcry against 'aid with strings', but surely the 'strings' objected to are political reins. The new British Ministry of Overseas Development can only be effective if it is given the resources to distribute. But unless such resources are used discriminatingly they will become as sterile as in the past. The Ministry needs to be tough along socialist principles. It made a constructive start in 1965 by publishing a White Paper laying down a philosophy of aid for the first time. (Though it is difficult to see how its proposal to recruit professional experts from Britain to serve in the developing countries can be reconciled with the new immigration policy designed to attract similarly trained people from the Commonwealth nations to this country.) Aid must be concentrated where there is seen to be a genuine attempt to plan combined agrarian-industrial revolutions, where the co-operative method of agriculture and industrial production has been introduced, and where administrations are reasonably honest and dedicated. Instead of building cloisters for African universities every support should be given to village schools and agricultural colleges; instead of luxury urban hospitals, rural clinics should be encouraged; in place of expensive tractors, carts, hoes, spades should be bought. Above all, foreign aid must break loose from the acceptance of existing sovereign states as the units for development. It is sheer waste of resources to support the building of separate iron and steel industries in neighbouring countries. Here the Economic Commission for Africa is giving an outstanding lead. It would be far more productive and a great deal more helpful to the majority of African peoples to support the E C A regional, multi-national efforts at development (including an integrated iron and steel industry for East Africa) than to encourage the wasteful prestigious projects of many individual African states. Meanwhile, in the field of primary products, on the export of which most African states will have to depend for many years to pay for imports, export quotas, production controls and the removal of taxation or import restriction on tropical products should be priorities for any socialist government. If the Labour Party is serious in breaking the hold of world prices on African economics, some effort will have to be made to lower tariff barriers and offer protection to their infant industrial exports.

The social and economic revolution needed to break the strangle-hold of African poverty can only come from idealism, self-sacrifice and dedication. We cannot call on Africans to practise such qualities unless we are willing to participate in them ourselves. The same rule applies to African leaders. Whether the African revolutions develop peacefully or violently depends on the character of the co-operation between the developed and the developing world and on the speed with which African leaders return to social justice as the objective of independence. They might well reread Franz Fanon's words, 'The bourgeois leaders of underdeveloped countries imprison national consciousness in sterile formalism. It is only when men and women are included on a vast scale in enlightened and fruitful work that form and body are given to that consciousness. Then the flag and the palace where sits the government cease to be the symbols of the nation. The nation deserts these brightly-lit, empty shells and takes shelter in the country, where it is given life and dynamic power. The living expression of the nation is the moving consciousness of the whole of the people, it is the coherent, enlightened action of men and women. The collective building up of a destiny is the assumption of responsibility on the historical scale. Otherwise there is anarchy, repression and the resurgence of tribal parties and federalism. The national government, if it wants to be national, ought to govern by the people and for the people, for the outcasts and by the outcasts. No leader however valuable he may be can substitute himself for the popular will, and the national government, before concerning itself about international prestige, ought first to give back dignity to all citizens, fill their minds and feast their eyes with human things, and create a prospect that is human because conscious and sovereign men dwell therein.' (Frantz Fanon, *The Wretched of the Earth*, MacGibbon and Kee, p. 103.)

APPENDIX I (See Chapter Three, 4)

THE RICHARD TOLL RICE-GROWING SCHEME IN SENEGAL

In 1949 Senegal undertook a more modest project than that of the Niger Office. All the same, 6,000 hectares of irrigated land in the Richard Toll rice-growing scheme, in the lower valley of the Senegal River near Saint-Louis, still cost three billion CFA francs, or a million old francs per irrigated hectare. The average yields are twenty-six quintals per hectare, sold here for seventeen francs a kilo; but there is not much possibility of cultivating cotton here. Conceived during the years of war scarcity, the project has cost far more than envisaged, because of inadequate preliminary studies, and a narrow agricultural engineering viewpoint. An invasion by small grain-eating birds, the Quelea, threatened to ruin the entire project. Mechanized rice cultivation, the rule here, remains very largely a deficit enterprise. Wild rice is invading the rice fields increasingly, and the 1961 harvest was a very difficult one.

Only one small sector of 300 hectares was turned over to settlers in 1957. Methods of selecting the settlers were extremely questionable, as they were based on political considerations. Some of the settlers began to operate with paid workers or share-croppers; this tendency had been apparent at the Niger Office as far back as 1950.

The land development service prepared the ground with tractors, and advanced seeds. The settlers have not maintained the canals or the drains properly, nor have they maintained their rice fields correctly. They harvested 18·5 quintals in 1960 (as against 27 in 1959) and paid nine quintals of rent per hectare. Their net return per day of work (about forty days per hectare) was thus more than 400 CFA francs in 1960, more than 700 francs in 1959. This is much higher than that of many Mediterranean peasants. In the rest of the country, the average daily income of the Senegalese peasant is between 70 and 160 francs.

The result is that very high public expenses have enabled a few favoured people to secure an income without working for it. Those that work themselves obtain an income three to five times higher. This fact was often put forward to justify granting more funds to the Niger Office. The role of these credits in fact was to create among the rural population a new group of privileged people, a kind of rural middle class to swell the ranks of the urban middle class created by other F I D E S funds.

APPENDIX II (See Chapter Five, 4)

CONTINUOUS CULTIVATION: PIGS AND MILK IN THE SAKAY, MADAGASCAR

In 1953 the Bureau for Agricultural Development (BDPA) was put in charge of installing settlers from Reunion Island on the heavily populated plateaux in western Madagascar. They lived miserably there on the prescribed lots, which were soon washed out by erosion because the incline was too steep. This was the last 'manifestation' of white colonization in Madagascar. Like Martinique and Guadeloupe, Reunion Island must from now on attack the anguishing problem of over-population from all sides at once: birth control, industrialization, and intensive agricultural development. Emigration alone cannot solve it.

Debatable as the entire operation was, it has technical results of the highest interest to Madagascar. These 'white' settlers, who resembled fine old pirates more than anything, were totally uprooted and in unfamiliar surroundings, but were further advanced technically and much more receptive to the advice of the experts than the Malagasies. After the failure of the first attempts at continuous cultivation, which did not 'rest' the soil during a long fallow period (particularly at Yangambi, research centre of the ex-Belgian Congo), the Congress of Goma concluded in 1948, prematurely, that fallow periods were absolutely necessary.

The hills or *tanety* of Madagascar were, as I mentioned before, generally thought to be infertile. The leader of the operation, Thomas, quickly realized that to achieve continuous cultivation (necessitated by the population explosion) without ruining the soil, two measures were essential: erosion prevention and organic fertilizers. He also realized that since they were 175 kilometres from the capital, the crops of this savannah zone, necessarily 'poor' (mostly manioc and corn, in the beginning), should be turned into animal feed right on the spot.

Aside from receiving large credits, the operation was facilitated by the high price of pork, which had become very scarce after an epidemic. I have discussed elsewhere[1] the rotation they adopted, which alternates corn, a leguminous plant (both for feed and green fertilizer) and manioc, for eighteen to twenty months, followed by three years of fallow, during which time leguminous plants grow along with wild grasses.

As it can be used for pasture, this 'controlled' fallow land is on a level with European meadows, on which grasses spring up after a crop is harvested. This practice originated with the English ley-farming system, whereby arable land was turned into pasture for varying periods. I have rebaptized it 'feed revolution' to encourage its spread. Agronomy can use modern publicity methods as well as any other field.

In 1961, a much more productive solution was discovered, with the magnificent success of three grasses in planted meadows.[2] Without fertilizer, a hundred tons of green grass was harvested per hectare in three mowings. This can feed enough cows to produce roughly 10,000 litres of milk, if they are also given supplementary protein. With fertilizers, fifty to sixty tons were obtained per mowing. The 'natural and permanent' meadows in the Auge country in France, which are too natural and permanent, have a ceiling of around 3,000 to 4,000 litres of milk per hectare from the cows that graze them.

[1] *Evolution des Campagnes Malgaches*, pp. 117–222.
[2] *Chloris gayana*, especially suitable for hay; *Brachiaria ruzizensis* which resists trampling well; *Melinis mintiflora*, which is hardier, very common in South America, and should be used as pasture with care, never over-grazed nor mown close to the ground.

The Pangola in Cuba (*Digitaria decumbens*) can supply cattle with enough to produce as much as 1,300 kilos of meat per hectare annually, on estates, with irrigation and fertilizer. This is twice the yield from the best sown grazing meadows in Europe, and the quadruple of our 'good' wild fields. The alfalfa fields of Mexico, as well as the Beauport Pangola in Guadeloupe, produce twice as much as the best fields in the Netherlands.

Results in the Sakay region confirm the idea that tropical livestock is in no way inferior to that of the temperate zone. I am persuaded that it will surpass it one day, when it catches up in techniques. There is no doubt that cattle thrive in the cool weather there, due to the height, which is 900 metres. Frisians, the most productive breed in the world, can be kept there if well fed. The BDPA dairy farm is already producing 3,200 litres of milk per season (the maximum is 6,000), and will go over 4,000 litres in five years. Milk is sold for twenty-five CFA francs a litre, but could be sold for twenty francs as early as 1966. Starting in 1970 the capital can be supplied with milk from its suburbs, which can compete with the imported milks.

At that point, the Sakay region will be in a position to start a dairy industry economically, supplying butter and cheese, then powdered milk, and later on concentrated milk. It would be a big mistake to stop at the stage of butter, and give the skimmed milk to the pigs, because the protein deficiency in human food intake is much more serious than the fat deficiency in the tropics. The European outlook, which calculates everything in terms of income, can be detected in this wastage. The tropical countries should also breed dairy cows whose milk has a high protein content, and not put the primary emphasis on butter content.[1] They should also start to save all the skimmed milk right away for the peasants' and herders' children.

Until now pig raising has not been profitable unless prices are high, around 100 CFA francs per live kilogram. This is because expensive imported proteins and meat and fish meals are fed to the pigs. In order to reduce costs, the leaves of leguminous plants,

[1] Cf. the study of P. Auriol on the protein content of milk in *Bulletin Technique d'Information des Services Agricoles*, No. 168, April, 1962.

together with banana leaves, can be used. Peanuts can be introduced in crop rotation systems and ground in a local oil factory. This would supply oil cakes, an economical source of proteins. It could satisfy human protein needs along with skimmed milk before being fed to the livestock.

The Sakay could undertake cotton cultivation, thereby orienting itself towards modern agriculture, which is characterized by the relative subordination of food crops, and subsistence economy, to industrial crops, feed crops and intensive livestock raising. The future development of the hills of central and western Madagascar, on at least two million hectares, already has a nucleus of agro-industrial development and a solid technical base to work with. The next step will be to spread the knowledge and techniques to the Malagasies themselves, in a more constructive way than Somasak has done.[1]

APPENDIX III (See Chapter Five, 4)

COTTON CULTIVATION BY PEASANTS WITH CADRES

In Ubangi Shari and Chad a method of developing cotton plantations, similar to one used in the neighbouring ex-Belgian Congo, made a very poor start in 1924–1929. The peasants were forced to plant cotton, and each adult had to work thirty-five to fifty ares (one are is 100 square metres). The cotton was carried on the peasant's head to far distant points of purchase, was often weighed on false scales, and the village chiefs, who were paid for all the cotton, could keep almost all the profit. During my 1949–1950 trip there, the crop was still obligatory even in areas too humid for it, where yields were not always even 100 kilos of cottonseed per hectare! However, markets were closer, the scales inspected, and the growers themselves were paid directly for the cotton. The abuses

---

[1] In 1961, the amount spent on education and organization by this development company was higher than the value of the gross production of the peasants.

of the traders, which I still found in Madagascar in 1961–1962, had been suppressed, which proves that it can be done.

Given a choice between the depopulated 'fifth zone' studied in Chad to the west of Shari, and North Cameroon, I did not hesitate to propose the latter for an expansion in cotton cultivation. In 1960–1961, 28,500 tons of cottonseed were harvested there, on nearly 60,000 hectares, with a yield of more than 800 kilos in the best districts. The same year Chad, with twenty years of cultivation behind it, and a more favourable climate, had not gone over 350 kilos per hectare.

In March I took a good look at the CFDT (*Compagnie Française pour le Développement des Textiles*) at work in Mali, near Segou and Koutiala. Traditional methods of growing cotton yield no more than 175 kilos a hectare there. The small group of two hundred villagers that had followed the advice of the CFDT fairly well had just harvested an average of 800 kilos per hectare. The two best farmers had got 1,300 and 1,700 kilos. The agricultural station of M. Pesoba has even reached an average of 2,300 kilos on six hectares. The Tikem Cotton Research Station (IRCT) in Chad harvested the equivalent of four tons a hectare on a small experimental area.

The margin of progress possible in the savannah is thus enormous, despite the fact that the potential is less than in the great forest. To achieve such progress, the CFDT first of all obtained a monopoly on buying cottonseed, which meant that it was paid for accurately. Expansion of cotton cultivation is held back in Dahomey because corruption still exists in too many areas at the point of sale.

Next, the peasants were well trained, and given enough technical organizers so that the latter could watch the progress of each individual peasant. The first act of the organizers was to teach the peasants respect of the cultivation calendar, and particularly for early sowing (Chart II, Chapter Twelve, 2). Secondly, peasants were shown the need for a combination stable and manure shed, where oxen were quartered at night. The manure was properly watered, and a trained pair of oxen and a cart, which were needed to carry the manure to the fields, were turned over to the peasants on credit. The next step was feeding the oxen adequately during the period of heavy work at the end of the dry season, when feed is scarce. This stage of progress, more difficult to reach, involved storing hay reserves, from grasses cut in the bush at the end of the rainy season. When I saw about twenty haystacks in a Malian village, I felt that there were very real grounds for hope. Next came insect control measures. Let me take this up with another example.

APPENDIX IV (See Chapter Eleven, 2)

COTTON DEVELOPMENT IN CHAD – OUTLINE OF PRIORITIES

Once early sowing is recognized as essential, the next step is 'pre-germination', whereby seeds are soaked in water for a day. They gain three to eight days of growth and avoid the need for resowing if a drought occurs after planting. Next, the seeds must be superficially planted, only one to two centimetres deep, and correctly spaced, which will increase yields. Lastly, the three weedings, if done early, will be even more effective. The third alone, if it had been done throughout the cotton plantations in 1960, would have produced at least 20,000 tons more.

These four actions are a first stage in modernization, which could be achieved everywhere in two or three years if everyone, from politicians to technical experts, lends a hand. When this stage has been reached, the next stage can be begun with a reasonable chance of success. In many cases it will begin by substituting a pair of oxen and a plough for a hand plough. This speeds up preparation of the ground and makes rain water penetrate more deeply. Lastly, it will also speed up the weeding process: a small hand-held plough will be drawn by the oxen, which means that the land will be cleared of stumps. There are no good feed-producing fallow lands here; when the land is left fallow, only bushes grow up. Applications of manure to fertilize the land should be substituted for these fallow periods very soon. At the same time, the three insecticide treatments should become universal practice. They pay for themselves on fields that are sown early and well weeded. In conjunction with the other crop disciplines, they increase yields to around a ton of cottonseed a hectare. This technical level could be attained in most areas in the space of seven or eight years.

There is always the danger that ploughing will speed up erosion in sandy earth, when the incline is more than 1·5 per cent. This is especially true if the slope is very long, which is true around the Toubouri lakes. People must be taught to work at right angles to the slope, until they are trained to follow the contour lines of the slope exactly. It is too often thought that an experienced geometrician is needed to trace out these horizontal lines on the terrain. It is not true: with a clear plastic hose full of muddy water, attached at the two ends to pickaxe handles, and marked with an equal altitude gauge, two illiterate but intelligent peasants can manage perfectly with an hour's training.

The first peasant remains at the first stake. The other, after testing at various spots along the slope, plants the second stake at the point where the water is level with the gauge mark. This is the kind of simple technique that should be taught in African schools. Unfortunately, they still pride themselves on teaching students how to make straight lines, cut at right angles, true symbols of European civilization. On the plantations where peasants were forced to cultivate cotton, the fields were cut into squares, which contributed – and still does – to erosion. Certain seeds yield less after ploughing: therefore the ploughed land should be packed down again with a roller, at least along the sowing line.

The third stage of progress would collect, as has been done in China for four or five thousand years, all the available manure. The 'Kraal', or area enclosed by a fence of thorny bushes, where the herd spends the night, will be the best source of manure. Really good fertilizer can be made if stable-manure sheds are built. These are sheltered from sun and rain by a sheltered roof, and the animals spend the night there. The dung is periodically watered in the dry season. Good fertilizer that is not expensive – and it should not be made without taking cost into consideration – presupposes that water is drawn from wells, ponds or rivers cheaply, in other words with draught animals. If good fertilizer is applied in massive doses before insecticide treatments are given, the vegetation it stimulates encourages development of parasites, such as Diparopsis. The damage done may be more than the gains from the fertilizer. Applications of insecticides and manure-fertilizer must be made during the same stage, therefore. They should come two or three years after the second stage, and come into general use in a dozen years.

The fourth stage will start by building up feed reserves of hay and silage. It will then raise livestock not simply for draught animals, but also for meat and milk production. This will open the way for the second 'agricultural revolution', in which cultivation will be continuously productive at last, fallow periods eliminated, and agriculture and livestock raising carried on in close conjunction with each other. This stage can often be preceded by the use of mineral fertilizer, located along sowing lines, wherever experience has shown it to be effective in raising yields. This fertilizer is very expensive and requires the success of the three other stages first. One should count on at least twelve to fifteen years before it is in general use. It is not, however, too early to think about manufacturing certain fertilizers locally (Gauthiot falls in Chad). My outline is, of course, flexible and must be adapted to varying conditions. Often it will be advisable to carry on several stages at the same time.

APPENDIX V (See Chapter Twelve, 7)

SHEEP – GOOD UTILIZATION OF IRREGULAR FEED SUPPLIES

A great effort was made in Mali after the First World War by wool merchants in the north to develop sheep's wool, using Australian and South African methods. The projects, and the Tourcoingbam installation, had to be abandoned. Until around 1880 the wool of a sheep was worth twelve times the sheep itself, live weight. One reason was that the animals were kept alive until they were quite old, for the annual fleece, and the meat, which had a greasy taste, was worth less. Today a kilo of lamb, live weight, sells for more than the fleece in Europe; in Africa it is much more expensive than beef.

Sheep bred for wool are more difficult to raise in hot climates than the hardy local breeds, which have a hairy coat. When there is a good and easily accessible market for the meat, the latter breed would be preferable therefore. Their meat production can be greatly increased by 'industrial cross-breeding' with prize rams. However, females used for reproduction should be sired by local rams, in order to retain female herds of the hardy breed. They can be improved gradually, particularly for milk, measured by weight of lambs at weaning, and for meat.

Modern herds include a high proportion of ewes, quickly eliminate castrated males, and keep a few rams chosen for reproduction. The objective is the sale of young lambs, weighing between twenty-five and thirty-five kilograms, a weight that can be attained in four to six months. Breeding should be timed so that the lambs are born when rains have covered the savannah with vegetation. Wild feed resources would thus satisfy the bulk of the herd's needs, in the form of good quality grass; the needs are higher when ewes are nursing the lambs and when the weaned lambs are being fattened.

Six months later, when the lambs not kept for reproduction and old ewes have been sold, the herd would consist only of the reproducing core. Its feed requirements would be very reduced, as there would be fewer animals, with less demanding requirements. The curve of feed requirements drops from four to one, demonstrating that sheep adapt far better than cattle to the enormous seasonal variations in the wild savannah.

The great bulk of products would arrive on the market in the beginning of the dry season. In Moslem countries, sheep are killed in great quantities for the Ait el Khebir fete, which generally does not coincide with this period. Will governments ask the religious authorities to adjust the festival to seasonal production in each country? If so, this huge demand can be satisfied at less cost. In non-Moslem countries, the massive and concentrated supply can be absorbed – without resorting to freezers, which is far too expensive – if lamb and mutton supply a modest proportion of the meat consumed.

If feed is cultivated to complement the resources of the savannah, particularly in quality, production can extend over a longer period. Although meat production will still take first place, cheese from sheep's milk, much appreciated in the Mediterranean area, could be produced in notable quantities. This will not be to the detriment of the lambs, provided the ewes are fed better, and receive more proteins.

Wool remains an important secondary product, especially in the coolest mountain zones, like Ankaratra, south of Tananarive. There the pasturelands are scarcely utilized, and warm clothes are needed. Astrakhan fur is rapidly becoming popular, and the animals are well suited to tropical regions that are not too hot. An African-run enterprise to raise them failed in Chad, but Angola and south-western Africa are succeeding with settlers of European origin. They are giving the animals regular treatments against intestinal and pulmonary parasites. Sheep cannot survive negligence in the same way as cattle.

Enough of this small animal, which links us still to the far-off Mediterranean. Towards the coast, in areas where Islam has not yet penetrated – it is progressing fast – another animal can render great service.

APPENDIX VI (See Chapter Twelve, 7)

PIGS AND FOWL – LIMITED PRODUCTION, WITH INEXPENSIVE PROTEINS

The example of the Sakay region has shown the potential of pig raising as the basis of the agricultural development of savannah zones. In forest zones, where cattle are more difficult to raise, pigs survive well on wild feed, and utilize crop by-products or household garbage. Left to themselves, pigs grow very slowly and losses are high, because proteins are lacking and parasites become virulent. Under modern methods, pigs are enclosed in a cement yard and cleaned frequently with a great deal of water. Pigs cannot supply inexpensive meat, which is of such importance in developing countries, unless the protein complements which are given them are not too expensive.

This means that meat and fish meals must be produced on the spot; but, like skim milk and even peanut flowers, they must first satisfy human protein requirements. Technical experts who think primarily in European terms can be very dangerous in this kind of situation. Once human needs are filled – and those concerned must be assisted in formulating them – intensive pig raising will benefit from nearby concentrated feeds. I would suggest establishing some small peanut processing plants in the savannah, perhaps also oil palm factories in the forest zone. If pigs are fed on cakes with too much fat content, they will produce an oily lard. This can be avoided by feeding the pigs, for the last month of fattening up, manioc, corn and 'de-oiled' cakes.

Nevertheless, pigs are not resistant to great heat or excessive humidity, and I would hesitate to advise a large-scale development of pig raising. This is especially true if one is thinking in terms of large-scale production of food of animal origin. Africa simply does not yet have sufficient quantities of the vegetable products, particularly grains and tubers, and of the nitrogenous complements needed to feed the animals. The manioc surplus is an asset in this regard, because the plant does not demand much care, and its leaves have a high Vitamin C content.

Chickens found wandering in the bush are sold very cheaply in Africa, as a 'wild' product, somewhat like the Malagasy zebu. Cost price would be raised considerably, even more than for pigs, if expensive concentrated feeds are imported from Europe, and sheds built on a large scale. Ambitions now are limited to competition with imported 'French' chickens, and supplying fresh but very expensive eggs to the upper classes. One cannot start talking about a weekly 'chicken in the pot'[1] without first finding out whether or not the necessarily large grain surpluses exist. Otherwise the lack of grain, already aggravated by the fabrication of millet beer, will be even

[1] This promise of Henry IV, or rather Sully, was somewhat demagogic, given the grain resources of the period!

more serious, and peasants in poor regions will have a very difficult
time in lasting until the next harvest. However, Rhode Island Reds
can be easily raised in the 'back yard', and ducks, where ponds
exist, can easily feed themselves. Guinea pigs also live happily in
the yard. Many other secondary animals should be studied in this
regard. I would like now to say a last word on fisheries.

APPENDIX VII

FISH MEAL PROVIDES THE MOST ECONOMICAL PROTEINS

Tropical Africa now produces a million tons of fish, three times
more than in 1938. Half of it comes from the sea, on the west coast,
and the other from the interior waterways, lakes and pools. The
catch from the sea, however, is for the most part made by foreign
trawlers with refrigeration: French, Greek, Israeli, Italian, Japanese,
along the Mauritanian coast; even Soviet and Polish, in the Gulf of
Guinea; and Japanese and Nationalist Chinese, near Madagascar.
Transported fresh, in ice, the fish quickly becomes too expensive,
and the African peasant cannot afford it. Canned imports will be too
expensive for a long time, as will canned fish from national factories,
when it is produced. Portuguese peasants scarcely eat anything but
salted sardines, since they cannot afford the canned varieties with
their meagre incomes (seven kilos of corn per day's work).

Dried smoked fish is more widespread, and could be relatively
accessible, but the regulations make it a difficult process. By far the
most economical way of making fish generally available is through
manufacturing fish meal, fine or even coarse. In the framework of
the world-wide fight against hunger, the FAO is mounting a campaign to popularize it that is very useful. The 250,000 tons of
sardines and other fish caught in Angola are mostly made into meal;
yet this is exported to Europe, where it is fed to cattle, pigs and fowl.
The same aberration of the liberal economy discussed in the case of

the peanut cake holds true here, but it is more serious, because fish meal supplies the most precious amino-acids for young children, pregnant women and nursing mothers.

In the equatorial zone, where livestock raising is so difficult, the Belgians hoped to supply economical local proteins by fish farming, notably with *Tilapia*. The enormous efforts they made with organization and propaganda produced only meagre results: 4,500 hectares of ponds produced around 2,250 tons of fish annually in the ex-Belgian Congo; much less in the former French Equatorial Africa or in the Cameroons. The habit of feeding the fish every day, with leaves (potato, manioc) from plants produced on the edges of the ponds, is acquired here with more difficulty than in the south of China. Nevertheless, this resource should not be neglected: activism could play a very useful role in encouraging it.

TABLE OF EQUIVALENT MEASURES

1 mm	=	·039 inches
1 cm	=	·394 inches
1 metre	=	1·09 yards
1 kilometre	=	·62 miles
1 are	=	100 square metres
1 hectare	=	2·47 acres
1 kilo	=	2·20 lbs.
1 quintal	=	approximate 1 cwt
1 metric quintal	=	100 kilograms = 220 lbs.
1 tonne	=	·98 tons
1 litre	=	1·75 pints

CURRENCY

£ = 13.75 french NF in 1962 (average for year)

£ = 2.80 dollars in 1962 (average for year)

£ = 139.15 Belgian francs

CFA franc = $0·004 (or $1=247 CFA francs) in 1962

SELECTED BIBLIOGRAPHY

1. WORKS ON UNDERDEVELOPMENT AND RELATED PROBLEMS

ARDANT, G *Le Monde en friche*. Paris: Presses Universitaires de France. 1959

BARRE, R *Le Développement économique, Analyse et Politique*. Cahiers Institut de Science Économique Appliquée. Series F, No. 11, 1958

BETTELHEIM, CHARLES *L'Inde Indépendante*. Paris: A Colin, 1962

CHOMBART DE LAUWE, PAUL HENRY *Les Paysans Soviétiques*. Paris: Éditions du Seuil, 1961

CIPOLLA, C M *Economic History of World Population*. Penguin Books

CLARK, COLIN *The Conditions of Economic Progress*. London: Macmillan, 3rd ed. 1957; New York: St Martin's Press, 1957

DOBB, MAURICE HERBERT *An Essay on Economic Growth and Planning*. New York: Monthly Review Press, 1960. Routledge & Kegan Paul, 1960

DRABKIN-DARIN, HAIM *Patterns of Cooperative Agriculture in Israel*. Tel Aviv: published by the Department for International Cooperation, Ministry of Foreign Affairs, for the International Association for Rural Planning, 1962. Jewish Agency for Israel, 77 Great Russell Street, London, WC1

Food and Agriculture Organization of the United Nations. *FAO Africa Survey; report on the possibilities of African rural development in relation to economic and social growth*. Rome: 1962

FURTADO, C *Development and Underdevelopment*. California University Press: Cambridge University Press, 1965 and 1967

KARDELJ, EDWARD *Les Problèmes de la politique socialiste dans les campagnes*. Paris: N.E.F., 1960

LEBRET, LOUIS-JOSEPH *Suicide ou survie de l'Occident*. Paris: Éditions Ouvrières, 1958

LEDERER, WM J & BURDICK, EUGENE *The Ugly American*. New York: Norton, 1958. London: Gollancz, 1959

LEWIS, WILLIAM ARTHUR *The Theory of Economic Growth*. London: Allen & Unwin, 1955 cloth, paperback 1963; Homewood, Illinois: R. D. Irwin, 1955

MENDE, TIBOR *Entre la peur et l'espoir*. Paris: Éditions du Seuil, 1958

MOUSSA, PIERRE *Les Nations prolétaires*. Paris: Presses Universitaires de France, 1959 (English edition available: *The Underprivileged Nations*. London: Sidgwick & Jackson 1962. New York: Peter Smith, 1962)

MYRDAL, GUNNAR *An International Economy, Problems and Prospects*. New York: Harper, 1956 (no English edition)

Asian Drama: an inquiry into the poverty of nations. Allen Lane: The Penguin Press, London

Economic Theory and Underdeveloped Regions. London: Duckworth, 1957. Published in the United States with the title: *Rich Lands and Poor; the Road to World Prosperity*. New York: Harper, 1957, 1958

NURKSE, RAGNAR *Problems of Capital Formation in Underdeveloped Countries*. New York: Oxford University Press, 1962. Oxford: Blackwell, 1957

PERROUX, FRANÇOIS *La Coexistence pacifique*. Paris: Presses Universitaires de France 1958

L'Économie du XXe siècle. Paris: Presses Universitaires de France, 1961

Les Mesures des Progrès économiques et l'idée d'économie progressive. Cahiers Institut de Science Économique Appliquée, first series, 1956

Théorie du Progrès économique, Trois outils d'analyse pour l'étude du sous-développement. Cahiers Institut de Science Économique Appliquée, Series F, No. 1, 1955

PROU, CHARLES *Établissement des programmes en économie sous-développée*. Paris: Centre d'Études des Programmes Économiques, 1961

ROSTOW, WALT WHITMAN *The Stages of Economic Growth, a non-Communist manifesto*. Cambridge: University Press, 1960.

SAUVY, A and others. *Le Tiers-Monde, sous-développement et développement*. Paris: Presses Universitaires de France, 1956 and 1961

TIAGUNENKO, VIKTOR LEONIDOVICH *Contribution aux problèmes de la situation des pays sous-développés dans la production capitaliste mondiale*. Moscow: Revue soviétique, 1958

TINBERGEN, JAN *The Design of Development*. Baltimore: Johns Hopkins Press, 1958. Oxford, 1958

2. WORKS ON AFRICA OR 'COLONIAL' PROBLEMS

D'ARBOUZIER, G *L'Afrique vers l'unité*. Éditions St-Paul, 1962

CHEVERNY, J *Éloge du colonialisme*. Paris: Julliard, 1961

DIA, MAMADOU *Réflexions sur l'économie de l'Afrique noire*. Paris: Présence Africaine, 1953.

FANON, FRANTZ *Les Damnés de la Terre*. Paris: F. Maspero, 1961. Published in English under the title: *The Wretched of the Earth*, Grove Press, 1965. MacGibbon and Kee, 1965

FAVROD, CHARLES HENRI *Le Poids de l'Afrique*. Paris: Éditions du Seuil, 1958

L'Afrique Seule. Paris: Éditions du Seuil, 1961

GENDARME, RENÉ *L'Économie de Madagascar. Diagnostic et Perspectives de Développement*. Paris: Éditions Cujas, 1963 (banned in Paris)

HATCH, JOHN *A History of Postwar Africa*. André Deutsch, London, and Frederick A. Praeger, New York, 1966.

JEANSON, F *La Révolution algérienne, Problèmes et perspectives*. Milan: Feltrinelli, 1962

JOOS, LOUIS C *Brève histoire de l'Afrique Noire*. Issy-les Moulineaux: Éditions St-Paul, 1961

LACOUTURE, JEAN *Cinq hommes et la France*. Paris: Éditions du Seuil, 1961

RABEMANANJARA, JACQUES *Nationalisme et problèmes malgaches*. Paris: Présence Africaine, 1958

SENGHOR, L S *On African Socialism*, n.e., Praeger, New York, and Pall Mall, London, 1965.

SURET-CANALE, J *Afrique noire, occidentale et centrale*. Paris: Éditions Sociales, 1961–4

VIGUIER, P *L'Afrique de l'Ouest vue par un agriculteur*. La Maison Rustique, 1960

3. JOURNALS

Afrique

Civilisation et Développement, Institut de recherches et de formation en vue du développement. (I.R.F.E.D.)

Croissance des Jeunes Nations

Jeune Afrique, Tunis

Présence Africaine, Paris. Published also in English translation.

Tiers-Monde. Problèmes des Pays Sous-Développés. University of Paris: Institut d'étude du développement économique et sociale. Presses Universitaires de France.

SPECIAL ISSUES

Esprit, Juin 1957, 'Les Maladies infantiles de l'indépendance'. October 1961, 'De l'Assistance à la solidarité'.

Cahiers Africains No. 5, 'Le Sénégal en marche'

Études Socialistes Janvier 1962, 'Spécial Sénégal'

BIBLIOGRAPHY ON ENGLISH-SPEAKING AFRICA

BALOGH, THOMAS *The Mechanism of Neo-Imperialism*. Bulletin of the Oxford University Institute of Statistics, Blackwell

CHISIZA, D K *Realities of African Independence*. Africa Publications Trust, 1960. Published in America under the title *Africa – What Lies Ahead*. African–American Institute, New York, 1961

CLARK, RALPH *Aid in Uganda – Programmes and Policies*. Overseas Development Institute, 1966

FAO *Africa Report*

HESELTINE, NIGEL *Remaking Africa*. Museum Press, 1961

JAMAL, A H *The Critical Phase of Emergent African States*. East African Publishing House, 1965

LITTLE, I M D *Aid to Africa*. Pergamon Press, Oxford, 1964

LITTLE, I M D, and CLIFFORD, J M *International Aid*. Allen and Unwin, 1965

ORR, JOHN BOYD, and LUBBOCK, DAVID *The White Man's Dilemma*. Allen and Unwin new edition, 1964. Distributed in U.S. by British Book Centre

OVERSEAS DEVELOPMENT INSTITUTE *British Aid Series* (five vols.)

UNITED NATIONS *Economic Bulletins for Africa*

WILLIAMS, PETER *Aid in Uganda – Education*. Overseas Development Institute, 1966

WORSLEY, PETER *The Third World*. Weidenfeld and Nicolson, 1964

INDEX

Abala (Niger), 234
Abidjan (Ivory Coast), 85, 128, 140, 224, 240; flour mills, 116; bicycle assembly, 117
Activism. *See* Rural activism
Addis Ababa conference (1961), 297
Afghanistan, 275, 280
African common front, proposal for, 264–6
African Common Market, a need for, 104, 263–4
Africanization, prematurely enforced, 93–5, 170, 225
Agrarian reform, 125, 250
Agricultural Engineering, Department of, 54
Agricultural Provident Societies, 216
Agricultural Services, 54, 62, 65, 141, 216
Agriculture: underdeveloped, 30–3; need for priority in planning, 99; accelerated development as corollary to industrialization, 104–5; equipment and fertilizers, 112–14; process of decolonization, 123–5; land tenure, 125–31; tenant farming, 131–3; and dowry system and gerontocracy, 133–5; and exploitation by Moslem priests, 135–8; close crop supervision, 139–40; track farming and animal proteins, 150–1; education in, 195–202; unified Department of Rural Development required, 204–5; rural activism, 205–10; and credit, 211–15, 219–20; co-operatives, 215–22; trade bureaus and marketing boards, 222–6
See also Cocoa; Coffee; Livestock; Oil palm; Peanuts; Peasantry; etc.
Ahidjo, President, 85
Alcohol: introduced by Europeans, 36–7, 39; spread of alcoholism, 48–51, 114, 163
Algeria, 79, 122, 253, 262, 267; Provident Societies, 67
Alliance for Progress, 270
Alucam. *See* Edéa
Alumina, 107, 108
Aluminium, 106, 107
Ambavalo, 219
Angola 36

Antilles, 109, 110
Antsirabé (Madagascar), 118
Apithy, President, 79, 190
Ardant, G., 232, 281–2
Argentina, 275, 280
Armaments, amount spent on, 278–9
Army: joint army needed, 79; a menace to African development, 236n.
Arusha Declaration, 285, 291
Asiatic bamboo, 162
Assalé, President, 85
Association of African Coffee Producers, 65
Aswan Dam, 165
Australia, 127, 279

Babel (veterinary doctor), 74
Baboulène, J., 254
Balogh, Thomas, 103n.
Bamako (Mali), 92, 117, 128, 163, 241, 243
Bananas, 39, 60, 71, 152; control needed through the ripening stage, 147–9
Banda, Dr Hastings, 295
Bandiagara (Mali), 242
Bangui (Congo Brazzaville), 118, 121, 264
Bartoume-Moussa, Dr, 37
BDPA (Bureau pour le Développement de la Production Agricole), 134
Beauport (Guadeloupe), 179
Belgium, 267
Belhé, M., 93
Ben Bella, 262
Benin union (proposed), 79
Bergmann, Dennis, 149
Beriberi, 115
Bethlehem Steel, 276
Betsabetsa ('wine' from fermented cane sugar juice), 109
Bicycles, 117
Bismarck, Otto von, 85
Blohorn oil palm plantation, Cosrou, 102
Blum, Léon, 77
Bobrowsky, Czeslaw, 256
Boltz, Father, 40–1
Bonabéri (Cameroons), 148, 149
Bouaké (Ivory Coast), 118, 157
Boulel-Kaffrine (Senegal), 58
Boyd Orr, Sir John, 266

11